The Battle of Fort Sumter

On April 12, 1861, the long-simmering tensions between the American North and South exploded as Southern troops in the seceding state of South Carolina fired on the Federal forces at Fort Sumter in Charleston harbor. The battle of Fort Sumter marked the outbreak of Civil War in the United States. The attack provoked outrage in the North, consolidated support for the newly inaugurated President Lincoln, and fueled the onset of the war that would consume and reshape the country.

In this concise narrative, Wesley Moody explores the long history of tensions that lead to the events at Fort Sumter, the details of the crisis and battle, the impact of Fort Sumter on the unfolding Civil War, and the battle's place in historical memory. Supplemented by primary documents including newspaper coverage, first-person accounts, letters, and government documents, and supported by a companion website, this book provides students with a nuanced understanding of both the long-term and immediate origins of the American Civil War.

Wesley Moody is Professor of History at Florida State College, Jacksonville.

Critical Moments in American History

Edited by William Thomas Allison, Georgia Southern University

The Battle of the Greasy Grass/ Little Bighorn
Custer's Last Stand in Memory, History, and Popular Culture
Debra Buchholtz

The Assassination of John F. Kennedy
Political Trauma and American Memory
Alice L. George

Freedom to Serve
Truman, Civil Rights, and Executive Order 9981
Jon E. Taylor

The Battles of Kings Mountain and Cowpens
The American Revolution in the Southern Backcountry
Melissa Walker

The Cuban Missile Crisis
The Threshold of Nuclear War
Alice L. George

The Nativist Movement in America
Religious Conflict in the 19th Century
Katie Oxx

The 1980 Presidential Election
Ronald Reagan and the Shaping of the American Conservative Movement
Jeffrey D. Howison

The Louisiana Purchase
A Global Context
Robert D. Bush

The Fort Pillow Massacre
North, South, and the Status of African Americans in the Civil War Era
Bruce Tap

From Selma to Montgomery
The Long March to Freedom
Barbara Combs

The Homestead Strike
Labor, Violence, and American Industry
Paul E. Kahan

The Flu Epidemic of 1918
America's Experience in the Global Health Crisis
Sandra Opdycke

The Emergence of Rock and Roll
Music and the Rise of American Youth Culture
Mitchell K. Hall

Transforming Civil War Prisons
Lincoln, Lieber, and the Politics of Captivity
Paul J. Springer and Glenn Robins

The Battle of Fort Sumter
The First Shots of the American Civil War
Wesley Moody

The WPA
Creating Jobs and Hope in the Great Depression
Sandra Opdycke

The Battle of Fort Sumter

The First Shots of the American Civil War

Wesley Moody

NEW YORK AND LONDON

First published 2016
by Routledge
711 Third Avenue, New York, NY 10017

and by Routledge
2 Park Square, Milton Park, Abingdon, Oxon, OX14 4RN

Routledge is an imprint of the Taylor & Francis Group, an informa business

Library of Congress Cataloging in Publication Data
Names: Moody, Wesley, author.Title: The Battle of Fort Sumter : the first shots of the American Civil War / Wesley Moody.
Description: New York, NY : Routledge, 2016. |
Includes bibliographical references and index.
Identifiers: LCCN 2015040934| ISBN 9781138783461 (hardback) | ISBN 9781138783478 (pbk.) | ISBN 9781315768687 (e-book)
Subjects: LCSH: Fort Sumter (Charleston, S.C.)—Siege, 1861. | Charleston (S.C.)—History—Civil War, 1861–1865. | United States—History—Civil War, 1861–1865—Causes.
Classification: LCC E471.1 .M66 2016 | DDC 973.7/31—dc 3
LC record available at http://lccn.loc.gov/2015040934

ISBN: 978-1-138-78346-1 (hbk)
ISBN: 978-1-138-78347-8 (pbk)
ISBN: 978-1-315-76868-7 (ebk)

Typeset in Bembo and Helvetica Neue
by Florence Production Ltd, Stoodleigh, Devon, UK

Printed and bound in the United States of America by Publishers Graphics, LLC on sustainably sourced paper.

To John, Sarah and Patrick who
were very patient while dad wrote

Contents

Series Introduction

Welcome to the Routledge *Critical Moments in American History* series. The purpose of this new series is to give students a window into the historian's craft through concise, readable books by leading scholars, who bring together the best scholarship and engaging primary sources to explore a critical moment in the American past. In discovering the principal points of the story in these books, gaining a sense of historiography, following a fresh trail of primary documents, and exploring suggested readings, students can then set out on their own journey, to debate the ideas presented, interpret primary sources, and reach their own conclusions – just like the historian.

A critical moment in history can be a range of things – a pivotal year, the pinnacle of a movement or trend, or an important event such as the passage of a piece of legislation, an election, a court decision, a battle. It can be social, cultural, political, or economic. It can be heroic or tragic. Whatever they are, such moments are by definition "game changers," momentous changes in the pattern of the American fabric, paradigm shifts in the American experience. Many of the critical moments explored in this series are familiar; some less so.

There is no ultimate list of critical moments in American history – any group of students, historians, or other scholars may come up with a different catalog of topics. These differences of view, however, are what make history itself and the study of history so important and so fascinating. Therein can be found the utility of historical inquiry – to explore, to challenge, to understand, and to realize the legacy of the past through its influence of the present. It is the hope of this series to help students realize this intrinsic value of our past and of studying our past.

William Thomas Allison
Georgia Southern University

Figures

Acknowledgments

A special thanks is due to the librarians at Florida State College at Jacksonville. Especially Barbara Salvage, Anthony Harmon and Barbara Markham, whose research help and ability to procure the really hard to find references, made this book possible. My colleague, Joann Carpenter kindly and patiently read my manuscript. Her suggestions were extremely helpful and this book is much better thanks to her help.

Timeline

1670	Charleston, South Carolina founded
1688	First Quaker meeting spoke out against slavery
1690	South Carolina began planting rice and importing slaves
1739	Stono Rebellion
1758	Society of Friends declared slavery a sin
1775	First meeting of an abolitionist society
1775–1783	American Revolution
1776	British invasion of Charleston is defeated
1787	U.S. Constitution adopted
1791–1804	Haitian Revolution
1793	First fugitive slave law passed
1793	Cotton gin invented
1800	Prosser Slave Revolt in Virginia
1808	The United States banned slave imports from overseas
1812–1815	War of 1812
1819	Missouri Compromise
1823	Charleston police formed
1828	Jackson elected President of the United States
1828	Democratic and Whig parties formed
1829	Construction of Fort Sumter begun
1831	Publication of *Appeal to the Colored Citizens of the World*
1831	Nat Turner Slave Revolt
1831	Slave revolt in British Jamaica
1831	Nullification Crisis
1833	American Anti-slavery Society Formed
1837	Financial Panic of 1837
1846–1847	U.S. War with Mexico

1847	Wilmot Proviso proposed
1849	California Gold Rush
1850	Compromise of 1850
1850	*Slavery Justified* published
1854	Republican Party formed
1856	Kansas/Nebraska Act Passed
May 21, 1856	Lawrence, Kansas burned by proslavery forces
May 22, 1856	Charles Sumner beaten by South Carolina congressman Preston Brooks
November 4, 1856	Buchanan elected President of the United States
1858	Lincoln–Douglas Debates
October 25, 1858	Seward gives "irrepressible conflict" speech in New York
October 16–18, 1859	Harper's Ferry Raid
November 6, 1860	Lincoln elected President of the United States
November 19, 1860	Anderson took command at Fort Moultrie
December 7, 1860	Don Carlos Buell delivered orders to Anderson at Fort Moultrie
December 8, 1860	South Carolina congressmen met with Buchanan
December 14, 1860	Francis Pickens became Governor of South Carolina
December 20, 1860	South Carolina declared independence from the Union
December 24, 1860	South Carolina Commissioners arrived in Washington D.C.
December 26, 1860	Anderson transferred his command to Fort Sumter
December 27, 1860	Fort Moultrie and Castle Pinckney seized by South Carolina
December 27, 1860	Buchanan refused to meet South Carolina's Commissioners
December 29, 1860	Floyd resigns as Secretary of War
December 29, 1860	Buchanan refused to order the evacuation of Fort Sumter
January 5, 1861	*Star of the West* expedition launched
January 9, 1861	Confederate batteries fire on the *Star of the West*
January 11, 1861	Pickens ordered the evacuation of Fort Sumter. Anderson refuses
February 3, 1861	Women and children evacuated from Fort Sumter, sent to New York
March 1, 1861	The Confederacy assumed control of military affairs in Charleston
March 3, 1861	Beauregard took command of Confederate forces in Charleston
March 4, 1861	Lincoln inaugurated as President of the United States
April 10, 1861	Fox expedition launched
4:30 AM April 12, 1861	Confederate opened open fire on Fort Sumter
2:30 PM April 13, 1861	Robert Anderson surrendered Fort Sumter
April 14, 1861	Anderson's command evacuated Fort Sumter
April 15, 1861	Lincoln calls for seventy-five-thousand troops to suppress rebellion
April 19, 1861	Anderson and his men arrived in New York
July 21, 1861	First major land battle of the Civil War
February 18, 1861	Charleston captured by Union troops
April 9, 1865	General Robert E. Lee surrendered

April 15, 1865	Anderson raised the U.S. flag over Fort Sumter in an official ceremony
April 15, 1865	Lincoln assassinated
June 23, 1865	Last Confederate army surrendered in Oklahoma
1898	Fort Sumter reactivated for Spanish American War
1948	Fort Sumter made a National Monument

CHAPTER 1

Origins of Civil War

At just before 4:30 in the morning of April 12, 1861 a mortar shell exploded over Fort Sumter. The men and officers of the First Artillery United States Army had silently watched the explosive shell streak across the dark night sky. It exploded high overhead harmlessly showering the fort's parade ground with bits of iron. There were a few moments of eerie silence before the full barrage was unleashed upon Fort Sumter and its occupants. The men inside the massive stone walls of Fort Sumter had not been caught by surprise. Following the gentlemanly laws of nineteenth century warfare they were informed an hour earlier when the Confederate batteries would open fire. This was the opening of the American Civil War, a conflict that would cost the lives of as many as eight hundred and fifty thousand people and fundamentally changed the United States of America.[1]

Fort Sumter was the key to a defensive system to protect Charleston from the type of naval invasion the British had launched against the United States during the Revolution and the War of 1812. This early morning attack was not by a foreign foe but from the city the fort was built to defend. Five months earlier South Carolina had exercised what it claimed to be its right to "withdraw from the Federal Union" and "resumed her position among the nations of the world, as a separate and independent State."[2]

Like any independent nation, South Carolina could not accept a foreign nation controlling the entrance of its major port. Unfortunately for the leaders of this new nation, the newly elected administration in Washington D.C. took a very different view of South Carolina's declared right to leave the Union formed under the U.S. Constitution. With compromise impossible and Fort Sumter an irritant that could not be ignored, South Carolina found itself with no option but to take military

Building of Fort Sumter

Following the War of 1812, Congress approved eight hundred thousand dollars for the building of a series of fortifications along the U.S. coast. This fortifications program was known as the Third System. President James Madison appointed a board of engineers to identify locations for the new forts. The board identified more than two hundred sites on the Atlantic, Gulf and Pacific Coasts that needed permanent stone fortresses. Only about fifty were ever built and most were still unfinished at the start of the Civil War.

Fort Sumter was part of this Third System. Construction began in 1829. The first step was to build an island in the middle of the harbor. Tons of shells and waste rock from New England quarries were piled into the harbor. Nearly a million dollars were spent before dry land broke the surface. Before the first shipload of New England granite spilled into the harbor the Federal government had to win a lawsuit against a local resident who claimed he had been given sole right over the land in the harbor by the state of South Carolina.

Even after the lawsuit was settled the tides slowed work on the foundation. Occasional yellow fever and malaria outbreaks also slowed the work. Work was also slowed by finances. During economic downturns the government had to cut spending on projects like Fort Sumter. U.S. Senators and members of the House of Representatives fought for the limited funding to build the harbor defenses in their district. South Carolina did not push, for the idea of a strong Federal garrison was already distrustful to South Carolina by the 1830's.

After thirty years work, only the outside structure was finished. Of the planned one hundred and forty guns only fifteen were in place and the interior barracks were still unfinished. As tensions rose in 1860 the Corps of Engineers rushed to finish before it came to open hostility.

Fort Sumter was well designed and well placed. For four years of war, Fort Sumter beat off several invading fleets, including those made up of ironclads, exactly what it was meant to do.

action against the eighty six man garrison. The actions of both sides in Charleston would play an important role in this war and its eventual result.

1860 PRESIDENTIAL ELECTION

The causes of the conflict inside Charleston harbor and the wider war that followed date to the very beginning of this nation. The breaking point, however, for most Southerners and especially the people of South Carolina was November 6, 1860. The election of the Republican Abraham Lincoln as president, without the votes of a single Southern state, convinced them that their influence within the Republic was waning and their only recourse was to leave.

The 1860 presidential election was a bitter four way fight that put a new political party in the White House within six years of its formation. The meteoric rise of the Republican Party within so short a time was caused by the same issues that led to the Civil War itself. Among these slavery was the main issue that caused the sectional tension between North and South and created the political gap that the Republicans filled. Modern apologists for the Confederate cause identify a number of issues that created the sectional crisis, from economic issues to political philosophy. While there is truth in these arguments, if one even scratches the surface of any of them slavery is there. The economics of the agrarian South differed greatly from those of the industrializing North or even the agrarian Midwest. However, the major difference was the dependence on slave labor versus free. To discuss Antebellum economics without the slavery issue being front and center is misleading. The role of the central government is probably the most often cited reason for the Civil War given by those trying to avoid the slavery issue. It is undeniable that the issue of "States' Rights" was first and foremost in the minds of most Southerners before the war. One can easily find throughout the writings of leading secessionists numerous references to the importance of the balance between State and Federal power as a cause for the Civil War. One has to carefully edit to disguise that the major concern over Federal power was that it would fall into the hands of abolitionists.

THE ISSUE OF SLAVERY

The tension had been present as early as the nation itself. Slavery would continue to grow as an issue following the creation of the United States for three major reasons. The economic expansion of the United States was like nothing the world had ever seen. Tobacco continued to be a very profitable industry in South Carolina, North Carolina and Virginia. Cotton, however, would come to dominate, making up seventy five percent of the United States' total exports in 1860.[3] While the generation of the Founding Fathers had been able to look at slavery as a necessary evil that would die a natural death in a changing world for economic reasons, as slavery became more profitable, their descendants defended slavery as a moral good and the lynchpin of a democratic society.

Another reason that slavery grew as a political issue was the growing numbers who saw slavery as a moral concern that could not be ignored. The abolitionist movement is as old as the nation itself. The Society of Friends, better known as Quakers, was the backbone of the early abolitionist movement in the English speaking world. Individual Quaker meetings spoke out against slavery as early as 1688, and in 1758 slavery was declared a sin by the Society of Friends as a body. At the first meeting of the Society for the Relief of Free Negroes Unlawfully Held in Bondage, the first American abolition society, in 1775 most of the attendees were Quakers.[4]

> The Society of Friends, commonly called Quakers, were founded by George Fox in England in 1647. They were banned and persecuted in Britain and her American colonies. The Quakers were pacifists and heavily engaged in most reform movements.

The abolitionist movement grew beyond the Quakers. As a conflict with Great Britain neared and the popularity of European Enlightenment writers grew, the Quakers found that their neighbors in the North were becoming much more receptive to their anti-slavery message. To many New England patriots it was becoming obvious that slavery was a gross violation of Locke and Montesquieu's natural law. At the inaugural meeting of the Society for the Relief of Free Negroes Unlawfully Held in Bondage in April of 1775, days before the first shots of the American Revolution at Lexington and Concord, the famous Enlightenment pamphleteer Thomas Paine was present as a founding member. Before the war ended, leading patriots such as Benjamin Franklin, Patrick Henry, James Otis, Alexander Hamilton and even the Virginians James Madison and Thomas Jefferson had questioned the morality of slavery. The belief grew among New England Protestants that the war with England was divine retribution for their sins and there would be neither peace nor independence until African slavery had ended.[5]

Peace and independence came and slavery survived in the new nation. The institution did however appear to be coming to an end in the decades following the Revolution. All Northern states had either banned slavery or set in place laws for gradual emancipation by 1804. Although the price of tobacco declined and the number of private manumissions grew, slavery still remained a strong institution in the South. No abolition society existed south of Virginia and no serious anti-slavery legislation was mentioned in the Deep South. Although "all men are created equal" and enlightenment ideas were very important to the Revolution, the defense of private property was extremely important and was what Southerners pointed to as the important outcome of the war.[6]

The South's representatives at the Constitutional Convention of 1787 arrived in Philadelphia with the defense of slavery a top priority. Slave owning Southerners were not paranoid in their fear of abolitionists lurking in the Federal Convention. While the Convention was meeting, the Confederation Congress passed the Northwest Ordinance which among other things banned slavery in the territory north of the Ohio River and east of the Mississippi River. Some French settlers in the region were slave owners but the Congress ignored their petitions.[7]

The U.S. Constitution, as originally ratified, was filled with compromises on the issue of slavery. In order to gain Southern support for the Constitution, Northern representatives accepted some major concessions. Although less of an issue in 1787 than it would become in later years, Article IV, Section 2 of the Constitution required the return of runaway slaves. The Three Fifth's Compromise counted slaves in the U.S. Census that determined representation in the House of Representatives. Southerners, of course, wanted to count the slaves the same as free citizens in order to increase their representation in the new government. The Constitution also prevented Congress from passing a law to ban the international slave trade before 1808. It furthermore gave Congress the power to pass a fugitive slave law, which they would in 1793. The debates at the Constitutional Convention over the issues of slavery showed the growing anti-slavery sentiment in the North and the writers' numerous euphemisms for slavery were evidence that slavery was viewed negatively by a large portion of the population.[8]

THE ABOLITIONIST MOVEMENT

The abolitionist movement faced a number of setbacks in the days of the early Republic. The bloody excesses of the French Revolution soured most Americans on any kind of radical reform. The successful slave revolts in the French colony of Saint-Domingue, modern day Haiti, were the stuff of nightmares for slaveholders. This was followed in 1800 by a failed slave revolt led by a free black in Virginia named Gabriel Prosser. Although the revolt never moved beyond the plotting stage there were more than thirty hangings in response. The weakness of the abolitionist movement was perhaps best illustrated by Kentucky's entrance into the Union as a Slave State with so little difficulty and the Congress's passage of the original fugitive slave law.[9]

Perhaps there was no greater setback to the abolitionist movement than Eli Whitney's invention of the cotton gin in 1793. As every school child knows, Eli Whitney's invention had a profound effect on the economy and the nation as a whole. Although patent issues kept him from profiting as much from his machine as he might have, his invention made cotton an extremely valuable commodity. The increase in the value of slave labor was also astronomical. As the economic impact of slavery grew, the number of those who supported abolition shrank.[10] Western Europe, followed by the Northeastern United States was going through an industrial revolution that was based on the production of textiles. This caused a high demand for cotton that further increased the institution of slavery.

The abolitionist movement did have its successes, as Congress banned the international slave trade. There were a large number of Americans who supported this ban but saw absolutely nothing wrong with slavery itself. Although this seems a rather intellectually dishonest position to take, it did allow many Americans to take a moral stand on the issue without it having an immediate effect on their lives or the economy. Following in the same line was the American Colonization Society. The Society, founded in 1816, pushed for the voluntary freeing of slaves followed by a return to Africa. This they hoped would help overcome the concern about the dangers of a large free black population. Besides the plan being wildly impractical from a purely logistical point of view, very few freed slaves were interested. The vast majority of slaves were born in the United States as were their parents and grandparents. This was the land of their birth and Africa was an unknown land. The colonization movement had mixed results and it can be debated whether there were long term effects on the abolitionist movement. It has been argued that the colonization movement allowed people who were not ready to offer their full support to abolition and civil rights to at least take incremental steps. This was a setback to the abolitionist movement because people could sooth their consciences without making too radical a stand. James G. Birney, former slave owner turned abolitionist, felt the Colonization Society was "an opiate to the consciences" and kept its members from feeling "deeply and keenly the sin of slavery."[11] However, the fact that so many members went on to become radical abolitionists in the next few decades leads one to believe that the colonization movement led to the conversion of these men to more drastic beliefs.

The American Colonization Society founded the nation of Liberia in 1822 as a place to settle freedmen. Its capital Monrovia is the only foreign capital named after a U.S. president.

During the 1830's the abolitionist movement took a more radical turn. The idea of a gradual ending of slavery was abandoned for the goal of immediate emancipation. Exactly why this change occurred is a debated point, and as with any large social movement made up of so many individuals it is extremely difficult to pinpoint exact causes. The eminent Lincoln scholar David H. Donald provoked a storm of controversy when he suggested that the change could be explained simply by stereotypical youthful rebellion.[12]

Every generation seems to think that theirs is the most unique and revolutionary. The world always seems to be changing and a golden age being left further in the past. To those descendants of New England Puritans in the early 1830's setting out on careers as clergymen and missionaries, it must truly have seemed a world traveling in the wrong direction. The country, especially pious New England, was consumed with the acquisition of material wealth. Jacksonian democracy could only be described as revolutionary and for many New England Protestants was truly the "reign of King Mob" with the Democratic Party appealing to the lowest common denominator, the drunken illiterates of the frontier and the rapidly growing cities. How else could one explain the presence of a duel fighting slave owner in the White House?

These young religious men found themselves increasingly unable to take positions as ministers in isolated New England communities. There was, however, more opportunity and more demand for moral crusaders. Revivalism broke out across the country as did a growing sense of a need to reform society. Older generations denigrated the movement that led to hundreds of new Christian denominations, most of which were led by men with little or no education. Although a strong voice and the "Holy Spirit" might be all you needed to preach on the frontier, New England had a more organized system. The demands of this religious reawakening did open up the Congregationalist seminaries to men who a generation earlier would have been excluded because they were not from the elite sect of society. These new ministers also found themselves in vocations that had not existed for that earlier generation. Rather than taking their places in the pulpit, they became editors of newspapers, school teachers, agents for newly created benevolent societies and ministers at large. They were the nation's first full time social activists.[13]

The 1820's also saw the beginning of a wave of reform movements. No institution, from education, health care to the treatment of the mentally ill, was safe from the eyes of the early nineteenth century reformer. Alcohol consumption and prison systems also attracted a great deal of attention. There have been countless volumes on the origins of these movements. The sense of patriotism that emerged following the War of 1812 motivated many to strive to make the nation a more perfect place. God had obviously played a role in the country's unlikely success and if its citizens refused to be their brother's keeper we were obviously unworthy of Divine influence.

William Lloyd Garrison

William Lloyd Garrison was born in 1805 in Newbury Port, Massachusetts. He was the fourth child of a struggling housekeeper whose husband had abandoned her when Garrison was two. At thirteen his mother secured him an apprenticeship at the local newspaper. In 1826, Garrison went out on his own, editing a series of newspapers in New England. These early attempts were unsuccessful. While most editors were concerned about the number of subscribers Garrison used his papers as a tool of moral crusade.

This changed when he found his audience. In 1828, he joined the *National Philanthropist*, a Boston paper, where his style of moral writing was appreciated. In the same year, he coedited the weekly Baltimore paper, *Genius of Universal Emancipation*. His calls for immediate emancipation and his attacks on slaveholders landed him in a Baltimore jail. His time incarcerated made him a celebrity in the abolitionist community.

In 1831, Garrison started his own paper, *The Liberator*. Garrison, through his paper, called for immediate emancipation and complete civil rights for former slaves. If that was not radical enough in the 1830's, Garrison also called for the equality of the sexes.

Garrison often received death threats. He barely escaped an angry mob in Boston in 1836. His newspapers were burned by U.S. Post Offices in the South and possession of *The Liberator* in some parts of the South was a hanging offense.

Before the war, Garrison believed the Free States should secede from the Union instead of keeping common cause with slaveholders. With the election of Lincoln, Garrison became strongly pro-Union. He believed that was the best way to end slavery.

After the war he slipped into a quiet retirement. He only occasionally wrote pro Radical Republican articles for newspapers. He died in New York City in 1879, his life's work completed.

Arguments have been made that the growth of an urban middle class created a population that simply had the time to become involved. There has also been a great deal written about the changing role of women in society in the early nineteenth century. Upper middle class women would be a driving force behind most of these reform movements.[14]

One of the major reasons for the explosion of reform movements during this period was the abandonment of the Calvinist belief in predestination during the Second Great Awakening by most Protestant denominations. This brought about the return of the pre Calvin idea that the afterlife was merit based. Obviously, if your actions on Earth would guarantee either eternal reward or damnation, what better way to earn the former than to serve your fellow man by reforming society? If you were looking to serve "the least of these my brothers," who better than the enslaved African?

Events in the year 1831 would both make slavery the focus of these reformers and make Southerners much more concerned about the effects of an abolitionist movement. Only a few years earlier, former slave David Walker, wrote his now infamous *Appeal to the Colored Citizens of the World.* Living and writing in Boston, Walker called for slaves to rise up and kill their owners. More troubling than the words of Walker was the Nat Turner Revolt in Southampton County, Virginia in 1831. The largest slave revolt in American history was the nightmare come true for Southerners whether they owned slaves or not. As all Southerners knew, when a violent slave insurrection occurred the slaves would not bother to ask where the sympathies of their potential victim lie. The year 1831 also saw sixty thousand slaves on the sugar plantations of British Jamaica rise up in an unsuccessful revolt.[15]

In 1832, a war of secession almost broke out thirty years before the Civil War. Often called the Nullification Crisis, South Carolina, under the leadership of the father of Southern Nationalism, John C. Calhoun, attempted to nullify a U.S. law and threatened to leave the Union. Because of the lack of support from the other Southern states and the aggressive action taken by President Andrew Jackson, South Carolina relented and open conflict was avoided. Although the law in question dealt with protective tariffs, state sovereignty was the real issue and South Carolinians were very vocal that States' Rights was the surest way to defend slavery.[16]

To men like William Lloyd Garrison, Wendell Phillips and Theodore Weld, the events of 1831 were sure signs that society was on the verge of collapse. One did not have to look too closely to see that slavery was the cause of this unrest and only immediate abolition could save the nation. The abolitionists of the 1830's were radical compared to those of earlier decades. They had abandoned the idea of gradual emancipation and called for immediate and total emancipation. This more comprehensive goal came about not only because this was a more reform minded generation, but perhaps, more than anything, because they saw the intellectual inconsistency in gradual emancipation. It is difficult to make the argument that slavery is wrong while offering a solution that would leave men and women currently enslaved in that situation for the rest of their lives. The argument that slavery is wrong and has to stop now was simply a much easier argument to accept intellectually. With culture, tradition and even economics against you, the moral and intellectual arguments could not be abandoned.

The one and only political issue for these men and women was the immediate and complete end of slavery. There was no room to compromise when it came to this moral evil. The radical abolitionists made up only a minority of the population even in the New England states, but they were an extremely vocal group. In Philadelphia in December 1833, American abolitionists formed the American Anti-Slavery Society. With only sixty two members, they called for an immediate end to slavery based on the belief that every person should be "secure in his right to his own body, to the products of his own labor, to the protection of the law" and "to the common advantages of society."[17] From these humble beginnings, the American Anti-Slavery Society grew to over two hundred thousand members.

THE ANTI-ABOLITIONIST MOVEMENT

Slave owning Southerners, and those who aspired to be, were already concerned that the Federal government was going to interfere with their Peculiar Institution. As abolitionists became more radical with their demand for an immediate end to slavery, Southerners, out of fear, became more radical as well.

As stated earlier, it is impossible to assign a single motivation to millions of people. However, one is hard pressed not to see slavery as the main or major underlying issue in Southern politics in the forty years that predated the American Civil War. The defense of slavery was the issue that allowed most Southerners to put aside their differences and unite behind a common cause.

The defense that emerged to counter the growing tide of abolitionism was far from the almost apologetic defense of slavery offered by previous generations. Slavery, it was argued by Southern politicians, editors and the slaveholding class, was a positive good. Africans were better off enslaved than living free in their homeland. It was a "benevolent institution, and the happiest and best ever designed for a laboring population."[18] The wage labor system of Northeastern factories was unfavorably compared to the South's Peculiar Institution. It was suggested that the Northern working class would be better off under a Southern style labor system. James Hammond argued in his famous "Cotton Is King" speech in Congress that both North and South had slaves but that the South's "slaves are hired for life and well compensated; there is no starvation, no begging, no want of employment among our people, and not too much employment either." Meanwhile the slaves in the North "are hired by the day, not cared for, and scantily compensated, which may be proved in the most painful manner, at any hour in any street in any of your large towns."[19]

Slavery, it was argued, also protected democracy. Without it, the working classes with their superior numbers would vote in radical populist change. In 1850, George Fitzhugh wrote *Slavery Justified*. He was born in northern Virginia to a family of modest means. Fitzhugh failed at every vocation he tried until he ventured into the world of radical proslavery literature. In *Slavery Justified*, Fitzhugh argued that the ideas of liberty and equality were relatively new. That in itself is not a radical argument. "All men are created equal" was a new and shocking statement when Thomas Jefferson wrote it only seventy four years earlier. Abraham Lincoln in his famous Gettysburg Address would make the same argument that the idea of freedom was a radical new idea that deserved to be defended. Where Fitzhugh disagreed with those two great men was in his belief that liberty and equality were a failed experiment. Fitzhugh saw in the North, mobs, unions, strikes, armed resistance to the law and "jealousy of the rich by the poor."[20] All these things Fitzhugh argued were absent in the peaceful quiet South. Fitzhugh, as did many Southerners, saw the Peculiar Institution as an American feudal system that guaranteed an orderly society.

Race, of course, was also an important part of the proslavery argument. These racial arguments couched themselves in scientific terms but, at best, were pseudo-scientific. Africans were believed to be an inferior race. According to the *New Orleans Medical and Surgical Journal*, Africans' brains were smaller and were more directly wired to their nerves, insinuating that their actions were not necessarily the result of conscious thought, but were more primal. This also caused Africans to suffer from some peculiar diseases. "Drapetomania" was believed to cause some slaves to want to run away and "dsaethesia" was associated with what was referred to as "rascality."[21] Africans were not believed to be inferior in all ways. It was the prevailing belief that they were better suited to work in hot, unhealthy climates. This was a dubious honor indeed considering the reward was a lifetime laboring in cotton fields and on sugar cane plantations. Although race and class arguments were not necessarily exclusive, it was racial factors, proslavery advocates would argue, that earned Africans their place at the bottom of the class structure.

The proslavery arguments that emerged in response to radical abolitionism and the ideas of Southern nationalism are difficult to separate and one can quickly find oneself in a "chicken or the egg" type thought experiment. If slavery was a positive good that was under assault from outside forces, then a Southern nation based on the principles of a slave owning society was the natural answer. Furthermore, those whose end goal was a Southern nation for reasons other than slavery found that slavery and the fear of abolitionists was the one issue that unified most Southerners.

Arguments for the necessity of Southern institutes of higher learning fell on deaf ears unless presented as a defense against the youth of the South having "their minds poisoned by fanatical teaching and influences against the institution of slavery," which kept "the flesh-eating, blood drinking, gluttonous, lazy debased, brutal hordes" under control.[22] There was little call for purely Southern literature, except from a small minority, until "the pure stream of literature has been corrupted by the turbid waters of Abolition."[23]

POPULATION GROWTH AND POLITICAL SHIFT

Although prior to John Brown the vast majority of abolitionists were pacifists, the great fear of Southerners was that abolitionism would cause slave revolts. Surrounded and outnumbered by slaves, the poisoned meal or the fire set in the night was as great an anxiety as a general uprising like Nat Turner's. Slaves, according to Southerners, were not smart enough to realize they were being forced into bondage unless they were told this by an abolitionist. The danger of a single abolitionist spreading their vile message of equality was bad enough, but the damage that could be done if the central government fell into the hands of those people was unthinkable. As the Civil War approached, the danger of an abolitionist dominated government grew.

For the first decades of the nation's history America's population shifted south and westward. This loss of control by the North caused New England Federalists to consider secession in the closing days of the War of 1812. Just the suggestion of separation ended the Federalists as an organized party when the war ended on a successful note. The same kind of demographic shift was now affecting the South. In 1790 the population of the nation was almost evenly split between North and South. By 1820 the South was only forty six percent of the population. This may seem like an insignificant change but it translated to the South holding only forty two percent of the seats in the U.S. House of Representatives and a similar huge disadvantage in the Electoral College. Only the fact that Southern states could count three out of every five slaves in the census kept the numbers as close as they were. This trend showed no sign of changing. Ironically, slavery was both the cause of and the solution to this problem. Free societies grow faster than those with a slave labor force. When immigration is part of the picture, the difference is even more extreme. Immigrants moved to where they could find unskilled work. That work in the South was done by slaves thus limiting the opportunities for new arrivals. Westward expansion of slavery was therefore necessary to keep up with the population growth in Free States but also to maintain the all-important tie in the Senate.

THE MISSOURI COMPROMISE

The first crisis over the expansion of slavery came with Missouri's application for statehood in 1819. Northern congressmen were probably not as concerned with the moral issues associated with the expansion of slavery as they were with the political issues. The fight over Missouri had a great deal more to do with the desires of the residents of the U.S. capital than it did with the rest of the nation. Although the South was in the minority in the House of Representatives and the Electoral College, Northern politicians felt that they were already overrepresented because of the Three Fifths Clause in the Constitution. If Missouri became a state, the slaveholding states would hold a two seat advantage in the U.S. Senate. The New York delegation put forward the demand that Missouri ban slavery in their constitution before it would get support for its bid for statehood. Southerners of course, were outraged. The fear was that if Northern states could force Missouri to emancipate their slaves the established states might be next.[24]

The Southern politicians were not as outraged as their successors would be in the 1850's. The issue was settled with the Missouri Compromise. Maine was approved for statehood at the same time, maintaining the balance in the Senate and the territory north of what became known as the Missouri Compromise Line. This was not an even split, and with it the majority of the Louisiana Purchase was made off limits to slavery. This passed with a majority of Southern votes. The sectional crisis was obviously still a few years off. There were those, however, who saw this as the beginning of a dangerous conflict. Even while Congress celebrated the passage of the Missouri Compromise as the solution to a growing crisis, an older generation, typified by Thomas Jefferson, believed it all but guaranteed the coming of a civil war and the destruction of the Union. Jefferson felt it was only drawing the battle line of the coming destructive war.[25]

THE BIRTH OF POLITICAL PARTIES

Another man who saw the growing dangers of sectionalism was future President Martin Van Buren. From 1815 until 1828, there were really no political parties. The Federalists and the Democratic-Republicans were proto-parties for lack of a better term. There was no organization like later political parties. When the Federalists were destroyed from self-inflicted wounds including the Alien and Sedition Acts (1798) and the infamous Hartford Convention, there was no need for the Democratic-Republicans.

With no other political enemies, political competition became defined as the North versus the South or Slave States versus Free. This divide was much more dangerous than the political factions that George Washington had famously warned about in his 1796 farewell address. Van Buren, working with presidential candidate Andrew Jackson, organized what is considered the first modern American political party. According to the New York born Van Buren, the return to a two party system would furnish "a complete antidote to sectional prejudices by producing counteracting feelings."[26] Had other factors not so heated the sectional issues this may have been successful. It did work until after the war with Mexico. The Missouri Compromise was perhaps given more credit than it deserved for the lack of an armed sectional crisis by 1850.

Initially, the political landscape was divided along the lines of personality. The Democrats were the party of Jackson. The entire Democratic Party machine, which thanks to Van Buren was rather complex, worked to elect Jackson in 1828. Their opponents could simply be described as anti-Jackson. They took the name Whigs. In British politics the Whigs were traditionally the party opposed to the monarch having too much power. The modern American Whigs took the name as both an allusion to the American Revolution and to make the not so subtle point that Jackson was a potential tyrant.

Although he redefined the role of the president as the leader of the nation, Jackson dispelled the fears of his critics and in the tradition of George Washington went home after his second term. The aging Jackson was still very active in the party he came to love until his death in 1845.

When Martin Van Buren replaced Jackson as president and head of the Democratic Party, neither he nor his opponents could demand loyalty based on personality alone. The parties came to represent the two sides of the debate that dated back to the 1787 Constitutional Convention. In the tradition of the Federalists, the Whigs believed in a strong central government and a liberal interpretation of the idea of the implied powers of the Constitution to improve the infrastructure of the country. The Democrats, in the tradition of Thomas Jefferson's Democratic-Republicans, believed in a weak central government and a strict constructionist view of the Constitution.

Although each of the parties was stronger in certain regions than in others, they were by no means sectional parties. On regional issues, candidates could confidently adopt the position of the local constituency. Only every four years did the parties have to present a united front to their voters. As the Whigs were strongest in the North, especially in the east, they typically ran candidates from the West. The Kentuckian, Henry Clay was the Whig presidential candidate twice. The Whigs had the most success with Western war heroes. Generals William Henry Harrison and Zachary Taylor were the only two Whigs elected president. If the candidate was a slave owner, like Taylor, so that Southern slave owners could be confident in a policy of noninterference with their property, it was an added bonus.

After the presidency of Tennessean James K. Polk in 1844–1848, the Democratic Party followed suit and nominated a string of candidates from Northern Free States. Northerners could vote for a Democratic presidential candidate confident that they were not supporting a party whose major purpose was the defense of the Peculiar Institution, just as Southerners could vote for the Whig candidate confident that they were not supporting an abolitionist party.

This may have worked and sectional tensions might have been postponed for much longer had it not been for war with Mexico and the addition of more than a half million square miles of new territory. After Texas' defeat of Mexico and the tenuous peace that followed, Texas was an independent slaveholding republic on America's southwestern border. As much as modern Texans take pride in their short lived status as a republic, what Texans wanted in 1836 was to enter the Union.

Van Buran's plan to ease sectional tension did not survive Texas. With an election coming Jackson did not touch the Texas issue until after the votes were cast. His fear was that any move toward annexation would make the Democratic Party appear to be the party of Southern slaveholders. Even after the election of his chosen successor as president, Jackson took only the tepid position of supporting diplomatic recognition.[27]

The financial crisis of 1837 consumed much of Van Buren's administration and led to the election of the first Whig president, William Henry Harrison in 1840. Unfortunately for the Whigs, Harrison was the shortest serving president in U.S. history, dying just over a month after his inauguration. After a potential Constitutional crisis, Vice President John Tyler became president. A Virginian with very strong Democratic leanings, he was chosen as vice president to help win Southern votes. As president, Tyler is remembered for annexing Texas at the very end of his sole term. This was a controversial move that his successor, Democrat James K. Polk, would have probably made anyway. The annexation of Texas led directly to war with Mexico. Polk's critics accuse him of deliberately bringing about war in order to gain territory. This is probably a bit harsh as Polk

In exchange for eighteen million dollars the United States was granted 525,000 square miles of territory. Those living in the newly acquired land were allowed to remain and become U.S. citizens or return to Mexico and receive land grants equal to what they lost. Most remained in the United States.

really wanted to purchase from Mexico the land the U.S. would eventually acquire through war. Although European experts predicted a disaster for the American military, the war was a decisive military victory for the United States. In the treaty of Guadeloupe Hidalgo America gained what is today the U.S. southwest.

SLAVERY AND THE TERRITORIES

Even before the acquisition of the Western land, the expansion of slavery into the new territory was being debated. David Wilmot, a Democratic from Pennsylvania, put forward what would quickly come to be known as the Wilmot Proviso. Attached to the appropriations bill that granted money for the purchase of territory from Mexico, the proviso called for slavery to be banned in all the territory purchased with those funds. Wilmot had mixed motivations as did most Northern Democrats who voted with him. The growing sense among Northerners that slavery was wrong cannot be discounted. Although a man like Wilmot was not so radical as to subscribe to William Garrison's *The Liberator*, when given an opportunity to vote yes or no to the issue of slavery, he opposed the Peculiar Institution. Wilmot, however, was also looking out for the good of the Democratic Party. President Polk's ties to the South seemed stronger than party loyalty. If Northern voters came to believe that Polk's war with Mexico was fought for the purpose of expanding slavery, it might well mean the end of the Democratic Party in the Free States. If the Democrats themselves, in modern political parlance, got ahead of the issue, they might be able to limit the damage Polk and the Southern Democrats would do to the party.

The Wilmot Proviso had no chance of becoming law. The Northern dominated House of Representatives passed it several times but it would always die in the evenly divided Senate. Even had a few Southern Senators crossed the line and voted with Wilmot, it would never have been signed into law by President Polk or any of his successors in the White House.

When the Mexican war ended with an overwhelming American victory, the legal status of new American territory was no longer a strictly academic question. The issue of statehood came up much faster than anyone could have predicted. To those that believed that it was America's

"Manifest Destiny" to stretch from "sea to shining sea," the discovery of gold in California must have been evidence of Divine favor. The Spanish and then the Mexicans had explored and lived on the land for more than three hundred years and Americans within a year of occupation had struck gold. The potential wealth drew over three hundred thousand people to the new territory, not only from the rest of America, but from Europe and Asia as well. Sleepy sundrenched California almost instantly became large enough that statehood was desired by its residents.

Although the issue of political control of the Senate and thus the national government was a strong motivating factor, many Southerners came to believe that the expansion of slavery into the territories was key to its survival. Modern economists have downplayed the importance of the expansion of slavery. Whether it needed to expand or not does not really matter – all that is important was that they believed it did. Northerners also came to believe that the expansion of slavery into the territories would limit their opportunities. Free labor would have a great deal of difficulty competing with the initial importation of cheap slave labor.[28]

Southerners' belief that slavery depended on its expansion into the territories was buoyed by the argument that abolitionists and, eventually, Northern politicians made that the first step in the destruction of slavery was obviously to stop its spread into the territories. If this was the chosen battlefront of the slavery question, then that is where Southerners would fight.

Newly elected President Zachary Taylor had a simple solution for the Whig party on the question of the expansion of slavery into the territories. Taylor had been the perfect candidate for the Whig party in 1848. He was the conquering hero. Born in Virginia and raised in Kentucky, Taylor owned a two thousand acre plantation with eighty slaves near Baton Rouge, Louisiana. Voters in the South knew their slaves were safe under Taylor and the Northern voters were convinced that he would follow the party line on the major issues. Having never held elected office nor made any statements on public policy, Taylor could be whatever the voters wanted him to be. Taylor's solution was to avoid the entire territory question by having the vast majority of the new lands apply for statehood before Congress could debate the issue. If the acquired land were never organized into formal territory then the question of slavery in those areas would not be a Federal issue but would be a State concern.[29]

Unlike the vast majority of the men debating this issue, Taylor was not only familiar with the nature of this new land but as a plantation owner understood that economy. Regardless of what the government did, slavery would not be imported into the southwest. The conditions would simply not make it profitable. The argument over slavery in the new territory was simply bluster. Taylor believed that if the issue was a *fait accompli* by the time Congress reconvened, there would not be a political fight.

We can only speculate about the success of Taylor's plan. California and New Mexico did not cooperate with a quick application as Taylor had hoped and the issue of slavery fell right into the lap of Congress. The issue of slavery had the potential of tearing both political parties apart along sectional lines. It was not just the territorial question that was dividing the Free States from the Slave States. Northern politicians were demanding the end of the slave trade in Washington D.C. A person could stand on the steps of the Capitol building and hear humans being sold at auction. For a nation founded on Republican principles this was unacceptable. Although this was an issue that affected few Southerners, to accept a ban on slavery in the District of Columbia was to admit that slavery was not a positive moral good. Southerners were demanding a tougher fugitive slave law. Southern slave owners and their agents were finding it more and more difficult to recover their lost slave property. Their efforts were constantly being frustrated not only by Northern citizens but by local officials and law enforcement. Southerners wanted a Federal law that gave stiff penalties for those officials who refused to aid in the recovery of runaways. This was a law that Northerners found especially repulsive. Bounty hunters were an abusive group who often kidnapped free blacks and took them South to slavery. Few slave owners cared if they got the right man.[30]

THE COMPROMISE OF 1850

In 1850, with Taylor's solution for the territorial issues dead, Senator Henry Clay brought forward his own plan. The elderly Kentuckian had helped craft the Missouri Compromise and had written the agreement that had ended the Nullification Crisis twenty years earlier. Clay believed that a compromise that dealt with all the major issues between the two sections could end the growing hostility. The old Kentuckian found that the opponents of compromise were much stronger and more numerous than they had been thirty years earlier. Clay's proposed compromise failed quickly in Congress. His only support was Southern Whigs and Northern Democrats, two groups that were the most concerned about national unity and thus party unity.

President Taylor was as much an obstacle to the passage of the compromise as was sectional tension. The old soldier had authored his own compromise and refused to consider any other options. No congressmen would take the political risk of voting for a controversial bill if there was no way the president would sign it. That Clay was prematurely taking credit for the compromise did not make his rival any more willing to budge.

On July 9, 1850 President Zachary Taylor died in his bed in the White House. He was only the second U.S. president to die in office. After attending the groundbreaking ceremony at the Washington Monument in the brutal heat and then perhaps overdoing it on a dairy based dessert, the sixty six year old Taylor died of what doctors at the time called Cholera Morbus. His death of symptoms that were consistent with poisoning at a time of heightened sectional tension would fuel conspiracy theories that would eventually lead to exhumation in 1991.

Millard Fillmore became the new President of the United States. The New York Whig was a strong supporter of the Compromise. He replaced Taylor's entire cabinet with more moderate men. Clay also left the capital. The Washington D.C. summer had seriously affected the old man's health and he did not want to leave the city the way Taylor had. Stephen Douglas, a Democrat from Illinois took up the leadership of the Compromise in Congress. Working together, Fillmore and Douglas were able to pass the Compromise of 1850. They broke the omnibus bill into separate parts. This allowed the moderates who supported the bill to vote for each part and the partisans to vote only for those parts of the bill they already supported.[31]

Those who had championed the Compromise of 1850 believed that they had solved the nation's sectional crisis. They thought that their Compromise, like the Missouri Compromise thirty years earlier, would put these issues to rest for a generation. They could not have been more wrong. The peace lasted less than three years.

BLEEDING KANSAS

A number of issues led to what was dubbed by the press "Bleeding Kansas." Party politics, the transcontinental railroad and of course the expansion of slave territory all played a role. With the rapid growth of California and the rest of the West Coast, a railroad connecting the nation's two coasts seemed not only a great economic opportunity but also a governmental necessity. If the two halves of the nation were not connected, California, with its growing wealth, and the East might go their separate ways. There were also national security issues involving the nation's ability to move its small army quickly across the country. The economic benefits were countless. Not only would it link West Coast money to East Coast goods but the possibility of the Europe/Asia trade traveling by train from New York to San Francisco could make both those ports the busiest and most financially profitable in the world.[32]

Although the railroad would be a private enterprise, it would need government assistance. Not only would the railroad need to be given the land that the railroad itself would be built on, the company would need land near the tracks that could be sold to raise the necessary capital. Since it was the government giving away the land, it controlled the decision about where the railroad would be built. The very influential Illinois Democrat Stephen Douglas wanted the railroad to begin in Chicago. This would not only benefit his constituents but would make the land he owned in southern Wisconsin a great deal more valuable. The problem with the northern route that Douglas desired was that it would necessitate the government organizing territory which would not have been necessary if a southern route had been chosen.[33]

The new territory that would be set on the path to statehood was north of the Missouri Compromise Line and would thus be made up of Free States. This would further throw off the balance in the Senate to the disadvantage of the Slave States. Southern congressmen had no reason to vote for Douglas' railroad bill. The Illinois senator adjusted his bill to give them exactly what they wanted.

After the admission of Texas and Arkansas, there was nowhere left for slavery to extend. It was for this reason that newly elected President Franklin Pierce pushed for expansion into the Caribbean and Central America. Douglas altered his bill from creating a single Nebraska territory to creating a dual Kansas and Nebraska Territory. The status of the new territories would be determined by the territorial legislators who were chosen by the people. This came to be known as popular sovereignty. While Douglas believed that voters would likely create two free territories, Southerners believed that they were being given Kansas.

Both political parties thought they could benefit from a little controversy. To Democrats, like Douglas, the debate would be strictly Whig versus Democrat and would end internal party bickering. Although Douglas' bill, for all intents and purposes revoked the Missouri Compromise Line, Whig Senator Archibald Dixon of Kentucky proposed the bold political move of altering the Senate version of the Kansas/Nebraska Act to officially revoke the Line. This would allow Southern Whigs to campaign in 1856 as the true defenders of slavery. Northern Whigs could rally their supporters against the bill they would still portray as Douglas'. It would take some serious political gymnastics for the party to run two opposite campaigns at the same time but the Whig leadership was confident.[34]

In the end, neither party realized just how explosive the issue had become. Northern voters would punish both parties for the passage of the Kansas/Nebraska Act. It led to the destruction of the Whig party and the Northern Democrats seriously lost influence among their voters. There were ninety one seats in the House of Representatives held by Northern Democrats when the Act was passed. After the next election there were only twenty five.

The violence that broke out was also unexpected. Midwestern farmers who came to Kansas for the land and New Englanders who came for the dual benefits of the land and the opportunity to help stop the spread of slavery outnumbered Southern proslavery settlers as Douglas expected. However, during the election hundreds of armed proslavery Missourians flooded across the border into Kansas. They seized polling places and insured a proslavery Territorial legislature. Anti-slavery settlers who came to be known as Free-Staters formed their own government in Lawrence. President Pierce saw the Free-Staters as an illegitimate illegal government and ordered the U.S. Marshall to disband it. Pierce's orders were carried out with a great deal of violence by a small army of newly deputized Missouri border ruffians. The Free-Staters struck back against proslavery settlers. What followed became all-out war in Kansas, and although pale compared to what was about to come, the violence in Kansas was described as civil war at the time. By the time the U.S. Army restored order more than fifty people had been killed in Kansas.

The growing split between the Northern and Southern wings of the Democratic Party and the decline of the Whig party opened the way for the creation of a new political party. For many Northerners, events in Kansas demonstrated that there needed to be a change in the political order. The question was, to which of the two newly formed parties would these disillusioned voters turn?

Founded in 1854 in either Wisconsin or Michigan depending on who you ask, the Republican Party had the strongest support among Midwesterners. The party's main issue was preventing the spread of slavery into new territories. The violence in Kansas had offered a serious political advantage to the new party.

The major challenge to the Republicans was the Native American Party, or after 1855 simply called the American Party, they were more commonly known as the Know Nothings. Both groups agreed that the current state of American politics was flawed. Where they disagreed was the cause. To the Know Nothings the problem was the professional politicians and the immigrants that voted for them. The waves of immigrants that came in the 1840's and 1850's seemed to the Know Nothings to refuse to assimilate either culturally or politically. That a growing percentage of these new arrivals were Catholic made matters worse. The Know Nothings had the dual fear that the immigrants would either vote as they were ordered by the Pope or would become the basis of the kind of corrupt political machines that would dominate major American cities for the rest of the century.

The Know Nothings never gained much traction in the South or Midwest simply because there were not a lot of immigrants in those areas. However, they had enough followers in the Northeast to make impressive gains in the 1854 and 1856 elections. Events in Kansas and on the floor of the U.S. Senate would convince Northerners that the slave owning aristocracies of the South were a bigger threat to American democracy than Catholics and foreigners.

The day after the attack on Lawrence, Republican Senator Charles Sumner was beaten savagely by South Carolina Representative Preston Brooks on the Senate Floor. Sumner had given a passionate anti-slavery speech that Brooks had interpreted as a personal attack against his relative Senator Andrew Butler also of South Carolina. The premeditated attack nearly killed Sumner. To Northerners, this violent response to a political speech was the perfect example of Southern Tyranny.[35]

1856 PRESIDENTIAL ELECTION

These dual attacks occurred just a month before the first Republican national convention giving the young party a great deal of hope going into their first presidential election. Taking a page from the Whig playbook, the Republicans nominated John C. Fremont. Like Harrison and Taylor, Fremont was a popular and famous soldier and also a Westerner. Like the two generals, the forty three year old was also a political novice. His fame came through his service with the U.S. Army Corps of Topographical Engineers. The "Pathfinder" had mapped the way for Western settlers. Gold was discovered on the California ranch he had just purchased making him one of the richest men in the country.

The Democrats ran Pennsylvania moderate James Buchanan against Fremont. He was a veteran politician who had recently served as the American ambassador to Great Britain. This gave him the advantage over other Democratic hopefuls of having nothing at all to do with the Kansas/Nebraska Act. One other advantage Buchanan had in the general election was the very plausible and vocal threat that the Southern states would secede if a Republican was elected president. When the votes were cast enough voters decided that it was simply not worth the risk. More men, however, voted against Buchanan than voted for him. Had the Know

James Buchanan

James Buchanan was born near Mercersburg, Pennsylvania in 1791. His father was a wealthy merchant and farmer who emigrated from Ireland at the end of the American Revolution. James Buchanan was the oldest son of eleven children.

Buchanan graduated from Dickenson College and began practicing law at the age of twenty two. He joined a militia unit during the War of 1812. Buchanan was the last president born in the eighteenth century and the last president to be a veteran of the War of 1812, although his unit never saw action during that war.

At twenty three, Buchanan entered public service. He was elected to the Pennsylvania House of Representatives where he served for five years. He maintained his very successful law practice which allowed him to accumulate a sizeable fortune.

Around 1819, Buchanan began seeing Ann Caroline Coleman, the daughter of a wealthy iron merchant. The father did not approve of Buchanan, and the match probably would not have worked even had she not died at an early age. A distraught Buchanan vowed he would never marry. He was the only president who never married.

In 1820, Buchanan was elected to the U.S. House of Representatives where he would spend his next ten years. As a reward for his work on behalf of Andrew Jackson's presidential campaign in Pennsylvania, Buchanan was made ambassador to Russia. He was successful as a diplomat, helping through an important trade agreement between the two countries.

On his return, Pennsylvania sent him to Washington as their Senator. He served in the Senate until President James Polk appointed him Secretary of State. With a war with Mexico and a potential war with Great Britain, this was a difficult post. Buchanan handled it ably but found himself turned out with the election of Zachary Taylor and the Whig party in 1848.

When the Democrats returned to the White House in 1852, Buchanan was given the prestigious post of Ambassador to Great Britain. This position gave him an advantage in securing the Democratic nomination in 1856. He could bear no share of the blame for the Kansas/Nebraska fiasco as there was an entire ocean between him and the decisions that led to that bloodshed.

In 1856, he narrowly defeated the first Republican presidential candidate, John C. Fremont to become the fifteenth president of the United States. It was an unhappy and stressful four years. When Lincoln was elected in 1860 Buchanan was relieved to hand over the reins of power. Not only did he have a sectional crisis to deal with, but his reckless foreign policy almost brought about conflict with Britain, Spain, Mexico and even Paraguay. Perhaps though, he hoped a foreign conflict might unite the country as Lincoln's Secretary of State suggested in the first month of the Republican administration.

In retirement, Buchanan rarely left his Pennsylvania home. He was not a popular figure in the North and was blamed, not unfairly, for the poor position the Union found itself at the beginning of the war. His 1868 memoirs blamed the Civil War on Lincoln and the Republicans – he and his party were blameless. He died the same year and has since haunted the bottom of the list in any ranking of U.S. presidents.

Nothings not run a viable candidate, former president Millard Fillmore, this election and history could have been much different.

Many Whigs were cautious about joining a new party. One such Whig politician who was concerned about attaching his political future to the Republicans was Abraham Lincoln. A self-educated frontier lawyer, Lincoln had served a single term in the U.S. House of Representatives. Like many Northerners, what seemed like Whig acquiescence to the Kansas/Nebraska Act convinced Lincoln that his loyalties should change.[36]

LINCOLN–DOUGLAS DEBATES

The Illinois lawyer's first opportunity as a Republican was the impossible task of challenging Democratic Party titan Stephen Douglas for his senate seat. Although Lincoln was defeated, the campaign would greatly benefit his career and the Republican Party. Lincoln forced his opponent into a series of impromptu debates across the state. The transcripts were carried in newspapers across the country. Not only did the debates make Lincoln a known figure but because he expressed the Republican ideology better than anyone else, he helped Republicans win elections across the North. The debates also forced Douglas to take public positions that would hurt him in the 1860 presidential election. If Douglas came out for popular sovereignty on the slavery issue, his support among Northern voters would diminish significantly. If he came across in any way as anti-slavery it would be impossible for him to get enough Southern support to gain the Democratic nomination. Douglas emerged from the debates having damaged his political reputation with both Northern and Southern voters. That should not, however, reflect negatively on Douglas' political ability. It is highly unlikely that any candidate could have said anything that would have made them acceptable to both North and South in 1860.

1860 PRESIDENTIAL ELECTION

In 1860 Southern Democrats decided that the election of another "dough faced" politician like Pierce or Buchanan was unacceptable. The time had come for a candidate who was unapologetically proslavery. Their ideal candidate was John C. Breckenridge. The Kentuckian and sitting vice president was from a slave owning family and would eventually serve as a Confederate general and as the Confederate Secretary of War. To the Northern Democratic Party leadership Breckenridge could not have been a worse choice. They believed that it was highly unlikely that he could win without the support of Northern voters. If the Pennsylvanian Buchanan had not carried his home state he would not have won. The thirty nine year old Kentuckian was not nearly as radical as the elements of the Democratic Party that nominated him.

The two factions could not agree on a candidate and the Democratic Party split. Holding a new convention the extremist wing of the party nominated Breckenridge and adopted a radical proslavery platform. The rest of the party nominated Stephen Douglas. With two Democrats in the race it was highly unlikely that either candidate could secure a majority. Perhaps Northern Democrats hoped that Southerners would come to their senses prior to the election and withdraw Breckenridge.

Southern Democrats hoped that with no one candidate taking a majority in the Electoral College, the election would be thrown into the House of Representatives. The Northern congressmen could be more open to a Breckenridge presidency than the voting public. There were Southern radicals who believed that the South must break away from the Union. Electing a Democratic president whether it was Douglas or Breckinridge was only forestalling the inevitable, the end of the Peculiar Institution and the destruction of the Southern way of life. The only way the South would be safe from the tyranny of the Northern majority was to leave the Union and form its own nation. The election of an abolitionist Republican might be just the push to convince the majority of Southerners that disunion was the only option.[37]

John C. Breckinridge's hope that the 1860 election would be thrown into the House was further buoyed by the entrance of John Bell of Tennessee as the fourth candidate in this election. He narrowly beat Sam Houston of Texas for the nomination of the Constitutional Union Party. Made up mostly of Southern Whigs and Know Nothings the party's platform was anti-sectional and promised to follow the strict letter of the Constitution. They were not strong enough to actually win. The leadership hoped they could cause the election to be decided by the House of Representatives where a compromise could be reached.

For only their second presidential election the Republicans nominated Abraham Lincoln. Although he had gained national attention with his debates against Douglas, Lincoln was not a frontrunner when the Republican convention opened in Chicago. His popularity was mostly in the Midwest. The frontrunner, William H. Seward, had a number of issues that would make it difficult for him to win the general election. As the 1856 election had shown, the party needed Know Nothing votes to be successful. Lincoln had argued against the policies of the Know Nothing party in a way that would not drive their supporters away from the Republicans. Seward had bitterly attacked the nativists in speech and print.

That Seward was a New Yorker would hurt him in the Ohio Valley where the Kentucky born Lincoln would be strong.

As today, the country in 1860 had strong populist leanings and Lincoln's humble origins and success fueled by his own hard work would be very popular among the old Jacksonian Democrats. Lincoln was also a Whig in the tradition of Henry Clay and supported internal improvements such as roads, canals and dredging that would "encourage the development of the industrial interests of the whole country."[38] As history would bear out, the Republican convention made the right choice. Although Lincoln did not cast a vote for himself, enough other men did to make him the sixteenth President of the United States.[39]

Predictably Breckinridge took the Deep South. Bell took the Border States of Virginia, Tennessee and Kentucky. One can easily understand those states voting for the most moderate candidate considering nearly half of all Civil War battles would be fought in those three states. Lincoln won California, Oregon and made an almost clean sweep of the Northern states. That the new president had been elected without the support of a single Southern state, reinforced by the fact that Lincoln had not even appeared on the ballot in ten Southern states, made Southern fears of a tyranny based on a Northern majority seem much more imminent. In the end the choice by the Southern Democrats to nominate their own candidate and split the party mattered little. Had Lincoln only had one opponent, and everyone who voted against Lincoln had voted for the other candidate, Lincoln would still have won the election.

The election of Abraham Lincoln was the end of a chain of events that convinced enough Southerners that they should no longer be a part of the Union. On December 20, 1860 South Carolina declared it was no longer part of the United States. She was quickly followed by Mississippi and Florida. The events outlined in this chapter led to this secession crisis. It would be the events over the next five months concerning an unfinished fort inside Charleston harbor in South Carolina that would determine the nature of the Civil War itself.

NOTES

1 David Detzer, Allegiance, Fort Sumter, *Charleston and the Beginning of the Civil War* (New York: Harcourt, Inc., 2001) 272–273.

2 J. Watson Webb, *Declaration of the Immediate Causes Which Induce and Justify the Secession of South Carolina from the Federal Union* (Charleston: Evans and Cogswell, Printers to the Convention, 1860) 1.

3 U.S. Department of Commerce, Bureau of the Census, *Historical Statistics of the United States* (Washington D.C: U.S. Government Printing Office, 1975) volume 2, 899.

4 Jennifer Rycenga, "Quakers and Antislavery" in Peter Hinks and John McKivigan, Editors, *Encyclopedia of Antislavery and Abolition* (Westport: Greenwood Press, 2007) 550.

5 James Brewer Stewart, *Holy Warriors, the Abolitionists and American Slavery* (New York: Hill and Wang, 1976) 17–20.

6 Stewart, *Holy Warriors*, 25

7 Andrew R.L. Clayton, "The Northwest Ordinance from the Perspective of the Frontier" in *The Northwest Ordinance 1787, A Bicentennial Handbook* (Indianapolis: Indiana Historical Society, 1987) 22.

8 Stewart, *Holy Warriors*, 27.

9 Stewart, *Holy Warriors*, 28–29.

10 John McCardell, *The Idea of a Southern Nation. Southern Nationalists and Southern Nationalism, 1830–1860* (New York: W.W. Norton and Company, 1979) 24–25.

11 James G. Birney quoted in Stewart, *Holy Warriors*, 43

12 Robert Allen Skotheim, "Notes and Documents. A Note on Historical Method: David Donald's 'Toward a Reconsideration of Abolitionists'" *The Journal of Southern History* vol. 25, no. 3 (August, 1959) 356–365.

13 Stewart, *Holy Warriors*, 37.

14 Lori D. Ginzberg, *Women in Antebellum Reform* (Wheeling, IL: Harlan Davidson, Inc., 2000) 1–25.

15 Charles Johnson and Patricia Smith, *Africans in America, American's Journey through Slavery* (New York: Harcourt Brace and Company, 1998) 307–309.

16 William W. Freehling, *Prelude to Civil War, The Nullification Controversy in South Carolina 1816–1836* (New York: Harper and Row, 1966) 49–56.

17 American Anti-Slavery Society, 1833, quoted in Stewart, *Holy Warriors*, 52.

18 Charlton W. Tebeau, *A History of Florida* (Coral Gables: University of Miami Press, 1975) 244.

19 James Henry Hammond, "Speech of Hon. James H. Hammond, of South Carolina, On the Admission of Kansas, Under the Lecompton Constitution: Delivered in the Senate of the United States, March 4, 1858," Washington D. C., 1858 (Special Collections, American Antiquarian Society, Worcester, MA).

20 J. McCardell, *The Idea of a Southern Nation*, 86.

21 McCardell, *The Idea of a Southern Nation*, 82.

22 C.K. Marshall, address delivered December 18, 1851 at Oakland College, Mississippi, quoted in McCardell, *The Idea of a Southern Nation*, 204.

23 *Debow's Review* (1858) 305–306, quoted in McCardell, *The Idea of a Southern Nation*, 155–156.

24 Michael F. Holt, *The Fate of Their Country: Politicians, Slavery Extension, and the Coming of the Civil War* (New York: Hill and Wang, 2004) 5–7.

25 "Thomas Jefferson to John Holms", April 2, 1820, *Thomas Jefferson Papers* (Library of Congress). "Jefferson to William Short", April 13, 1820, *Thomas Jefferson Papers* (Library of Congress).

26 Martin Van Buren, quoted in Holt, *The Fate of Their Country*, 7.

27 Robert V. Remini, *Andrew Jackson* (New York: Twayne Publishers, 1966) 212.

28 Holt, *The Fate of Their Country*, 29–31.

29 John S.D. Eisenhower, *Zachary Taylor, The American Presidents Series* (New York: Times Books, 2008) 127–129.

30 Holman Hamilton, *Prologue to Conflict, the Crisis and Compromise of 1850* (Lexington: University of Kentucky Press, 1966) 22.
31 Holt, *The Fate of Their Country*, 133.
32 Hamilton, *Prologue to Conflict*, 133. David Howard Bain, *Empire Express, Building the First Transcontinental Railroad* (New York: Viking, 1999) 13–19.
33 Bain, *Empire Express*, 68.
34 Holt, *The Fate of Their Country*, 102–104.
35 William James Hull Hoffer, *The Caning of Charles Sumner, Honor Idealism and the Origins of the Civil War* (Baltimore: Johns Hopkins University Press, 2010) 1–6.
36 David Herbert Donald, *Lincoln* (New York: Simon and Schuster, 1995) 190–191.
37 McCardell, *The Idea of a Southern Nation*, 330.
38 1860 Republican Party Platform, quoted in Charles A. Beard, *American in Midpassage* (New York: The Macmillan Company, 1939) 366.
39 Donald, *Lincoln*, 255.

CHAPTER 2

The Capital of Secession

In 1865, when General William T. Sherman's army marched nearly unopposed into South Carolina after his successful capture of Savannah, he wrote the Army Chief of Staff, Henry Halleck that his men had an "insatiable desire to wreak vengeance upon South Carolina. I almost tremble at her fate."[1] The yearning of the officers and men of Sherman's army to get revenge on South Carolina for the coming of the war was not unfounded. The heart of the secessionist movement was South Carolina and the heart of Antebellum South Carolina was Charleston.

Charleston was one of the earliest true urban centers in what is today the United States. It was settled in 1670 by ninety three Englishmen who named their new home after their king, Charles II. The land had previously been claimed by the Spanish and Native Americans. This would cause a great deal of conflict for this new colony. Within a decade, the city of Charleston had more than a thousand residents and was one of the principal seaports of North America.

SLAVERY AND CHARLESTON

In 1690, Charleston farmers began growing rice. It was a very lucrative crop, but it was also extremely labor intensive. The importation of large numbers of West African slaves began in earnest to meet the demand. By 1700, black residents outnumbered whites. The white residents of Charleston feared this new majority. They were justified in their fear. On September 9, 1739 between twenty and sixty African slaves, many of whom had been enslaved in the highly Catholic Kingdom of Kongo, what is today Angola, rose up against their owners in an attempt to escape to Spanish St. Augustine. They assumed they would be welcomed by their coreligionists in Spanish Florida. The revolt was brutally put down and South Carolina passed a series of laws to better control their slaves. The memory of what came to be known as the Stono Rebellion would haunt white South Carolinians for the next one hundred and thirty years.[2]

When thirteen of Britain's North American colonies declared their independence in 1776, South Carolinians were more concerned with the effect the war might have on slavery than they were with the British military. Harsh punishments were inflicted on slaves who were suspected of collaborating with the British and, although the army was greatly outnumbered, South Carolina fiercely rejected any call by the Continental Congress to enlist slaves.[3]

In 1776, a British force under the joint command of Admiral Peter Parker and General Sir Henry Clinton attempted to capture Charleston. The British amphibious assault was beaten back by a combination of troops from the Continental army and local militia. The key to the American defenses was a palmetto log and dirt fort built on Sullivan's Island. The fort unexpectedly withstood the naval bombardment and the British plan quickly unraveled. The palmetto tree became the state symbol of South Carolina and would become a very powerful symbol throughout the South during the Civil War.

General Charles Lee did not believe the palmetto log fort would survive the heavy guns and ordered the fort evacuated. The local militia disobeyed his order and remained in the fort.

Charleston, like most of post-Revolutionary America, struggled with just how far to carry the ideals of the Enlightenment that came to symbolize the Revolution. The wealthy rice and indigo planters of South Carolina wanted to maintain as much as possible rule by the elite while the growing class of merchants and skilled laborers wanted a more democratic society. Events such as Shays' Rebellion in Massachusetts and, on a much larger scale, the bloody excesses of the French Revolution led to the creation of much stronger state governments and a stronger central government than had existed at the end of the American Revolution. The balancing act between efficient effective government and personal freedom and liberty will remain a constant theme not only in South Carolina's history, but American history as well for the foreseeable future.

Economically, post-Revolution Charleston was doing wonderfully. In 1800, it was the fifth largest city in the new United States with almost nineteen thousand people. As demand for rice and cotton grew, the port city of Charleston benefited greatly and the city's African population grew substantially.

The U.S. Constitution empowered Congress to ban the importation of African slaves after 1808. When the Constitution was ratified, all states, with the exception of Georgia, had already banned the trade. With the growing profits in the labor intensive cotton, rice and indigo crops the South Carolina legislature narrowly approved reopening the international slave trade in 1803. During the five years before the trade was again banned by Federal law, nearly forty thousand slaves were brought through Charleston. In this period, merchants poured their new found wealth into land and slaves, joining and expanding the planter class.[4]

The city passed a series of laws to control the slaves that now greatly outnumbered the city's white population. These laws were designed to make it impossible for slaves or free blacks to create any organized resistance. Slaves had to have a written pass to leave their owner's land, to own a firearm, to trade on their own account or for free blacks to immigrate into South Carolina. In 1823, a police force was created to enforce these laws as well as a fire department. Besides open revolt, slave owners feared arson more than anything else.[5]

Although Charleston was an extremely busy seaport in the first half of the nineteenth century, it was very different from most of America's major ports. Wealthy planters made Charleston their home, as opposed to the modern idea of working in the city and commuting from the suburbs. While their money was made on the plantations in rural South Carolina, they lived part of the year away from "work" in Charleston. Although these planters built huge beautiful homes and spent a great deal of money on their luxurious lifestyle, overall they stifled the Charleston economy. While industry naturally grew in other American seaport towns, Charleston's part time residents used their wealth and influence to preserve the city's quiet charm. The railroad was kept out and steam powered mills with their unsightly smoke were forced into the outskirts of town. Not only did the planter elite fear the noise and pollution industry would bring, but also the possible changes to Charleston society it was bound to bring with it. Slaves were more than sixty percent of the city's work force and the vast majority of them were employed in domestic service or other service industries catering to the elites.[6]

CHARLESTON AND ITS SOCIAL CLASSES

Many post Civil War writers describe an idyllic Charleston with perfect harmony among its residents, black and white, free and enslaved. This, however, was not an accurate depiction. Not only did the vast majority, if not all, of slaves naturally resent their lack of freedom, but, as the events in the coming Civil War would show, they were waiting for their opportunity to act. Among Charleston's white residents, there was a great deal of fear that their slaves would rise up in resistance or just in revenge. The city council offered a standing reward of $2,000 for information regarding slave revolts and arson, the most common form of slave resistance. Between 1825 and 1858, there were ninety one fires labeled arson by the *Charleston Courier*.[7]

Charleston was divided as much along social and cultural lines as it was along racial lines. Half the wealth of Charleston was in the hands of about three percent of the population. Most of that wealth came from cotton and tobacco plantations well outside of the city. Theirs was the world of balls and the latest fashions from Europe. Their lives were dedicated to the pursuits of leisure and what the sociologist Thorstein Veblen called conspicuous consumption.

The rest of white society was a very diverse group ranging from skilled laborers, or mechanics, as they were then known, to transients and prostitutes. There was no middle class to speak of. Charleston's elite looked down on them more than they did the black population. They viewed them as a bad influence on the city's black residents. As one Charleston resident complained "they teach our negroes to steal, sell them liquor, do everything to corrupt and demoralize them."[8] Most of this population were immigrants, with the Irish and Germans making up a large percentage. There were unsuccessful efforts to limit immigration. The white working class and poor resented the elite and their slaves. Not only did the elite do all they could to prevent the growth of the kind of industries that would most benefit the working class, but those jobs that did exist were often taken by slaves. Although slaves were forbidden by law to hire themselves out, there was little effort by city officials to prevent it. The elite had little sympathy for the white poorer classes and would have much preferred a city made up of only the wealthy planters and their black servants.

In an attempt to solve two problems simultaneously, the city founded the Charleston Marine School in 1859 to train sailors. The school would not only remove the lowest elements of white society from Charleston's streets but would also limit the number of Northern sailors who came to the city and spread their abolitionist ideas.[9]

CLASS STRUCTURE AND AFRICAN AMERICANS

There were three classes of blacks in Charleston. There were, of course the slaves. Their situation differed depending on who owned them and what their jobs were, although most had a better situation than their

Saint-Domingue Slave Revolt

Perhaps no other event in history so affected the minds of Antebellum Southern whites as the slave insurrection in what is today Haiti. The French colony of Saint-Domingue occupied a small section of the island of Hispaniola with the Spanish colony of Santo Domingo. French Saint-Domingue was one of the few French possessions left after the disastrous Seven Years War. Although smaller than Massachusetts, the colony was extremely valuable. Half of the world's coffee was grown there and it produced more sugar than any other place in the world. Saint-Domingue was more valuable to France than the thirteen colonies had been to England.

There were nearly a half million slaves in Saint-Domingue, the vast majority doing the back breaking, miserable work of sugar cultivation. There were more than ten times as many slaves as there were free men. Slaves were controlled through the use of terror. Disobedient slaves were whipped, branded and worse. Because of the high death rate due to overwork and disease and the obviously low birthrate, there had to be a constant stream of new slaves. In 1791 more than half of the slaves had been born in Africa and the majority of the rest had parents born in Africa. Most new slaves came from the central African region, which had been suffering from brutal civil wars over the last several decades. Many of the new slaves were former soldiers and had been sold into slavery as prisoners of war.

Saint-Domingue was in a volatile situation but like so many other places in the world it took the French Revolution to light the fire. In Saint-Domingue there was a class of freed slaves and their descendants. Most of the freedmen were the illegitimate offspring of slave owners and had been granted freedom and a little land. Some had become quite wealthy and successful. This class demanded the same kind of equal treatment and rights that were being granted in revolutionary France. When this was denied they took up arms against the colony's elite. Both sides used and armed their slaves against their opponents. The war simply got away from the original combatants. The freedmen and small plantation owners, recognizing the power of the revolting slaves, sided with them against the elite. The elite, desperate and willing to do anything to restore the old order, tried to enlist the aid of the British. The French Republic, afraid of losing their valuable colony, recognized the freedom of the slaves and granted them citizenship if they would fight to keep Saint-Domingue French. The colony remained French while the famous leader Toussaint L'Ouverture attempted to deal with the issues of emancipation.

When Napoleon Bonaparte seized power in France in 1800 he attempted to reinstate slavery. The colony launched a war of independence which after much bloodshed and the defeat of two French invasions resulted in the Republic of Haiti.

In 1804 after the war of independence the General of the Haitian Army Jean-Jacques Dessalines declared himself emperor of Haiti. The emperor had been born a slave but quickly rose through the ranks of the revolt. Among his many controversial actions, Dessalines ordered the execution of all whites in Haiti, including those who had aided the slave revolt and the war of independence. Between three thousand and five thousand people were killed over the next two months. Survivors fled to the United States with their tales of murder and atrocity. The stories of the French survivors became the nightmares of prosperous American slaveholders and abolition became a synonym for slave revolt and massacre.

plantation counterparts. Among the free blacks there were two classes. There were free men and women who struggled to survive doing menial work in a situation little better than slavery. There was also what was called the Brown Aristocracy, which in alliance with the planter class, had become successful even to the point of owning slaves themselves.[10]

Charleston's elite depended on slavery. Their wealth was the product of slave labor on their plantations and it was slaves who carried out the daily chores that supported their lavish lifestyles. As the abolitionist movement grew in the North, the anti-abolitionist movement grew accordingly. Perhaps nowhere was the movement as radical as it was in Charleston and the rest of the state. To South Carolina planters, the abolitionist movement was more than a challenge to their lifestyle, it was a threat to their very lives. In areas of South Carolina, Mississippi and Louisiana, where slaves and freedmen outnumbered whites, sometimes as much as nine to one, abolitionism meant only one thing, savage and bloody servile insurrection. When New England abolitionists professed pacifism to Southern planters, it appeared to them as an obvious lie. In their eyes, the only possible result of the abolitionist message when it reached slaves was violent revolt as had happened in the French colony of Saint-Domingue. Slave owners believed the abolitionists were putting the "torch and poison" into the hands of their slaves.[11]

SOUTH CAROLINA'S REACTION TO ABOLITIONISTS

For South Carolinians, in a frame of mind to see it, there were plenty of signs that abolitionists were planning death and destruction for the South. On October 25, 1858, one of the leaders of the new Republican Party, William H. Seward of New York, gave what quickly came to be known as his "irrepressible conflict" speech at Rochester, New York. Although he proved that he was no radical during the Fort Sumter crisis, this speech made him much feared in the South. It was a brilliant speech that briefly traced the history of slavery and free labor and showed how, as transportation and communication improvements brought the country closer together, the two labor systems would inevitably collide. Of the entire speech, it was only those two words, "irrepressible conflict," that struck the psyche of the South. It was a prophetic speech, but to Southerners it was simply a Republican admission that their policy would be one of brutal subjugation. To one Southern newspaper editor, the speech was proof that "hostility to the South and its institutions is widening and deepening. Those who tell you otherwise are themselves deceived or they willfully deceive you."[12]

If any doubt remained in South Carolina and the other Southern states that abolitionists and their political party meant to destroy the Southern way of life in blood and fire, it disappeared with John Brown's infamous Harpers Ferry Raid. While men like William Lloyd Garrison took the radical step of demanding an immediate and uncompensated end to slavery, John Brown took perhaps the next logical step of abandoning pacifism. To Brown, slavery was an evil practice and whatever was done to abolish it was justified. Brown also took another radical step. Up to this point, although there had been a great deal of talk about abolishing slavery, the real fight had been stopping its expansion into the territories. In 1859, Brown abandoned the policy of containment and decided to deliver a blow in an area where slavery was long established, Virginia.

THE HARPERS FERRY RAID

Brown's plan was daring and straightforward. He and eighteen followers would cross the Potomac River from Maryland into Virginia and seize the Federal arsenal at Harpers Ferry. With the nearly hundred thousand U.S. government muskets and rifles Brown planned to arm the local slaves. Brown believed this would be the spark that would begin a general slave revolt that would end in a black republic. He even carried a new constitution in his breast pocket in case the need should arise.[13] This plan reflected every fear and prediction the South had made about abolitionists since the beginning of the movement.

The plan had a number of glaring flaws that brought about its ultimate failure. Brown tried to recruit the famous black abolitionist Frederick Douglass. Brown assumed Douglass would guarantee that slaves would join his army. Douglass refused the invitation and tried to dissuade Brown from entering a "perfect steel trap" that "once in would never get out alive."[14] What Douglass understood was that the Southern response would be swift and brutal. What Brown tried to bring about was the worst fear of all Southerners if not most Americans, another massacre like Saint-Domingue. Douglass knew there would be an overwhelming response.

There were numerous issues with the plan. As events would show, Harpers Ferry was a very easy place to become trapped in and an impossible place to defend. The slaves did not flock to Brown like "buzzing bees" as he had predicted. This was partially because Brown had chosen for his slave insurrection a place with the smallest slave population in Virginia. Also for slaves to come forward, they had to believe that the revolt was real and that it had a chance to succeed. Slave owners, because of their paranoia about revolts, tested the loyalty of their slaves in many creative ways. It was a wise slave who was wary of any talk of organized plots. Slaves also knew, as Frederick Douglass did, that slave revolts usually ended badly for their participants. It would be best to wait and see if the plan had any chance of success before joining. Of course, it did not. Not only was the plan flawed, but Brown made numerous decisions during its execution that brought about failure. This has led some eminent Civil War historians to question whether Brown intended from the beginning to make himself a martyr for the cause.[15] That in the end Brown's raid started the chain of events that resulted in the abolition of slavery makes this theory very attractive; however, that Brown could have predicted what followed seems an impossibility.

Brown's plan hinged on word reaching the nearby slaves. This guaranteed that word would reach state and federal authorities as well. Virginia and Maryland militias had the small party trapped in the stoutly built fire engine house before the sun set. The unpleasant task of storming the building and freeing hostages was left to a detachment of U.S. Marines.

Within two weeks, Brown and his fellow raiders were tried and found guilty of treason against the state of Virginia. In a little over a month he was hung. Although the majority of Northerners condemned Brown's actions those who supported him were very vocal, calling him a "noble and self-sacrificing hero."[16]

In South Carolina, and other areas of the South, Brown's raid was a validation of what they believed all along. The initial reports of the raid were greatly exaggerated, with some newspapers claiming eight hundred men had been with Brown. Along with Brown and his followers, authorities seized a cache of papers. The documents showed Brown's link to prominent abolitionists and the Republican Party. The Harpers Ferry Raid was by no means sanctioned by the Party, but that New Englanders with leadership roles in the Republican Party were also giving money and aid to Brown was enough of a connection for most Southerners. More troubling to the people of South Carolina was that among these documents were maps of the South that included U.S. Census data showing where the black population outnumbered the whites. "X"s dotted the maps that to Southerners could only mean that Brown's plan was to strike simultaneously across the Slave States. This also meant that the plot did not end with John Brown dangling at the end of a rope. Abolitionist agents must be lurking throughout the South working with freedmen and the lowest class of poor whites to incite slave revolts.

SOUTH CAROLINA'S RESPONSE TO BROWN

Although Charleston's leaders felt they had long been vigilant enough about the threat of insurrection, they redoubled their efforts in the wake of Brown. Vigilance committees and committees of public safety were formed all over the South. Slave patrols had long existed in the South to corral runaway slaves and prevent organized resistance, but the new organizations took on a greater determination. Anyone suspected of being an abolitionist was driven from the state. One did not have to have a Northern accent to suffer their wrath. Anyone whose comments could be described as critical of the Peculiar Institution could find themselves in a great deal of trouble. The committees, much more than their predecessors, were in effect enforcing orthodoxy on the slave question. By 1860, the view had become that if there existed any divide among whites about this all important question issue it would invite revolt by the slaves.[17]

The city of Charleston with its mixed population of slaves and freedmen had a unique set of problems. The urban environment could be a lot more complex than its plantation counterpart. What Charleston's white residents began to realize after the Brown raid was that for decades, along with lax enforcement, slaves and freedmen had been pushing the limits of the Negro Acts that had been passed since 1740. By the 1850's many of these laws were being completely ignored. After 1834, it was illegal to teach a black person to read; however, every morning one could see the children of slaves and freedmen with books tucked under their arms on their way to the religious schools that took all comers and to schools run by the freedmen themselves. Private manumissions were also banned unless the owner had permission from the state assembly to free his slave. The law was obviously being ignored as the free population of Charleston continued to grow.

Slaves were also banned by law from trading on their own account or hiring themselves out. Any observer at the Charleston market could see that slaves were selling their own goods for their own benefit. White laborers constantly complained that they were having to compete in the labor market with slaves operating in the free market system.[18]

Along with groups of vigilantes, the Charleston city police department, a force of around two hundred and fifty, began trying to erase the earlier deficiencies in enforcing the Negro Codes. They began a house to house search of the homes of more than three thousand two hundred free slaves who lived in Charleston for any evidence of a connection to Northern abolitionists. The Brown Aristocracy found themselves under closer scrutiny by local officials. Traditionally they had been protected by the planter class, but in the atmosphere after John Brown's raid, no one would speak out in their defense. Freedmen who could not produce solid evidence of their status were enslaved. Many of the black laboring class fled the state.[19]

SECESSION

Besides making the people of South Carolina more cognizant of race relations and the presence of the outsiders, the raid convinced many that they were no longer safe in a union with Northerners, especially if the new Republican Party were to seize control of the Federal government in the upcoming presidential and congressional elections. While John Brown waited in a Virginia cell for his final punishment, the South Carolina General Assembly convened in Columbia, the state capital. Everyone was confident that the body would take some action. Just how drastic that action would be was the question. Governor William Gist had already made it extremely clear where he stood on the issue in a public letter – South Carolina should leave the Union. The North had simply gone too far. There was agreement among the representatives that disunion was the appropriate response to the events in Virginia and the changing political climate in the North. The disagreement lay in how and when it should happen. There were those, like the governor, who were for immediate secession. There were those who believed South Carolina should leave as soon as a Republican was elected president and those who believed that they should wait for that president to commit an unconstitutional attack on slavery or the South. Others argued that South Carolina should wait and allow other states to take the lead in order to insure that all the Southern states leave the Union. In the end, the session took only moderate action. Although the representatives officially condemned a great many things, they agreed to participate in the upcoming Democratic convention to insure the nomination of a strongly pro-Southern and proslavery candidate.

When the rest of the nation went to the polls on November 6, 1860, South Carolina voters could only wait. South Carolina was the last state where the legislature cast the state's votes for president in the Electoral College. This did not matter in 1860 as it is highly unlikely that anyone besides Breckinridge would have captured South Carolina's eight electoral votes.

When the legislature met in Columbia to vote for the president, Governor Gist suggested that they begin making preparations for a convention that would officially end South Carolina's connection with the American union. He also recommended that the state raise ten thousand soldiers. The latter suggestion was ignored and it was not until a week after Lincoln's election that, by a unanimous vote, a law was passed to create a statewide convention to discuss the issue of secession. Elections were held and one hundred and sixty nine members met in Charleston to debate the issue. Although the majority were for immediate secession, there were those who argued the state should wait and see what actions other states took or even wait for a multi-state convention. After a delay and a relocation to Charleston due to a smallpox outbreak in Columbia, on December 20, 1860, the one hundred and sixty nine members of the South Carolina convention voted unanimously to "dissolve the union now subsisting between South Carolina and other states, under the name of the United States of America."[20]

The convention also issued a "Declaration of the Immediate Causes which induce and justify the Secession of South Carolina from the Federal Union." The point of this document was to argue that the action South Carolina took was not revolutionary, but was completely legal and had precedent. The thirteen colonies had won their independence as thirteen independent nations. They were recognized as such by King George III in the 1783 Treaty of Paris. These thirteen nations entered independently into first the Articles of Confederation and then the Constitution in 1787. Now in 1860, a "sectional party" had seized control of the central government that was hostile to the laws and traditions of the fifteen slaveholding states. Because of the violations of the U.S. Constitution that would obviously follow the election of Lincoln, South Carolina was using its prerogative as a free independent state and severing her ties with the rest of the Union.[21]

South Carolina never intended to remain an independent state. Southern nationalism had always been more of a goal than an individual states' rights.[22] It was obvious, however, that the Palmetto State would have to take the lead. Before South Carolina had seceded, Governor Gist had written the other six Deep South cotton states to ask if they would leave the Union with a Republican victory. The results were mixed but no state was willing to go first. The most positive answers were from

Mississippi and Florida whose governors pledged their states would follow South Carolina out of the Union.

The first move was up to South Carolina and she had taken it. The declaration of South Carolina's independence was celebrated well into the night in Charleston. Militia companies paraded, military bands played throughout the city, fireworks exploded, bonfires burned and the Palmetto flag waved everywhere in the place of the "Stars and Stripes."

At least one South Carolina resident was in no mood to celebrate. James Lewis Pettigru was seventy one years old and the former State Attorney General. He said on the day the American flag was removed from the state capital that he had seen "the last happy day of his life." Pettigru remained intensely loyal to the Union amidst extreme public pressure. He was also very quotable and perhaps is best remembered for his quote that his state was "too small to be a nation and too large to be an insane asylum."[23]

SOUTH CAROLINA'S COMMISSIONERS TO WASHINGTON D.C.

Even had the central government been willing to allow the breakup of the Union, South Carolina's secession opened up a number of complicated issues. Under the United States Constitution, certain powers and responsibilities were given to the central government and certain powers and responsibilities were given to the state governments – the definition of a federal system. How would the transition to an independent nation take place? Did South Carolina expect the Federal government to continue these duties until the state was in a position to take them over? Would U.S. dollars still be legal script for the time being? What happened to Federal property in the state especially those with multi-million dollar improvements such as the U.S. Army's coastal defense system?[24]

These were the issues that a three man delegation from South Carolina came to Washington D.C. to negotiate in December of 1860. The commission was made up of three of South Carolina's most prominent citizens, Robert W. Barnwell, James H. Adams and James L. Orr. Their most pressing duty was "to treat with the government of the United States for delivery of the forts, magazines, lighthouses and other real estate."[25] Barnwell had been a U.S. Senator and was the former president of the University of South Carolina. Adams was governor of South Carolina from 1854 to 1856 during which time he had championed the reopening of the African slave trade. Orr had been the Speaker of the U.S. House of Representatives and governor of South Carolina.[26]

GOVERNOR FRANCIS PICKENS

The three elder statesmen were on a train to Washington on December 24. Events in Washington and Charleston would make their mission a lot more complicated. First, the new governor of South Carolina had taken it upon himself to open the very negotiations they were sent to carry out. This he had done poorly. Francis Pickens had only been governor for three days when his state issued its statement of disunion. The fifty five year old was the grandson of Revolutionary War general Andrew Pickens and had been active in politics since his early twenties. Most recently Pickens had been the U.S. Ambassador to Russia. The state legislature chose the

Francis Pickens

Francis Pickens was governor of South Carolina for only a short time but it was during one of the most critical stages of South Carolina's history. He was born in 1805 in St. Paul's Parish, South Carolina. He was part of one of the first families of South Carolina. His grandfather had been a hero of the America Revolution, his father had been governor of South Carolina and one of his cousins was the prominent political leader, John C. Calhoun.

Pickens attended South Carolina College, later renamed the University of South Carolina. In 1829 he began his law practice, although the majority of his income came from his plantation. In 1832 he followed in the family footsteps and entered politics. He served in the South Carolina House of Representatives for a single term before he was elected to the U.S. House of Representatives for nearly a decade. While in the House, he was a strong supporter of slavery and state sovereignty in the best Calhoun tradition. In 1844 he left the national capital to once again serve in the South Carolina House of Representatives.

In 1857, he failed in his attempt to become a U.S. Senator. President Buchanan rewarded him for his long service to the Democratic Party by appointing him Ambassador to Russia. He served in that post until he returned to South Carolina in 1860 because he felt the state needed his leadership during the coming secession crisis. He was chosen to be governor of South Carolina by the General Assembly by secret ballot. The people of South Carolina did not directly vote for the president or their governor. His term as governor was marked by South Carolina's secession and the Fort Sumter crisis. He left office in 1862.

After the War, Pickens served in the South Carolina constitutional convention that was part of President Andrew Johnson's Reconstruction policy. It was Pickens who introduced the motion to annul the act of secession. Pickens, like most planters, never recovered financially from the war. He died, financially destitute on his plantation, in 1869.

governor in Antebellum South Carolina and they had been wise to choose a professional diplomat for the post at this moment. Unfortunately for them, they chose the wrong diplomat. Pickens proved to be rash in the coming months when patience would have served his cause better.

Traditionally the position of governor in South Carolina had been that of a figurehead. The state legislature wielded the real power. This relationship, however, changed when the state tried to leave the Union. Governor Pickens' command of the militia took on real significance in the next several months. As the chief executive of an independent state, Pickens' role was more like that of the president. As chief diplomat of South Carolina, he wrote the President of the United States with his demands. All Federal property in South Carolina was to be handed over immediately. The aggressive and undiplomatic tone of the letter was counterproductive and made President Buchanan much less sympathetic to South Carolina's cause.[27]

PRESIDENT BUCHANAN

President James Buchanan had three full months of his presidency left after the November election. "Old Buck" had been a public servant all of his adult life. Buchanan's four years as president had been highly stressful with what seemed like a constant stream of crises. After the election, his goal was to avoid another major crisis. He was satisfied with biding his time until his successor assumed the office. Buchanan believed that South Carolina did not have the legal right to secede. He also believed that the Constitution did not authorize the Federal government to keep a state in the Union against its will. Buchanan did not want to see the Union dissolve. He placed the fate of the nation in the ability of Congress to reach a compromise that would satisfy the South.

The president, like many politicians in both the North and South, believed that secession was only a play to get added protections for slavery in law before the new president took office. Except for a few professional politicians, like Buchanan, no one was in the mood to compromise (Figure 2.1). The majority of the Northern public felt they had been giving in to Southern slave owners for way too long already. This was best illustrated by their overwhelming support of Lincoln, the candidate most disagreeable to the South. More Southerners might have been willing to compromise, but events were in the hands of men like Pickens whose goal had become a permanent break between North and South.

Buchanan has been criticized by many modern historians for not taking aggressive action at this critical moment.[28] This is an unfair criticism.

Figure 2.1 Political cartoon spoofing Buchanan's weak handling of the crisis. (Courtesy of the Library of Congress)

Buchanan had been chosen president because he was a diplomat and unlikely to take drastic action. One of the ways the authors of the Constitution attempted to protect individual liberty was to create a government with more than one branch. The idea was that for one branch to become despotic, it would have to do so at the expense of the other branches. Potential tyrants fighting one another in the halls of government would be unable to trample on the rights of the common man. The history of political power in this country has been the fight between presidential and congressional power. It has swung like a pendulum between the two. Andrew Jackson dominated the government while the Gilded Age presidents bowed to a powerful Congress. During Buchanan's presidency, Congress was dominant and it is unlikely Buchanan could have taken more of a leadership role. Buchanan was by training and temperament a diplomat. As such, his goal was to postpone conflict until a peaceful solution could be worked out. If the postponement carried him into retirement all the better.

Buchanan was also hampered by a split and hostile Cabinet. As the leader of a national political party, Buchanan chose a Cabinet made up of Southern and Northern Democrats. This all but guaranteed that some of his closest advisors were men who were hostile to the preservation of the Union, including two future Confederate generals and the future head of the Confederate Secret Service, not to mention his own vice president who would be the Confederate Secretary of War. One of those future generals was John B. Floyd, his current Secretary of War and the man who was in charge of the forts in Charleston. Buchanan was not getting the best information or advice from many in his cabinet.[29]

MAJOR ROBERT ANDERSON

Besides Pickens' clumsy attempt to negotiate, one other thing that seriously complicated the mission of the South Carolina delegation was the fifty five year old professional army officer who had only recently been put in command of Charleston's harbor defenses (Figure 2.2). Major Robert Anderson was born on the outskirts of Louisville, Kentucky in 1805. The son of a Revolutionary War officer, Anderson entered the United States

Figure 2.2
Major Robert Anderson, a professional army officer whose goal was to avoid Civil War. (Courtesy of the Library of Congress)

Military Academy at fifteen. Anderson graduated high enough in his class to be assigned to the artillery instead of the infantry. Anderson served in every conflict the United States fought from his graduation from West Point to his retirement in the midst of the Civil War. He fought in the Black Hawk and Second Seminole Wars as well as the Mexican War where he was wounded and brevetted for valor. Already a deeply religious man, Anderson's combat experience had made him something of a pacifist by 1860.[30]

Robert Anderson

Robert Anderson was born in rural Kentucky in what is now suburban Louisville. His father, Richard Clough Anderson, had been an officer in the Continental army and had been rewarded with land and the position of surveyor in the territory of Kentucky. Richard Anderson was well connected. As Robert Anderson was growing up his family home was visited by the political and social elite of the new nation, men like James Madison, the Marquis de Lafayette, Andrew Jackson and Henry Clay just to name a few.

Anderson graduated from West Point in 1825. He saw action in the Black Hawk War, the Second Seminole War and in the Mexican War where he was seriously wounded during an assault on the Mexican position at Molino del Rey on the outskirts of Mexico City. He also served on the staff of Winfield Scott during the crisis with Britain over the Maine/Canadian border. He was an artillery instructor at West Point and on the military–civilian committee, along with Jefferson Davis, that overhauled the Military Academy curriculum.

Anderson was married to the daughter of General Duncan Clinch of Georgia. The Clinchs owned land and slaves in South Georgia some of which Anderson inherited. This has caused many to mistakenly doubt the loyalty of Anderson to the Union cause. Anderson's family in Kentucky were strict Unionists, his brother was driven from Texas for his loyalty to the Union. General Clinch, who Anderson greatly admired, was a Jackson Unionist and would probably have been a Union supporter had he been alive.

After the events at Fort Sumter, Lincoln appointed Anderson brigadier general in the regular army and he was given command of the Department of the Cumberland which was mostly made up of his home state of Kentucky. His job was to not only keep the Border State of Kentucky in the Union but to also raise and organize a military force to defend it. The events at Fort Sumter had already ruined his health, the stress of the new position only made it worse. He asked to be relieved in October 1861. He was replaced by William T. Sherman. Anderson never held a command again. After the war he moved to Nice, France where his small pension would go further. He died in 1871, his health having never completely recovered from the stress of the events at Fort Sumter.

Anderson owned several slaves that his wife inherited. He sold the slaves in 1860, more for financial reasons than moral. The buyer refused to pay since Anderson was "waging war against slavery."

Besides leading men into battle, Anderson served with Winfield Scott in 1837 when he prevented war with Britain along the New England and New York borders. Anderson was also Scott's aide when the general played a key role in settling the Nullification Crisis. Anderson learned from Scott how to be a soldier diplomat. It was for this reason that Scott assigned Anderson to the potentially explosive position as commander of the U.S. Army forces in Charleston.

Secretary of War John B. Floyd had other reasons for sending Anderson to this extremely important post. The loyalty of the Virginia born Floyd was unquestionably with the South. As the sectional crisis grew, Floyd moved weapons to arsenals in the South that would obviously be seized if war began. As late as December 1860, Floyd ordered cannons from a foundry at Pittsburg rushed south to the newly constructed forts at Galveston, Texas and Ship Island on the Mississippi coast. It was only when the citizens of Pittsburg, including the foundry workers themselves, many of whom might have had to face those very guns during the next four years, rose up in protest that the order was countermanded.[31]

It is likely that Floyd, the future Confederate general, believed that Robert Anderson would be as sympathetic with the Southern cause as he was. Anderson had married into the Southern aristocracy. His wife was the daughter of General Duncan Clinch. Through her he owned slaves and a Georgia plantation. As events will show, Scott was a better judge of character than Floyd.

FORT SUMTER

The system of forts that Anderson took command of in November of 1860 had the potential of being very powerful. However, the command was far from its full potential. Castle Pinckney was less than a mile from Charleston's docks. Instead of a full garrison, the castle was manned by an Ordinance Sergeant Skillen, his wife and their fifteen year old daughter. Skillen's job was to simply maintain the installation and its equipment. It was a position given to a soldier as a reward for a long and honorable career. Nearly two miles to the south of Castle Pinckney was Fort Johnson on James Island. Dating from the Revolutionary War it had all but been abandoned by 1860.[32]

The heart of Charleston harbor's defense was Forts Moultrie and Sumter. The strategy was that any enemy fleet approaching Charleston would have to use the main ship channel which passed directly between those two forts. No ship could survive the brutal cross fire. Fort Moultrie was located on Sullivan's Island almost due east from Castle Pinckney and the Charleston docks. Its walls were made of two layers of brick with fifteen feet of dirt in between. There had been a fort on that site since the Revolution. Fort Moultrie's guns could reach Fort Sumter, which sat on an artificial island in the middle of the harbor.

Construction of Fort Sumter had been authorized in 1829 as part of a series of forts along the Atlantic, Pacific and Gulf coasts. Construction of the massive fortification continued for over thirty years. When international tensions were high, the pace of construction increased, and when the country faced economic woes, building would come to a standstill. When the fort was finished and its garrison of six hundred and fifty men were manning its one hundred and forty six heavy guns, no ship could survive in the channel or the harbor without the consent of Fort Sumter's commander (Figure 2.3).[33] It was this fact that made the thought of Fort Sumter remaining in the hands of the U.S. Army so unpalatable to the secessionists of South Carolina.

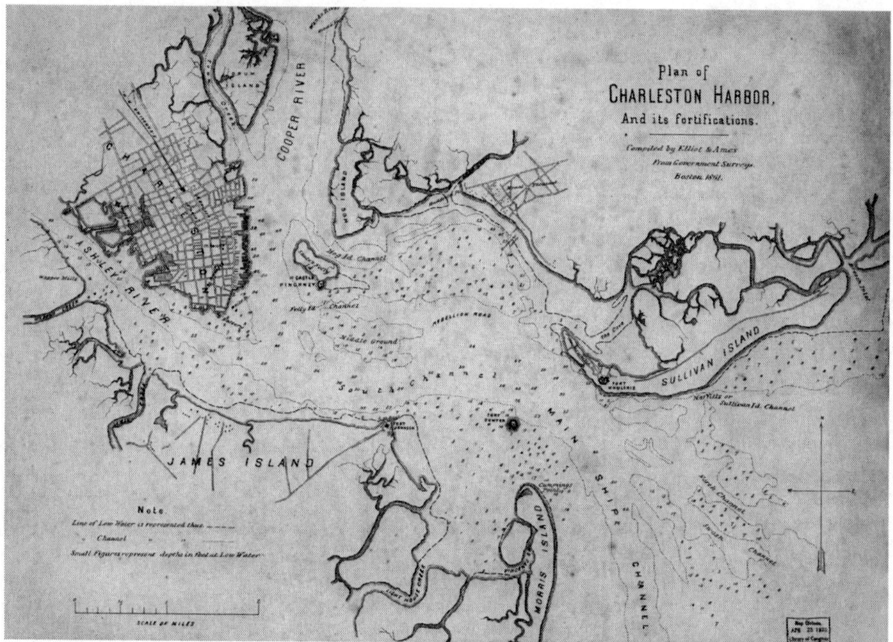

Figure 2.3 Map of Charleston Harbor and its defenses. (Courtesy of the Library of Congress)

By 1860, the structure was mostly complete, but the first gun had yet to be mounted. Nor did Anderson have anything close to the more than a thousand men he would need to fully man Forts Sumter and Moultrie. What Anderson had was two undersized companies from the First U.S. Artillery Regiment and the regimental band for a total force of ten officers and sixty four enlisted men. His two company commanders were Captains Abner Doubleday and Truman Seymour. Doubleday was a West Pointer and native New Yorker. He was also an abolitionist and supporter of the Republican Party. His presence with the garrison was especially galling to the people of Charleston.[34]

Seymour was also a West Pointer. He was the son of a Vermont preacher. Seymour had served as the Assistant Professor of Drawing at West Point. He was skilled enough to sell sketches of the upcoming crisis to one of the North's leading newspapers. Both men were combat veterans having served heroically in the U.S. war with Mexico. Unfortunately for Anderson, Seymour had recently been transferred from the Third Artillery, where he had served since 1825, to the First Artillery. He and his officers were not as familiar with one another as they normally would be.

Abner Doubleday

Born in western New York in 1819, Abner Doubleday was the grandson of a Revolutionary War veteran and the son of a U.S. congressman. He graduated from West Point in 1842 where his unapologetic abolitionism made him unpopular with Southern cadets and Northern moderates. Doubleday was in a distinct minority during his time at the academy.

Upon graduation Doubleday was assigned to artillery. He served in Mexico but received no honors or awards from the army.

After the events at Charleston, Doubleday was made brigadier general of volunteers. Assigned to the Army of the Potomac, Doubleday led troops in some of the biggest battles of the war: Second Manassas, Antietam, Chancellorsville and Gettysburg. He did not distinguish himself in any of these fights. He earned the nickname "forty eight hours" for his lack of initiative. This is ironic considering his great criticism of Anderson was for not taking more direct action more quickly. After Gettysburg Doubleday was stationed in Washington for the reminder of the war.

When peace came Doubleday served as a colonel in the infantry until his retirement in 1873. In 1876 he published *Reminiscences of Fort Sumter and Moultrie in 1860–'61*. The memoir is highly critical of his former commander Robert Anderson.

Doubleday is erroneously credited with inventing baseball. The story, which emerged after his death in 1893, was an attempt to hide the game's English origins.

Truman Seymour

A Vermont native, Truman Seymour was the son of a Methodist preacher. The twenty two year old Seymour graduated from the United States Military Academy just in time to fight in the U.S./Mexican War. He was honored with a promotion to brevet captain for his service. Seymour also saw action in Florida during the Third Seminole War.

After the events at Fort Sumter, he was again honored with a brevet promotion to major. Fitting his national status Seymour was given recruiting duty, an extremely important task especially at this early stage. He also served a short time building up the defenses of the capital. In April of 1862 he was made a brigadier general of volunteers. He served in George McClellan's Peninsular Campaign and also at the disastrous Second Battle of Bull Run. He commanded a brigade at Antietam, the bloodiest single day in American history. In 1863 he returned to Charleston and led the unsuccessful attack on Battery Wagner, made famous in the movie *Glory*, where he was wounded.

When he was again fit for duty he was given command of the invasion of Florida. Although Jacksonville was captured with little resistance his force was defeated soundly at the Battle of Olustee, the only significant battle in Florida. Seymour was removed from independent command and sent back to the Army of the Potomac in time for Grant's Overland Campaign. He was captured at the Battle of the Wilderness but was exchanged in time to participate in the siege of Petersburg and the final campaign of the war.

Although honored with the brevet rank of major general he was only a major in the much shrunken post Civil War army. He served mostly on coastal fortification duty until his retirement in 1876. Seymour moved his family to Florence, Italy and lived there quietly until his death in 1891.

FORT MOULTRIE

With the exception of the ordinance sergeant at Castle Pinckney and Captain John Foster of the Army Corps of Engineers with his civilian workers at Fort Sumter, Anderson's entire force was located at Fort Moultrie. It had fallen into a sad state of disrepair under his predecessor, Colonel John Gardner. There was ongoing repair work which left large gaps in the walls. The work was carried out by pro-secessionist local workers. Officers of the state militia strolled through the fort taking notes. Sand hills near the walls allowed perfect cover and concealment for infantry to fire into the fort. Blowing sand had created ramps against the wall of such slight grade that sentries often found cows roaming the ramparts. Even had Fort Moultrie been fully manned and in perfect condition, it would have been in only a slightly better situation. It was basically a sea battery designed to stop enemy vessels from approaching Charleston; it was extremely vulnerable to a hostile land force on the island.

According to one of its most famous residents, Edgar Allen Poe, Sullivan's Island was "very singular." The island was named after one of the officers of the first English expedition to what is now Charleston in 1670. Captain Francis O'Sullivan was an Irish soldier of fortune who was not very popular with his fellow officers. According to Poe the island "consists of little else than sea sand" and was "separated from the mainland by a scarcely perceptible creek, oozing its way through a wilderness of reeds and slime." In summer, the island was inhabited by the fugitives from Charleston, dust and fever."[35]

Edgar Allen Poe enlisted in the army under a false name in 1827. He served in the artillery in Boston and in South Carolina. In 1829 he left the ranks after securing a replacement to finish his enlistment. In 1830 he secured an appointment to West Point. He left the Military Academy after one year.

Despite Poe's unflattering descriptions of the island, it was a very popular resort destination for the elite of Charleston. The sea breezes over the island were a welcome relief from the heat and smell of Charleston in the summertime. The best families owned cottages on the island. The center of activity was the large two story hotel simply called the Moultrie House. Complete with a bowling alley and shooting gallery, it was one of the South's most famous resorts. Young unmarried army officers had long been a staple of social life on Sullivan's Island and a short stroll to Fort Moultrie to listen to the regimental band was a common activity.[36] Anderson himself had been a welcomed guest when he had been stationed at Fort Moultrie in the 1830's. When the milder temperatures of fall arrived, the garrison would find itself almost alone on the island again.

When Anderson took command, he carefully examined the situation and submitted a full report to the Secretary of War. As an experienced military professional, he made a number of unarguably true observations to his superiors. The local population was openly hostile to the Federal government and the presence of the U.S. Army. South Carolina forces planned to seize all Federal installations in and around Charleston. His current location could not be held unless the currently unoccupied Fort Sumter was garrisoned. Anderson recommended in his report that at least two companies be sent to occupy Fort Sumter and Castle Pinckney. If Fort Sumter fell into enemy hands, the other forts would be cut off from reinforcement or resupply. Castle Pinckney had lost value as a defense against incoming ships; however, a Federal garrison that close to downtown

Charleston would be a serious deterrent to any attack on Fort Moultrie. Not only did reinforcements need to be sent quickly, but they needed to be sent quietly. If South Carolina believed reinforcements were coming, they would occupy Fort Sumter and Castle Pinckney before Anderson could act. Anderson accurately pointed out this was not a purely military situation but a political one as well and he needed instructions from his civilian leadership.[37]

While Anderson waited for a response, the tension in Charleston only rose. The secession convention in Columbia had yet to meet but the local papers, especially the *Mercury*, stoked the fires of public sentiment against the incoming presidential administration and the occupants of Fort Moultrie.

Because of this, the biggest danger to Fort Moultrie became an armed angry mob. Fort Moultrie, as Anderson inherited it, could not be defended against a ground assault. Anderson's officers began to put the fort in a more defensible position. Captain Doubleday ran gun drill firing canister shot into the bay. He hoped the surface of the water being turned into froth by so many lead balls would give the locals pause before trying to storm the fort. Doubleday also placed "mines" around the fort. Since only he knew they were harmless, they had the desired deterrent effect.[38]

ANDERSON'S ORDERS

Anderson's orders were to put the garrison in a position to defend itself but also to take no actions that would inflame the locals. As Anderson would quickly discover, these were two orders that would be nearly impossible to carry out at the same time. Anderson also found it difficult to divine exactly what the current administration wanted him to do because they did not know themselves.

Anderson received two replies to his official report, neither of which was very satisfactory. The first from Floyd informed Anderson that all future correspondence should go directly to him. This effectively cut General Winfield Scott, a man of unquestionable loyalty to the Union, out of the loop. The second was from the U.S. Adjutant General Samuel Cooper and informed Anderson that there would be no reinforcements. According to this soon to be Confederate general, Anderson and his command were in no danger at Fort Moultrie.[39]

On December 5 Anderson crossed the harbor to meet with local leaders. Charleston's mayor and others promised they would do all they could to prevent an angry mob from attacking Fort Moultrie. However, everyone Anderson met with stressed the importance of the forts being handed over to them after the state seceded from the Union.[40] Their meaning was clear, if the forts were not handed over, they would be attacked not by a drunken mob but by state forces.

Anderson wrote again to the Secretary of War in an attempt to stress the dangerous position he and his garrison were in. Anderson wanted Floyd to clarify his rather contradictory orders. He desired to know how far he could go with his defensive preparations before it would be considered inflaming the locals. Anderson wanted to level the sand dunes and tear down the buildings near the fort. Both of these moves, Floyd believed, would be overly aggressive. Anderson through this line of query was attempting to correct the Secretary's understanding of the situation without directly challenging him. Anderson's flaw was that he assumed that Floyd was a man of honor who wanted Fort Moultrie to remain in possession of the U.S. government. Floyd was a politician in the most negative sense of the word. His instructions to Anderson were to basically do nothing until it was too late while still giving the appearance that Anderson had enough discretion so that failure could be blamed on the major.

On December 7 Floyd sent Major Don Carlos Buell of General Cooper's staff to deliver instructions personally to Anderson and report back on the situation. The Ohio born Buell traveled to Charleston by train. Although Buell was ordered to commit all the instructions to memory, they were not that different from what Floyd had already sent Anderson through the mail.

Buell was able to get a much better sense of the temperament in Charleston than anyone in the Buchanan administration. He traveled across the harbor to Fort Moultrie where he had a long conference with Anderson. Perhaps sensing that Anderson was being hung out to dry, Buell put Floyd's instructions in writing. The orders included permission to "put your command into either of" the forts "which you may deem most proper."[41] Although not in writing, Buell advised Anderson to make the move to a more defensible position. Neither Buell nor Anderson seemed to understand the firestorm the move would set off.

Buell returned to Washington where everyone was quite convinced that the U.S. Army in Charleston would do nothing. In the meantime, Anderson quietly spent the next two weeks planning his move. Anderson knew that if he stayed where he was he would be overrun. He and his men would do their duty and try to defend the fort but the resulting bloodbath would make war inevitable. The presence of two armed South Carolina steamers patrolling the ship channel was the last straw that convinced Anderson that he had to take action. Whether the ships were meant to keep him in place or to launch a seaborne attack on Fort Moultrie mattered little.

THE MOVE TO FORT SUMTER

On Christmas day 1860, Anderson put his plan into action. Charleston's residents awoke the next morning to the U.S. flag flying over Fort Sumter. He had made the decision to move his command to Fort Sumter. He hoped that since it was an island fortress and would be so difficult to seize, the South Carolinians would not attempt it. At the least it would postpone what was becoming inevitable. Anderson was trying to buy time so that hopefully a solution could be worked out by the politicians. Once shots were fired that would not be a possibility. He waited until the last possible moment to make his movement. Anderson had been following events in the local papers. He knew that South Carolina's three commissioners had left for Washington on Christmas Eve. He correctly assumed they would meet the president on December 26 and if they failed to convince the President to hand over the forts, they would probably send a telegram the same day to Governor Pickens who was likely to immediately launch an assault.

The three commissioners learned of Anderson's move as they made their last minute preparations to meet with the president. Along with Governor Pickens' extremely counterproductive letter to the president, Anderson's movement to Fort Sumter was going to greatly complicate issues for the commissioners and make the resolution they wanted nearly impossible to achieve in the short time left under the Buchanan administration.

NOTES

1 William T. Sherman to Henry Halleck, *The War of the Rebellion: A Compilation of the Official Records of the Union and Confederate Armies War*, hereafter cited as OR (Washington D.C.: Government Printing Office) Series 1, vol. 44, 799.
2 Mark M. Smith, "Remembering Mary, Shaping Revolt: Reconsidering the Stono Rebellion" *The Journal of Southern History* vol. 67, no. 3, August 2001, 513–534. Clayton E. Jewett, *Slavery in the South: A State by State History* (Westport, CT: Greenwood, 2004) 214.
3 Walter J. Fraser, *Charleston, the History of a Southern City* (Columbia: University of South Carolina Press, 1991) 154.
4 Fraser, *Charleston*, 188.
5 Jewett, *Slavery in the South*, 214.
6 Fraser, *Charleston*, 220.
7 Fraser, *Charleston*, 206, 234.
8 Quoted in Fraser, *Charleston*, 234.
9 Fraser, *Charleston*, 240–241.
10 Fraser, *Charleston*, 245.

11 Steven A. Channing, *Crisis of Fear, Secession in South Carolina* (New York: W.W. Norton Company, 1970) 22.
12 "The Issue" *Memphis Daily Appeal*, December 9, 1858.
13 David S. Reynolds, *John Brown, Abolitionist* (New York: Random House, 2003) 288–308.
14 Benjamin Quarles, *Frederic Douglass* (Athenaeum: New York, 1970) 178.
15 James McPherson, *This Mighty Scourge, Perspectives on the Civil War* (London: Oxford University Press, 2009) 30–36.
16 "Washington Irving and John Brown" *The Anti-Slavery Bugle*, December 24, 1859.
17 Channing, *Crisis of Fear*, 35.
18 Jewett, *Slavery in the South*, 214.
19 Fraser, *Charleston*, 242–243.
20 Quoted in Randall, *The Civil War and Reconstruction* (Boston: D.C. Heath and Company, 1953) 183–185.
21 Quoted in Randall, *The Civil War and Reconstruction*, 183–185.
22 John McCardell, *The Idea of a Southern Nation. Southern Nationalists and Southern Nationalism, 1830–1860* (New York: W.W. Norton and Company, 1979) 4–5.
23 James Petigru, quoted in Richard N. Current, *Lincoln and the First Shot* (Prospect Heights, Illinois: Waveland Press,1990) 73.
24 Randall, *The Civil War and Reconstruction*, 183–185.
25 Governor Francis Pickens, quoted in W.A. Swanberg, *First Blood, The Story of Fort Sumter* (New York: Charles Scribner's Sons, 1957) 94.
26 Fielding Garrison, "Robert Barnwell" in Allen Johnson, Editor, *Dictionary of American Biography* (New York: Charles Scribner's Sons, 1964) vol. 1, 640. John H. Edmonds, "James H. Adams" in *Dictionary of American Biography*, vol. 1, 71–72. Francis Ginkins, "James Orr" in *Dictionary of American Biography*, vol. 7, 59–60.
27 Bruce Catton, *The Coming Fury, The Centennial History of the Civil War* (New York: Doubleday, 1967 reprint; New York: Doubleday, 1961) 151.
28 Current, *Lincoln and the First Shot*, 23–25.
29 Catton, *The Coming Fury*, 123–125.
30 Robert Anderson, *An Artillery Officer in the Mexican War, 1846–7, Letters of Robert Anderson* (New York: Books for Libraries Press, 1971 reprint; New York: G.P. Putnam and Sons, 1911) 80.
31 Catton, *The Coming Fury*, 176.
32 Swanberg, *First Blood*, 7.
33 Roy Meredith, *Storm over Sumter, the Opening Engagement of the Civil War* (New York: Simon and Schuster, 1957) 26.
34 David Detzer, *Allegiance, Fort Sumter, Charleston and the Beginning of the Civil War* (New York: Harcourt, Inc., 2001) 41.
35 Edgar Allen Poe, *Goldbug* in *The Works of Edgar Allan Poe in One Volume* (New York: P.F. Collier and Son, 1927) 53. Frazer, *Charleston*, 1.
36 Detzer, *Allegiance*, 31.
37 Anderson to Colonel Samuel Cooper, December 1, 1860, OR, Series 1, vol. 1, 81.
38 Swanberg, *First Blood*, 43–45.
39 Cooper to Anderson, December 1, 1860, OR, Series 1, vol. 1, 82.
40 Swanberg, *First Blood*, 46
41 Don Carlos Buell to Robert Anderson, December 11, 1861, OR, Series 1, vol. 1, 88–89.

CHAPTER 3

Anderson's Bold Move

Major Robert Anderson made the decision to move his command to Fort Sumter without consulting or informing his officers or his superiors. For the move to be successful, it had to be a complete surprise. His original intention had been to make the move on Christmas Day, but rain and foul weather forced him to postpone until December 26. In 1776, Anderson's father, a captain in the Continental army, made the famous crossing of the Delaware with George Washington at Christmas.[1] One cannot help but think Major Anderson made that connection as he stared across the ship channel and thought about his own desperate situation.

Anderson knew that even the smallest hint that he was moving his force would cause South Carolina to quickly occupy Fort Sumter, if not attack Fort Moultrie. All of Anderson's preparations were intended to make it appear as if he were preparing to be attacked at Fort Moultrie, since the assumption was that the forts would be peacefully handed over by order of the president and South Carolina would be the beneficiary of any improvements.

Anderson's first move was to order Lt. Norman Hall, a recent West Point graduate, to take three of the command's boats, small flat bottomed sailing craft piloted by local men, and, along with six months supplies, carry the soldier's families, forty five women and children, across to the nearly abandoned Fort Johnson. As Hall was overseeing the work, he was approached by two citizens of Charleston who demanded to know what he was doing. The answer Anderson had prepared for him that the officers' wives were being sent North seemed to satisfy the two men who no doubt reported the movement to the growing state forces in Charleston. By noon, Hall's little flotilla was on its way to Fort Johnson. His orders were to wait at Fort Johnson in the boats until he heard the signal, the firing of two guns, and then hurry to Fort Sumter. If the captain of the

Norman J. Hall

Hall graduated from West Point just in time for the Civil War. The native New Yorker's first duty assignment was as a second lieutenant at Fort Sumter. After the events at Fort Sumter, Hall would command troops in some of the fiercest fighting in the Civil War.

Hall commanded artillery during General George McClellan's Peninsular Campaign and the subsequent Seven Days' Campaign. In July of 1862, he was given command of the Seventh Michigan Infantry. Colonel Hall led them at the Second Battle of Bull Run and the Battle of Antietam, the single bloodiest day in the Civil War. Hall, along with sixty percent of his command, was a casualty of the battle.

Hall returned to duty in time to be at the forefront of the disastrous Battle of Fredericksburg. At Gettysburg, Hall and his men were at the center of the Union line and beat back the famous "Pickett's Charge."

Gettysburg was the last of Hall's active service. The rigors of service and battle wounds had destroyed his health. He continued to serve the U.S. Army in an administrative role for the rest of his life. He died in 1867 at the young age of thirty.

boats got suspicious, he was to make a show of inspecting the barracks before letting the women move in.[2]

Anderson confided in Captain John Foster of the Corps of Engineers. Foster procured eight large boats to transfer the garrison of ten officers and sixty four men. The boats were hidden on the beach near the fort. Except for those few who had been let in on the secret, no one suspected Anderson's move. The men had spent the day strengthening the defenses on the landward side of Fort Moultrie. Mary Doubleday, the wife of Captain Doubleday, sent her husband to invite Major Anderson to evening tea. Although her husband was growing frustrated by Anderson's inaction, she would not forget her manners or social responsibilities. Doubleday was relieved to discover that instead of spending an awkward evening with his commanding officer, they would be taking action, something he had long advocated. Doubleday's orders were to take twenty men and seize Fort Sumter. South Carolina might have already placed guards or if South Carolina forces were alert they might respond before the rest of the U.S. forces could arrive. Doubleday's had the potential to be a dangerous mission.[3]

Doubleday ordered his men to form up. Once he was sure they were ready, he hurried back to his wife to tell her the news. She quickly packed her belongings and was escorted out of the fort. With a few other officers' wives, she had to find someone to take them in. Luckily she did have some friends in what would soon be enemy territory.

Once his personal affairs were taken care of, Doubleday reported to Anderson that his men were ready. The garrison marched the quarter mile to the shore. The men were loaded onto three boats. They set off in three separate directions to improve their odds of remaining undetected. Doubleday's boat would take the most direct path so it would arrive first. Once Anderson had made the decision to move the garrison, he was prepared to do what he had to do even if that meant opening the hostilities himself. At Fort Moultrie the garrison surgeon Samuel Crawford, Captain Foster and five enlisted men manned five preloaded heavy cannon. Their orders were to fire on the patrol boats if they attempted to stop the crossing. Firing on a state owned boat inside Charleston Harbor would have definitely started hostilities. Doubleday's boat came the closest to being detected by the guard boats. The steam powered ship came within a hundred yards of Doubleday and slowed significantly. The quick thinking Doubleday ordered his men to remove their wool army coats with their bright buttons giving them the appearance of ordinary workmen. The patrol boat passed by oblivious of the danger it had faced from the possibility of being destroyed by the heavy guns of Fort Moultrie.[4] Anderson had made his move before the patrol boats had taken up their nighttime vigil. The other boat was still at the docks in Charleston.

As planned, Doubleday and his men reached Fort Sumter first. They advanced through the main gate with weapons ready. The civilian workers in the fort outnumbered Doubleday's small force. He placed them under guard assuming most had Southern sympathies. The other two boats soon arrived. After unloading, they returned to Fort Moultrie to pick up the rest of the command. It took three trips, but by eight o'clock the entire command, with the exception of Lieutenant Hall and the families and the rear guard under Foster and Crawford, were at Fort Sumter. Anderson ordered a cannon to be fired. It was answered by Fort Moultrie. This was the two gun signal for Hall to come to Fort Sumter. Anderson had caught everyone completely by surprise. The captain of Hall's boats did not catch on until the signal guns were fired and Hall gave him the order to proceed to Fort Sumter. The captain, who obviously thought he was aiding in the first step of the complete evacuation of the forts, had to be restrained for the trip to Fort Sumter. His treatment at the hands of the young West Pointer and his sergeant surely got worse with each retelling.

ABANDONING FORT MOULTRIE

Once the women and children were on their way and the rest of the command were safely inside the walls, the rearguard carried out the last of the plan. All of Fort Moultrie's cannons were spiked – musket ram rods were hammered into the touch holes and broken off. This is only a temporary solution used by retreating armies to keep their own cannon from being used against them. The touchhole had to be drilled out before the cannon could be used again. The wooden carriages of the guns that faced Fort Sumter were burned and the actual guns were pushed off the walls. They then chopped down the flagpole and threw it in a ditch, a symbolic act that made it more difficult for South Carolina forces to fly the Palmetto flag that the garrison had come to despise. They were able to carry away all of the hospital supplies and most of the small arms. They were unable to bring over one month's supply of food or any of the garrison's fuel oil, two things that would be sorely missed in the months to come. Most of the officers' personal effects were also left behind. According to later claims made by the officers the value of what was left behind was nearly fourteen thousand dollars.

After the last of the men made it to the fort, Anderson retired to what would be his office for the next four months. He wrote two letters. As he had done on a regular basis for decades, he wrote his wife, Eliza, in New York that he was safely inside Fort Sumter and that "the whole force of South Carolina would not venture to attack us."[5] He next wrote to Adjutant of the Army General Samuel Cooper to report his situation. He had four months' supply of food and his entire command was safely inside the walls. He informed Cooper that he had taken this action "to prevent the effusion of blood."[6] Anderson had bought time for the politicians to work out a peaceful solution that would save the Union and restore the status quo. What Anderson did not realize was that the reaction to his move by the public, both North and South, would guarantee the coming of armed conflict. Beginning with Anderson's move across the harbor to the opening of the war itself, the events in Charleston were going to play a crucial role in the Northern attitude toward the war and the eventual Union victory. The famous Charleston diarist Mary Boykin Chesnut would write that Anderson's stealthy move to Fort Sumter guaranteed that the other cotton states would side with South Carolina.[7] Chesnut and many other Southerners saw Anderson's move as assuming "an attitude of hostility" that could only be viewed as threatening all the Southern states.[8]

CHARLESTON'S REACTION

The news of Anderson's move reached Charleston from several different sources. The patrol boat *Nina* which had taken up its position between Forts Moultrie and Sumter only after it was too late had passed close to

Fort Sumter on its return to the city. The crew and soldiers onboard were shocked to see U.S. soldiers standing guard on the ramparts. Civilian workers at Fort Sumter, who were loyal to the South, arrived back in Charleston with reports of the move. Residents of Sullivan's Island had gone to investigate the smoke from the fort only to discover Fort Moultrie abandoned and the gun carriages smoldering.

When Governor Pickens was informed of the events, he was furious. He had assured everyone that such a move was impossible. He showed restraint that was out of character and decided to investigate before acting. Colonel Johnston Pettigrew and Major Ellison Capers of the South Carolina militia were dispatched to Fort Sumter to determine the true state of affairs. Both Pettigrew and Capers would become Confederate generals and fight in some of the war's bloodiest battles.

The two men in the full uniform of the Charleston militia were politely shown into Anderson's office. Most of Anderson's officers were present for the meeting. Pettigrew asked if he could speak before these officers. Anderson answered in a friendly affirmative. He had no secrets from his officers. Pettigrew, who had refused a chair, informed Anderson that the governor was quite dismayed that Anderson had chosen to "reinforce" Fort Sumter. Anderson interrupted him. "I have not reinforced the fort. I have simply moved my command here."[9] The semantics did not matter to Pettigrew. He explained to Anderson that the former governor had informed the current governor that President Buchanan had pledged that the status quo would be maintained inside the harbor. Anderson's move had broken this pledge and "bloodshed might now be avoided no longer."[10]

Anderson knew of no such pledge. On December 8, before South Carolina's secession, the state's congressmen had met with the president. They told the president that although they could not speak officially, Anderson was in no danger of being attacked as long as he was not reinforced. They did not say that an empty Fort Sumter would not be seized. Nothing was put in writing and Buchanan always claimed he made no pledge. The South Carolina delegation, however, walked away from the meeting believing a pledge had been made. Buchanan probably told them that he currently had no intention of reinforcing Anderson and they took that as a promise that he never would.

Regardless, Pickens believed such a pledge had been made and his two representatives were there to demand that Anderson honor it and return to Fort Moultrie. Anderson refused. His position had been threatened at Fort Moultrie by the patrol boats filled with armed men. He had moved his command to Fort Sumter for their own safety. Perhaps sensing the meeting was becoming too heated, Anderson spoke the words that would unfairly color his actions over the next four months and for later generations. "In this controversy between the North and the South, my sympathies are entirely with the South. These gentlemen," referring to his officers, "know it perfectly well."[11] But he added his duty as an army officer came first. Although Anderson was no Republican or abolitionist, his Southern sympathies ended with secession. To Anderson, the officer and gentleman, the behavior of both abolitionists and Southern fire eaters was undignified. Just like during the Nullification Crisis of 1832, it would take cooler heads like his to prevent war. Anderson still hoped to buy time for the government to peacefully solve this crisis. His statement was meant to calm the situation and the two South Carolina soldiers.

Whatever his stated sympathies might be, Anderson refused to leave Fort Sumter and Pettigrew and Capers left very unsatisfied. Anderson's next act would better reflect what he believed than what he had said to those two men. Anderson ordered his command and the workmen to the parade ground. The regimental band was placed on the ramparts. The soldiers came to attention as the silver haired Major Anderson walked onto the parade ground with the U.S. flag he had personally carried from Fort Moultrie. The men were ordered to parade rest. The men and officers bowed their heads and removed their hats as the chaplain began to pray. Anderson kneeled. Chaplain Matthias Harris thanked God for their safe and successful transfer to Fort Sumter and asked that the flag would once again fly over a united country. When Harris finished, Anderson rose with great dignity and raised the flag. The band played "Hail Columbia." When Old Glory reached the top of the staff and unfurled in the cold strong breeze of the harbor, the men and officers broke into cheers. It was an extremely emotional moment for all that were there (Figure 3.1).[12]

> Anderson would keep the flag he raised over Fort Sumter with him throughout the war. He would raise it again over the fort after the end of the war, exactly four years after he was forced to lower it.

SEIZURE OF CASTLE PINCKNEY

Pickens believed Buchanan's pledge had created a truce and that Anderson's movement between two Federal forts violated that truce. This belief caused him to commit the first actual hostile act of the conflict. Colonel Pettigrew and as many men as he could fit on the patrol boat *Nina* steamed to Castle Pinckney. At the castle were thirty workmen, Lieutenant Richard Meade and Sergeant Skillen and his small family. As Pettigrew's men scrambled down the *Nina*'s gangplank onto the island, Meade ordered the gate

Figure 3.1 The flag raising ceremony at Fort Sumter after Anderson had transferred his command. (Courtesy of the Library of Congress)

Richard Kidder Meade, Jr.

Meade was the son of the prominent Virginia politician Richard Meade. He graduated second in his West Point class in 1857. He was assigned to the Corps of Engineers and served as an Assistant Professor at West Point for two years. After his tenure at the Military Academy he was sent to New York to improve the city's harbor defenses. He was there less than year before being assigned to Charleston.

After the events at Fort Sumter Meade left the Union along with his home state of Virginia. He was given the rank of major in the Confederate army. He served as an engineering officer on the staffs of General John B. Magruder and General James Longstreet. He died of an unrecorded disease, probably typhoid or tuberculosis, in Petersburg, Virginia in 1862. He was twenty six.

closed and barred. Charleston's residents, still angry about what they saw as Anderson's betrayal, strained to watch the action from the city's shore line.

After watching the landing with curiosity, the thirty workers retreated to their quarters, some going as far as hiding under their beds. Meade and, we can assume, Sergeant Skillen would have resisted had they any real means of doing so. They were hopelessly outnumbered as Pettigrew and his South Carolina men used the ladders they had brought to scale the walls. Colonel Pettigrew informed the lieutenant that he was taking the fort by the authority of the governor and would give Meade all the proper receipts for the public property under his command. The defiant Meade refused any paperwork from Pettigrew as he did not recognize the governor's authority. He would not offer his parole (a promise not to fight in exchange for not being held captive), nor would he recognize his status as a prisoner of war. Meade's legal stance was one the president elect, Abraham Lincoln, would have greatly approved. Meade did ask that Skillen and his family be treated with courtesy.

Pettigrew had not thought to bring a flag with him, so when the U.S. flag was lowered, he replaced it with the *Nina*'s flag, a red field with a lone star. The single star represented South Carolina as no longer being part of the constellation on the American flag, and red had long been the color of revolution. The fifteen year old daughter of the ordinance sergeant, Kate Skillen watched the proceedings with tears in her eyes. One of the militia officers reassuringly told her that she and her family would be safe. She snapped back that she was "not crying because I am afraid! I am crying because you put that miserable rag up there."[13] She then taunted the officer for bringing so many men to capture a position held by two soldiers and a teenage girl. One can only imagine that had Lieutenant Meade had the ability to resist, Kate Skillen would have gone down in history as another Molly Pitcher, working the cannons in defense of her country.

NEGOTIATIONS IN WASHINGTON D.C.

The abandoned Fort Moultrie was seized soon afterwards. Fear of the land mines that Captain Doubleday had pretended to bury made this a much slower process. South Carolina had now seized U.S. government instillations by force of arms. This action by Pickens greatly complicated the situation for those Southerners attempting to gain independence peacefully. South Carolina's three commissioners arrived in Washington on December 26 with that goal in mind. It was a two day trip by train. They were greeted by William Trescot, a thirty eight year old native of Charleston. A Harvard trained lawyer, Trescot had a successful career in the diplomatic service rising to the rank of Assistant Secretary of State under Buchanan. On several occasions, he had been acting Secretary of State. He had resigned the moment South Carolina left the Union, but in the months leading up to secession, he had been passing confidential information to the government of South Carolina. Now he was acting as South Carolina's unofficial representative and had arranged the commissioners' meeting with the president.

The meeting was set for the next day, December 27. Buchanan refused to recognize them as representatives of the independent nation of South Carolina. He would, however, see them as private citizens, a symbolic distinction that would have made little difference. Buchanan had agreed to pass their proposals to Congress. Their prepared proposal was straightforward. The land that the forts sat on had been given to the Federal government in 1805 for the express purpose of defending South Carolina. Now that South Carolina was out of the Union, the agreement no longer stood. South Carolina was prepared to be reasonable, at least in her mind, and reimburse the Federal government for all the cost of building the forts and other improvements on the land.[14]

As the four discussed strategy for the upcoming meeting with President Buchanan, Texas Senator Louis Wigfall burst into the house with shocking news from Charleston that Anderson had moved his command to Fort Sumter. Although he lived in Texas, the Charleston born Wigfall was a South Carolina man at heart. He had only heard rumors of Anderson's movements and had come to see if they were true. This news delivered by the highly excitable Wigfall put the other four men into a decidedly agitated state. As the five men discussed the implications of Anderson's

Louis T. Wigfall

Perhaps no one is more responsible for the violent outcome of events in April 1861 than Louis Trezevant Wigfall. He was born in South Carolina in 1816. He graduated from South Carolina College and opened a small law practice in Edgefield, South Carolina. Wigfall was a lot more interested in politics than the law. He joined the South Carolina militia, key to a political career in South Carolina, and served for a short time in the Second Seminole War. This was an experience that became more important with each retelling.

From the beginning Wigfall was a Southern nationalist. He believed the only way to protect Southern rights and their way of life was to leave the Union. This overwhelming belief was behind every political decision he made and earned him and men like him the nickname "fire eater." Wigfall was passionate about his beliefs, a heavy drinker and easily insulted. That combination led to fistfights, shootings and the occasional duel. He killed one man in a duel and severely wounded another. He used this reputation to intimidate political opponents.

In 1846 Wigfall moved to Texas and began another struggling law firm. He entered Texas politics where he was a bitter opponent of Governor Sam Houston, the hero of Texas independence and an Andrew Jackson Unionist. As a member of the Texas State Senate Wigfall supported the reopening of the international slave trade and the annexation of Cuba.

He was chosen to be one of Texas' two U.S. Senators in 1859. He was a leading secessionist and obvious critic of Lincoln. Showing a great deal of nerve, Wigfall remained in the U.S. Senate after Texas left the Union, where he was an outspoken supporter of the Confederacy. While still a sitting U.S. Senator, Wigfall was an aide to Confederate President Jefferson Davis, a member of the Confederate Congress and commander of a Texas battalion in the Confederate army. The U.S. Senate finally expelled him in July of 1861.

Wigfall served briefly in the Confederate Army before resigning to serve full time in the Confederate Congress. Wigfall was a major critic of President Davis, claiming Davis was to blame for the Confederacy's defeat by concentrating too heavily on the Virginia theater and ignoring the west, an argument that is not without merit. He also strongly supported strengthening the power of the central government in Richmond in order to win the war. An idea that contrasted sharply with his belief in State's Rights.

After the fall of Richmond and the surrender of Lee's army Wigfall returned to Texas to continue the war. To his dismay the Confederate army in Texas had already surrendered. He fled to Britain to avoid capture. He returned to the United States in 1872 and lived quietly in Maryland. He returned to Texas in 1874 and died in Galveston shortly after his arrival.

actions, Secretary of War Floyd arrived. They demanded answers from the secretary who was as shocked as they were. He insisted that they must be misinformed. He insisted that he had given clear and direct orders to Anderson to take no action.

Trescot in the meantime had received telegrams from Charleston confirming the news. Floyd returned to the War Department to fire off a message to Anderson. Trescot, along with the commissioners, traveled to the White House. Along the way, they collected two of South Carolina's strongest supporters in the Senate, future Confederate president Jefferson Davis of Mississippi and future Confederate Secretary of State Robert Hunter of Virginia. The six men met the president in his study. Although Buchanan attempted to open the meeting with pleasant small talk, Davis interrupted him in order to get straight to the point of the meeting. On learning that the president had not yet been informed of Anderson's move, and was perhaps the last person in Washington D.C. to know, Davis informed the president of the "great calamity" that had befallen them.[15]

A visibly distressed Buchanan assured the gathered Southerners that not only had Anderson's movement not been ordered, but was against his policy. Buchanan sent for Floyd to verify the report. He arrived shortly, obviously already on his way with the telegraph he had sent Anderson:

> There is a report here that you have abandoned Fort Moultrie, burned your carriages, and gone to Fort Sumter. It is not believed, as you had no orders to justify it. Say at once what could have given rise to such a story."[16]

It was an odd telegram for the Secretary of War to send. The message did not ask for verification nor did it send instructions as one would expect in a message from the Secretary of War to a subordinate in a politically problematic situation. Floyd clearly intended this message to distance himself from the major's actions. Floyd was already thinking about how the crisis and his role in it would be viewed in retrospect instead of how to solve it. It would have accomplished just as much if he had sent the telegraph straight to the press instead.

Floyd's major problem at the moment was that he had been asked to resign. Floyd was not being shown the door for the obvious reason that his actions in support of the secessionists, including insuring U.S. arsenals in the South were well stocked, were treasonous. He was asked to resign because of an unrelated financial scandal. One of the War Department's private contractors, a private company that mostly did business in the West, was on the verge of bankruptcy due to the financial crisis of 1857. The company's president had persuaded Floyd into issuing him promissory notes

John B. Floyd

John Buchanan Floyd was born to a prominent Virginia family in 1806. In 1829, he graduated from South Carolina College and began studying law in Virginia. In 1834, Floyd moved to Arkansas to make his fortune as a cotton planter. Floyd failed at this and returned to Virginia nearly broke and greatly weakened by illness.

Floyd turned out to be a much more successful lawyer than planter and he recovered from his Arkansas losses. In 1847, he entered politics and was elected to the Virginia General Assembly. In 1848, he was elected governor of Virginia. He served one term. In 1857, Floyd was named Secretary of War by James Buchanan. Floyd's time as Secretary of War is controversial not only because of his handling of the Fort Sumter crisis and the allegations that he purposely stocked U.S. arsenals in the South to the detriment of arsenals in the North. There was also financial malfeasance dealing with a contractor employed with the Indian Bureau. He was later exonerated on both charges, but this may have had more to do with the Federal Government having much more to deal with in 1861 than prosecuting Floyd.

On his resignation from Buchanan's cabinet, he was appointed brigadier general in the Confederate army. As a Confederate general, Floyd is best known for his unsuccessful defense of Fort Donelson. Before the fort fell to Ulysses Grant, Floyd and his command escaped, leaving General Simon Bolivar Buckner and his men to surrender. Floyd's actions at Fort Donelson destroyed what little military reputation he had. President Davis dismissed him from Confederate military service.

In April 1862, Floyd was appointed a general of Virginia militia. He was put in charge of recruiting partisans to wage war against Virginia Unionists. He died of natural causes in 1863, probably the aftereffects of his time in Arkansas.

for contracts not yet issued. These notes had no real value but the company was able to use them to secure funding from the banks. By 1860 this was no longer working and the company secured nearly nine hundred thousand dollars from the Interior Department using the Secretary of War's promissory notes in exchange. What had started as a bad idea had turned into something extremely illegal. Floyd had not profited personally from transactions but that did not change the illegality of his actions or the cost to American taxpayers.[17]

Floyd was asked to resign by Vice President John Breckenridge since Buchanan wanted to avoid the confrontation. Floyd was taking his own time in resigning and Buchanan was not pressuring him to act quickly. The president was allowing him to pick the opportune time to resign in order to save face – a very nice gesture had the country not been in the midst of a great crisis. In the meantime, however, he was allowing Floyd to act as Secretary of War.

Floyd's strategy was to make it appear as if he had resigned not because he was forced to but because he was making a protest against what he viewed as the administration's immoral handling of the Fort Sumter affair. The telegram he sent Anderson was Floyd setting up his exit strategy.

> Although Breckenridge would later serve as a Confederate general and Confederate Secretary of War he served the rest of his term as vice president loyally and is often credited with ensuring the orderly transfer of power between Buchanan and Lincoln.

The South Carolina commissioners, Trescot and the two senators pressed Buchanan to immediately order Anderson to move. He responded saying he would discuss the matter with his cabinet and allow Anderson an opportunity to explain himself. His visitors were most unhappy to be told that he was unwilling to immediately do as they wished.

BUCHANAN'S RESPONSE

An emergency cabinet meeting was called for the afternoon of 27 December. Although Floyd had been asked to turn in his resignation, Floyd was still attending cabinet meetings. Major Don Carlos Buell was summoned to the White House just in case the cabinet wanted some clarification about his meeting with Anderson. Before he entered the meeting an agitated Floyd commented to Buell that Anderson's actions had "made war inevitable." Slightly shocked, Buell replied "I do not think so, sir. On the contrary, I think that it will tend to avert war, if war can be averted."[18] The Secretary of War did not seem to have a clear understanding of what was at stake. More than half a million men would die in the next four years. His response to Buell showed that he was so caught up in his own view of events that he was surprised to learn that others thought differently. "But it has compromised the President!" was Floyd's weak response.

The meeting that followed was not the kind that Buchanan liked to hold. Floyd, who had not been invited took the lead in the meeting. He angrily denounced Anderson and argued that because of Anderson's rash actions the only possible option to avoid war was to completely give in to all of South Carolina's demands. The new Secretary of State had heard enough. Jeremiah Black had replaced Trescot who had been serving as interim Secretary of State. Like the president, Black was from Pennsylvania and the two men were longtime friends. Black had only recently served as the Attorney General so he was not a new face in the cabinet. Black approved of Anderson's move and stated that his actions were in accordance with his orders. If Black had meant this as a trap, Floyd stepped directly into it. Floyd angrily repeated that Anderson had violated the direct orders from the War Department. Black summoned Major Buell.

Don Carlos Buell looked after the best interests of his fellow Mexican War veteran and brother officer Robert Anderson. Not only had Buell provided a written record of Floyd's oral orders to Anderson, he made a second copy that he submitted to the War Department and that thus had to be endorsed by Floyd and the president. As Buell must have predicted, Anderson would have been sacrificed for the political benefit of others. With the order in front of them there was no way to argue that Anderson was in the wrong.

Of course, the question was what action to take now. To Floyd the solution was simple, the U.S. Army had to be withdrawn from South Carolina. Secretary of State Black, his replacement as Attorney General, the Ohioan Edwin Stanton, and the Kentucky born Postmaster General Joseph Holt vehemently disagreed. Stanton was a successful Ohio lawyer whose practice mostly involved arguing in front of the Supreme Court. He was strongly anti-secession and was asked by Lincoln to stay on in the War Department. Holt had only recently been the Commissioner of Patents and was a strong abolitionist. Black compared abandoning Fort Sumter to Benedict Arnold's attempt to hand over the American fortress at West Point to the British and he added "a president of the United States who would make such an order be guilty of treason."[19]

"Oh no! Not so bad as that my friend. Not so bad as that!"[20] The president answered. Black's point had struck home. Floyd's influence with the administration was over.

Buchanan is usually portrayed as having a change of heart, shifting from his Southern leaning advisors to men like Black, Seward and Holt whose sympathies lay in another direction. However, Buchanan had not changed. From the beginning his strategy had been to do nothing. When Anderson and his garrison were in the indefensible position at Fort Moultrie the do nothing strategy benefited South Carolina and was championed by Floyd. Now that Anderson was in Fort Sumter, Buchanan's strategy of taking no action seemed to be Buchanan taking strong action in defense of the Union and was strongly supported by part of his cabinet. Buchanan had not changed. Anderson had changed the situation.

The president still had to answer the South Carolina commissioners. Even had he not intended to give the pledge that the situation would not change the South Carolina congressmen believed he had, and Buchanan had done nothing to dissuade them of this belief. The president wanted to find a way to preserve his honor in the face of what seemed like a broken promise. It was Black who broke the spell that had Buchanan thinking only of the issue of his honor. Black threatened to resign if Buchanan did not take a strong stance with the commissioners. When Buchanan protested that "my personal honor as a gentleman is involved," Black shot back that as president his honor must be secondary to the laws of the nation and his oath of office. Buchanan relented and asked Black to draft recommendations for a response to the commissioners.[21]

Black and Attorney General Stanton did more than recommend a response, they crafted a complete response. The document the two men produced was direct and unyielding. The United States did not recognize South Carolina's independence, thus South Carolina did not have the right to be represented by diplomats. The United States would not enter negotiations over its own property. Fort Sumter would be held and Major Anderson was "a gallant and meritorious officer." The document concluded with the powerful statement "I am urged immediately to withdraw the troops from the harbor of Charleston. This I cannot do. This I will not do." Had these been Buchanan's own words and had he led his cabinet to this position instead of following, this might have been the defining statement of his presidency.

When the statement was presented to the full cabinet the Northern members were relieved that Buchanan had finally seen the light. Floyd and Secretary of the Interior Jacob Thompson were angry and frustrated. Floyd publicly resigned as a matter of honor, an opportunity he had been waiting for. He would soon return to Virginia to work toward convincing the people of Virginia to leave the Union as well.

The response was delivered to the commissioners nearly simultaneously with the news that Joseph Holt was the new Secretary of War. It was now obvious Buchanan would not order Anderson to move from Fort Sumter. The Southern influence had been removed from the cabinet.

Before the statement became public Georgia Senator Robert Toombs paid a visit to the president to inquire if he had made a decision. Buchanan asked the Senator why a fort at Charleston would matter to Georgia. "Sir, the cause of Charleston is the cause of the South." Toombs responded.

"Good God, Mr. Toombs, do you mean that I am in the midst of a revolution?" Was the president's shocked reply.

"Yes sir – more than that, you have been there for a year and have not yet found it out." Perhaps more than anything else this exchange shows the extent to which the old Pennsylvania diplomat was truly out of touch.[22] Although Buchanan and many professional politicians inside the District of Columbia did not really understand, to the rest of the North these events were very clear. Although politicians might call it compromise, frustrated Northerners regarded it as caving in and the men they sent to Washington had been doing it for as long as anyone could remember. Now that a real opposition party had emerged, the Great Slave Power was threatening to break up the Union. This bullying tactic had helped elect Buchanan in 1856. Even now there were men in the Republican Party trying to convince Abraham Lincoln to reach out to the Southern leadership to let them know he was willing to compromise.

THE NATION'S RESPONSE

After decades of retreat and giving in, someone finally said no. Not in words or newsprint, those things had proven worthless. Unsupported from Washington, Anderson had denied the Great Slave Power the control of Charleston Harbor. "A mighty throb of relief and exaltation went through all the land." This "brave and true officer" had finally stood up to the bully. Major Anderson had saved the Union.[23]

While newspapers across the North celebrated Anderson's bold defiance, there was also pessimism that "the miserable imbecile" in the White House would order Anderson back to the indefensible Fort Moultrie or worse yet, out of Charleston all together. If the president took this action, numerous newspapers called for nothing short of indictment for treason or impeachment.[24]

To Southern newspaper editors, Anderson had violated his orders and the sacred trust between the president and South Carolina. Most Southern newspapers attempted to separate Buchanan from Anderson's actions. Anderson had moved contrary to orders. To one South Carolina newspaper, it was "a gross breach of faith, and very derogatory to him as a man of honor."[25]

Northern Unionists saw this as their nation finally awakening to the dangers they faced and Southerners were optimistically hoping that was not the case. In their optimism, Southerners attempted to distance Buchanan from Anderson's actions. If it was, however, "the first step of the government toward coercion" it would "be met in that spirit."[26]

The events in Washington D.C. and Charleston were the major topic of discussion throughout South Carolina. One can only imagine what the state's African American community thought of the situation. The servant class had learned to keep their thoughts to themselves. They could not help but listen and were as well informed as anyone. There is no way to know if they were as optimistic about Anderson and the actions of the Federal government as the rest of Charleston was pessimistic. Most whites assumed they were silently plotting revolt and that once they were confident the white men were truly divided it would be time to strike. The South's African American community would prove more patient, but Southern whites were paranoid. As the Charleston elite strolled along Battery Park overlooking the harbor and Fort Sumter many sprinkled their conversation with French to prevent the listening slaves from understanding or, as William Trescot was reported to have said, "using French against Africa."[27] Unfortunately, like so many people in the history of the world we can only speculate on the thoughts of the "servants" on the Battery.

REINFORCING FORT SUMTER

Now that Buchanan's do nothing strategy had evolved into not ordering Anderson to abandon Fort Sumter, the major needed to be supported. General Winfield Scott, who had been kept away from Washington both by his own ill health and the hostility of former Secretary of War Floyd, approached the president with the request to reinforce Fort Sumter. The president assented and Scott began putting a plan into action. Initially the old general wanted to take two hundred men from Fort Monroe in Virginia, the closest body of U.S. troops to Charleston, and send them along with supplies to Fort Sumter aboard the U.S. Sloop of War *Brooklyn*. The *Brooklyn* was the most modern ship in the navy. This, however, started to seem like aggressive action to the president and he began to moderate. Buchanan felt it would not be polite to send the *Brooklyn* before the commissioners had an opportunity to read and respond to the letter that Black and Stanton had written. Of course, this was absurd as the letter stated South Carolina did not have the right to be represented by diplomats and yet Buchanan was postponing the government's actions to be polite to those very same diplomats. Also, the presence of the *Brooklyn* and several hundred soldiers would have affected the response of South Carolina, to the advantage of the administration. Buchanan also considered sending an officer to Charleston to meet with Anderson and determine if he needed reinforcements. This would further delay action.[28]

Unfortunately for the Union cause, it was at this moment that Winfield Scott began to back away from his earlier aggressive decisions. Scott worried about removing so many men from Fort Monroe at a time of crisis. Instead

> The *U.S.S. Brooklyn* was launched in 1859 and served until 1890. She was two hundred and thirty three feet long with a top speed of eleven knots (roughly thirteen mph). The *Brooklyn* needed a crew of over three hundred men and carried twenty one guns.

he decided to send men from the recruit depot in New York. He also decided to send the men and supplies aboard an unarmed civilian steamer. His belief was that a merchant ship would be able to reach Fort Sumter and unload its precious cargo before the government in South Carolina realized what was happening. Whether the general was being naïve or if this was just wishful thinking is anyone's guess. There was no way that a civilian ship could be hired, loaded with locally purchased supplies and armed uniformed men without anyone in a city filled with Southern sympathizers noticing and sending a telegram to Charleston. The Buchanan administration could not even keep it out of the newspapers. The *Brooklyn* sailing from a military installation would have had a much better chance of operating in secret. William Walker, the *Brooklyn*'s commander, would prove to be a dedicated officer during the Civil War and would not have been convinced to turn back as easily as a civilian ship master. Also had the South Carolina forces fired on a U.S. Navy vessel all doubts about what action Anderson should take would have been removed.

STAR OF THE WEST INCIDENT

Instead the army hired the *Star of the West*. She was a paddlewheel steamer built by Cornelius Vanderbilt for his Panama line. At two hundred and twenty eight feet long the *Star of the West* could comfortably carry the men and supplies to Charleston. A price of $1,250 a day had been negotiated which included the *Star of the West*'s crew and her captain, a naval veteran from the U.S./Mexican War. Traditionally a ship hires a local pilot to steer the ship into the harbor. This was, obviously, not an option. A New York pilot was hired who, although he had never been to Charleston, was confident he could pilot the *Star of the West* to Fort Sumter's wharf.

The *Star of the West* slipped away from her pier seemingly unnoticed on the evening of January 5. She picked up the two hundred soldiers under the command of First Lieutenant Charles Woods from Governor's Island, the recruit depot in New York harbor. Exactly where the secrecy was broken is unclear but rumors were in the newspapers and the streets of Charleston long before the ship reached her destination. There were enough Southern sympathizers in Washington D.C. that the news very well might have escaped from that city instead of New York.

The *Star of the West* reached Charleston harbor at around 1:30 in the morning on January 9. Captain John McGovern, the ship's civilian captain noticed that the signal buoys that marked the channel had been removed. Amazingly the captain was surprised by this and decided to wait until first light to enter the harbor. The decision would doom the *Star of the West*'s mission and make the coming conflict more inevitable than it had been.

NOTES

1 E.L. Anderson, *Soldier and Pioneer: A Biographical Sketch of Lt.-Col. Richard C. Anderson of the Continental Army* (New York: G.P. Putnam's Sons, 1879) 1–13, 20
2 W.A. Swanberg, First Blood, The Story of Fort Sumter (New York: Charles Scribner's Sons, 1957) 94–101.
3 Abner Doubleday, Reminiscences of Forts Sumter and Moultrie in 1860–'61 (New York: Harper Brothers, Publishers, 1876) 59–64.
4 Doubleday, Reminiscences, 65–66.
5 Roy Meredith, Storm over Sumter, the Opening Engagement of the Civil War (New York: Simon and Schuster, 1957) 61.
6 Meredith, Storm over Sumter, 61.
7 Mary Chesnut, Mary Chesnut's Civil War, C. Vann Woodward, Editor (New Haven: Yale University Press, 1981) 5.
8 E.A. Pollard, The Lost Cause (New York: Gramercy Publishing, 1996 reprint; New York: E.B. Treat and Co., 1866) 53.
9 Meredith, Storm over Sumter, 61.
10 Swanberg, First Blood, 103–105.
11 Doubleday, Reminiscences, 80.
12 Samuel Wyllie Crawford The Genesis of the Civil War, the Story of Sumter, 1860–1861 (New York: Charles L. Webster and Company, 1887) 112.
13 Quoted in Doubleday, Reminiscences, 73.
14 Swanberg, First Blood, 61–63.
15 Swanberg, First Blood, 111–112.
16 John B. Floyd to Anderson, December 27, 1860, The War of the Rebellion: A Compilation of the Official Records of the Union and Confederate Armies War (Washington D.C.: Government Printing Office) Series 1, vol. 1, 3.
17 Bruce Catton, The Coming Fury, The Centennial History of the Civil War (New York: Doubleday, 1967 reprint; New York: Doubleday, 1961) 173.
18 Buell quoted in Swanberg, First Blood, 113.
19 Edwin Stanton quoted in Swanberg, First Blood, 114.
20 Buchanan quoted in Swanberg, First Blood, 114.
21 Meredith, Storm over Sumter, 75.
22 Swanberg, First Blood, 117.
23 "Major Anderson's Master Stroke" Daily Cleveland Leader, December, 31 1860."From Washington D.C." The Cincinnati Commercial Appeal, December 28, 1860.
24 "Important from Charleston" Delaware Gazette, December 28, 1860. "The President Wavering" New York Daily Tribune, December 29, 1860.

25 "The Progress of Events" *Abbeville Press*, January 4, 1861.
26 "Washington DC" *Daily Nashville Patriot*, December 31, 1860.
27 Chesnut, *Mary Chesnut's Civil War*, 36.
28 Swanberg, *First Blood*, 117–121.

CHAPTER 4

Securing Sumter and the Birth of the Confederacy

Even before the emotional flag raising over Fort Sumter, Major Robert Anderson and his small garrison began to prepare the fort for an attack. Anderson had no way of knowing how South Carolina would react to his movements. His garrison might have been in a fight before the sun rose. Anderson and his officers expected a direct assault. Men landed on the island might be able to overwhelm the small garrison. Fort Sumter was built to fight an enemy at long range. Fully manned with all its cannons blazing, an enemy force would be unable to get anywhere near the fort. Because of this, it was not designed for a small force to defend it against an infantry attack. The old veteran Anderson would set about to change this.

PREPARING THE FORT FOR AN ASSAULT

The first obvious danger were the embrasures, the openings that the cannons were fired through. These forty two openings were closed and blocked as quickly as possible. No attack came that first night, when an assault would have had the best chance of success. Among the civilian workers, Captain Foster identified the men who were loyal to the Union and released the rest. It was those workers, who were sent away that confirmed Anderson's movement to the people of Charleston.[1] The men who remained would prove invaluable in aiding the garrison with the massive amount of labor necessary in making Fort Sumter battle ready.

Building materials lay everywhere. If the fort had been shelled the bricks and other supplies laying around would have been turned into deadly shrapnel. Soldiers had trouble navigating the parade ground with sixty six un-mounted guns, almost six thousand projectiles, stacks of bricks and the

John Gray Foster

A native of New Hampshire, John Foster graduated from West Point in 1846 at the age of twenty three. He was fourth in his class and was assigned to an engineering unit on its way to Mexico to serve under General Winfield Scott. Foster saw action at the siege of Vera Cruz and the battle of Cerro Gordo. He was brevetted twice for heroism and was wounded at Molino del Rey as was Robert Anderson. His service during the 1850's was routine with postings mostly in coastal defense forts like Forts Moultrie and Sumter.

Six months after the conclusion of events at Fort Sumter Foster was promoted to brigadier general of volunteers. He served in Ambrose Burnside's 1862 North Carolina expedition and was given command of the Department of North Carolina. A capable officer, he was given the larger and more demanding position of commander of the Department and Army of the Ohio. He held the command for only two months until his horse fell on him and his injuries forced him to resign his post. The war was almost over by the time he was healthy enough to return to duty. He was given the less than glamorous post of commander of the Department of Florida that he held until the end of the war.

He remained in the army after the war. He only rose to the rank of lieutenant colonel in the Corps of Engineers doing the same type of work he had done before the war. He produced a study on underwater demolition that was considered the definitive work on the subject for decades. In 1871 he was appointed assistant to the Chief of Engineers, a post he held until his death at the age of fifty one.

sand needed to make mortar. Only fourteen guns had been mounted and all faced the sea, not the enemy. The fort had three tiers, but the middle one was mostly unfinished. Among the living quarters, only the officer's quarters were finished. These were designed with small porches that opened on the outside of the fort. This was a very nice addition for the comfort of the officers but a serious weakness in the event of an assault.

If a determined storming party of a hundred men equipped with a few ladders attacked the fort in these early days it would have easily been taken. What saved the garrison during this period was the mistaken belief in Charleston that Fort Sumter was much more powerful than it actually was. The *Charleston Courier* proclaimed the fort could hold out against all of Charleston and easily level Fort Moultrie.[2]

The fort was designed for six hundred and fifty men. Anderson had less than seventy. The embrasures most necessary to mount cannons in were selected and the rest were bricked up. This took several weeks of hard labor. Some of the guns weighed as much as fifteen thousand pounds. The first priority was mounting the guns on the bottom tier, these would be of the most use against a landing party. The main gate also had to be secured. The huge gate faced toward Morris Island, where South Carolina would most probably build an artillery battery. The fort had been built to engage an enemy arriving from the Atlantic. All of Fort Sumter's weaknesses including the gate now faced the direction of the new enemy.[3]

The outside gate was two heavy iron doors. Once a visitor passed through those doors he entered a wide tunnel and came to a heavy wooden door that was raised by a series of ropes and pulleys. Both sets of doors were extremely vulnerable to artillery fire from Morris Island. If the doors were destroyed, Fort Sumter would be open to a sneak attack during the night. To counter this a large brick wall was built behind the innermost door. It had an opening large enough for one man to step through at a time. The visitor passing through that opening would find himself facing an eight inch howitzer loaded with canister shot. An attack force attempting to rush through the main gate would be cut to pieces by nails, musket balls and other fragments of metal that make up canister shot.

Anderson also wanted the huge ten inch columbiads on the upper tier. Their massive presence would be a serious deterrent. Raising the fifteen thousand pound guns fifty feet into the air was no easy task. The first columbiad was put into place without incident but the second snapped its ropes and fell fifty feet to the ground. Amazingly no one was killed. Once emplacing the guns was completed the ammunition still needed to be moved. Each projectile weighed one hundred and twenty eight pounds. One evening a couple of sergeants challenged the men's ability to lift and carry the heavy shot. After the contest that followed more than sixty iron balls had been carried to the top parapet. This became a nightly event for the remainder of the siege.[4]

The remaining columbiads were buried breech down in the parade ground as mortars aimed toward the city. This was an unorthodox tactic and so the obvious decision was made to test fire one. The big gun was loaded with two pounds of gunpowder, the normal charge being eighteen. The prediction was that the one hundred and twenty eight pound ball would travel less than a thousand yards. As it turned out the columbiad made a very efficient mortar. The officers and soldiers watched nervously as the shot streaked across the sky and fell just short of the city. The gun was not tested again and a delegation from the city was sent out to learn why they had been fired upon.[5]

> A columbiad weighed over fifteen thousand pounds and could send a one hundred and twenty eight pound shell almost five thousand yards.

The most likely spot for an enemy landing was the stone wharf. It faced the main gate and was obviously built to unload men and equipment. Two five gallon bottles filled with gunpowder were placed under the wharf. Each one had two separate fuses guaranteeing the structure would be destroyed if an enemy attempted to land. Also on the south wall was a nice paved area where an attacking enemy could stand and be safe from the fort's guns. To counter this a pile of rocks were pushed against the wall giving the impression of unfinished construction, but not giving any hint of the explosives hidden underneath that would rain stone down upon any attacking force.[6]

Unlike the star shaped fortress of an earlier generation a man could stand close to the wall and be out of the field of fire. Fort Sumter's defenders adopted a medieval solution to this problem. Wooden boxes, securely fastened, hung over the top of the walls. They were lined with iron plate to make them bullet proof. And holes in the bottom allowed a soldier to fire straight down. Hand grenades were improvised as well to drop through. Large stones that could have been used as stepping stones into the embrasures were rolled into the water.[7]

Captain Truman Seymour developed a simple but highly effective weapon. A barrel was filled with broken stones and a charge of gunpowder placed in its center. The device was detonated by means of a friction primer attached to a long cord. The barrel would be rolled down the wall and would explode at the end of the cord, measured for maximum effect. When Seymour's device was tested for the first time the majority of the garrison went to watch. This, of course, attracted the attention of the ships in the harbor and the men on Johnson Island who watched through field glasses. A description of the test also appeared in several Charleston newspapers. This and the other defensive improvements had a deterrent effect on South Carolina. A landing and infantry attack on Fort Sumter would cost many lives.[8]

SOUTH CAROLINA PREPARES FOR WAR

South Carolina was also busy preparing for the coming conflict inside the harbor. As commander and chief of South Carolina's armed forces, Governor Pickens set to work preparing his forces to do battle. Pickens operated under the assumption that Anderson would attack the city. This was a complete misunderstanding of the situation. Anderson was standing on the defensive. All of his improvements were aimed at beating back a ground assault. The major still hoped that the politicians could find a solution as long as shots had not been fired.[9]

The damage done to Fort Moultrie had to be repaired. Major Walter Gwynn of the South Carolina militia was placed in charge. The Virginia born Gwynn was a West Point educated artilleryman and a retired railroad engineer. He was, initially, given command of the workers who refused to stay at Fort Sumter. As it turned out, they were not any more interested in working at Fort Moultrie than they had been at Fort Sumter, as most did not return from their first lunch break. The issue had, obviously, been more a desire to stay out of the line of fire than loyalty to the Union or Southern causes. To replace them, Gwynn was loaned forty slaves by the South Carolina railroad (Figure 4.1). The gun carriages that Anderson's men had destroyed needed to be rebuilt and he wanted the wall strengthened. The sand dunes, which Anderson had so complained about, were now sorely needed back against the walls as they would greatly absorb the shock of Fort Sumter's heavy guns.[10]

Forty cadets from the Citadel, South Carolina's military academy in Charleston, were sent to Morris Island along with ninety militiamen. Under the command of Florida born Major P.F. Stevens, the superintendent of the Citadel, they were to construct a battery directly south of Fort Sumter. This battery would be in position to fire on any ship attempting to relieve Fort Sumter. Men on both sides worked feverishly to prepare for the fight. When the soldiers looked up from their work they could see men on the other side working just as hard.[11]

Figure 4.1 South Carolina forces putting cannons into place using slave labor. (Courtesy of the Library of Congress)

FORT SUMTER ISOLATED

Governor Pickens cut off Fort Sumter from all outside contact except for the mail. The command was not allowed to purchase fresh food or coal from Charleston. The mail which arrived had already been read in Charleston in search of secret orders. To Anderson's growing frustration, no such orders arrived. Anderson, however, was getting a quickly growing amount of fan mail from all over the North. A "Baltimore citizen" offered his services and gave his "heartfelt thanks" for Anderson's actions "for our beloved country."[12] L.R. Hunlbruth of Stanford Connecticut asked that "God bless you and give you wisdom and courage." He also told Anderson that he could "have no idea how much you have endeared yourself to the people of good old Connecticut."[13] A.G. Bradley of Boston wrote that Anderson's actions "made us feel as if we had a country yet."[14]

THE *STAR OF THE WEST*

Long before the *Star of the West* and its cargo of soldiers and supplies arrived rumors that a relief ship was in transit were common in Charleston. These were not general rumors but were very specific including the name of the ship, its time of departure and the exact nature of its cargo.[15] Washington D.C. could not keep a secret. When these rumors reached Fort Sumter they were dismissed by Major Anderson. He assumed that General Scott knew better than to send reinforcements in anything but a U.S. Navy vessel. He also assumed that if the government planned to take any action in the harbor he would have been informed. He had been, but the letter was still in the mail when the *Star of the West* arrived.

The *Star of the West* arrived during the night of January 8, 1861. With the channel markers removed and the normal navigation lights extinguished the ship's captain and her pilot decided to wait until dawn to enter the harbor. This would make it easier for them to see but also to be seen. When Captain McGovern ordered his ship into the channel he had no idea he was expected. Everyone involved in the planning had assumed that confusion and indecision among the South Carolina batteries would buy them enough time to complete their mission. Instead a member of Buchanan's own cabinet had tipped them off. The *Star of the West* encountered one of the city's patrol boats that had been waiting at the harbor's entrance. She signaled but when the *Star of the West* made no reply the little ship raced back to Charleston firing signal rockets. Everyone now knew what was going on except the officers and men of Fort Sumter.

The alarm was sounded on Morris Island and the Citadel cadets rushed to their posts. The camp was hidden behind the sand dunes so that all that could be seen from the water was the small red Palmetto flag flying over the batteries. When the *Star of the West* was still two miles away from Fort Sumter, but only a thousand yards from Morris Island, Major Stevens gave the order to fire. Senior Cadet George Edward Haynesworth pulled the lanyard that sent a twenty four pound iron ball high over the *Star of the West*. The first shot of the war had been fired.[16]

Captain Abner Doubleday was the officer on watch on the morning of January 9. He ordered the drummer to beat the garrison to quarters while he went personally to report to Major Anderson that a ship bearing the U.S. flag had been fired upon. Most of Fort Sumter's guns were manned before the second gun at Morris Island had been fired.

Captain McGowan had been given a large U.S. flag to raise in case he was fired upon. The flag was to be dipped and raised again as a pre-arranged signal to Fort Sumter. This, of course, was all in the letter that Anderson had yet to receive. To the gunners at Morris Island the wagging flag could only be an act of open defiance and they continued to fire. Of the more than a dozen shots fired before she was out of range only two actually struck the *Star of the West* and they did no real damage. Fort Moultrie fired a few shots when the ship was still a half mile out of range. When Captain McGowan saw the patrol boat *Clinch* moving to perhaps cut off his escape and with no aid coming from Fort Sumter he decided to retreat to the open waters of the Atlantic.[17]

The *Star of the West* incident illustrated just how poor a decision not sending a warship had been. The unarmed steamer had been able to enter and leave with little damage. Not only would Fort Sumter have supported, without question, a U.S. Navy ship, like the *Brooklyn*, but with the *Brooklyn* returning fire at the Morris Island batteries, the cadets' accuracy would have been even worse. Charleston harbor was far from sealed on January 9, and the administration had missed its opportunity to reinforce Anderson.

The men aboard the *Star of the West* and those men at Fort Moultrie and Morris Island were surprised that Fort Sumter had not opened fire in defense of a ship flying the flag of the United States of America. For Major Robert Anderson this was the hardest decision of his professional career. Had he known it was supplies and reinforcements for his garrison it probably would have affected his decision. However, the fact that the U.S. flag had been fired upon made Anderson and the majority of his officers and men want to open up with the full force of Fort Sumter. One soldier's wife had to be restrained from firing one of the big guns.[18]

On the other hand, as Lieutenant Meade urgently pointed out to Anderson, if Fort Sumter fired it would mean war and there would be no going back. Like many senior professional officers Anderson had the foresight to know what a bloodbath an American Civil War would be. We should forgive Major Anderson for being a little naïve and erring on the side of caution. However, most of his officers already understood that they had just witnessed the first shots of the war and had only watched. Anderson had chosen restraint. Perhaps, as Meade had suggested, the shots were the result of poor discipline among the South Carolina militia and not from official orders of the state. This was not an ungrounded believe. Only the day before a sentry on Castle Pinckney had mistakenly killed one of his own comrades and another militiamen had been shot in the leg during an accidental shooting.[19]

As the *Star of the West* steamed out to sea, Anderson called a council of his officers. Most were upset and frustrated. As the events of the past few moments began to sink in, the stoic Anderson grew angry at this insult and attack on his flag. Anderson suggested to his officers that they use the big guns of Fort Sumter to shut down Charleston harbor, something well within their power. The majority of his officers agreed on immediately closing down the harbor. Lieutenant Meade disagreed on the same grounds that he had stated earlier, it would mean war. Lieutenant Jefferson Davis, of no relation to the soon to be Confederate president, and Surgeon Crawford agreed with Anderson's proposed plan, with the exception that the opportunity for immediate action had passed and now the governor should be informed. Anderson agreed and sent Lieutenant Hall to Charleston with a dispatch for the governor.[20]

Anderson gave the governor the opportunity to repudiate the firing on the *Star of the West*. If not Anderson would "not permit any vessel to pass within range of the guns."[21] Hall was rowed ashore under a white flag. Charleston residents lined the shore still excited about the morning's events. The rumors about town were that Hall had come to deliver official word that the city was about to be bombarded.

On reading Anderson's letter Pickens gave Hall a written response and a military escort back to his boat. The governor's response was direct. South Carolina was no longer part of the United States and the *Star of the West*'s attempt to bring troops into the harbor was a hostile act against the sovereign nation of South Carolina. The message was also much more diplomatic than anything Pickens had written as governor. This new tone was probably due to the fact that the *Star of the West* had entered and successfully exited the harbor. Even though she had not unloaded her cargo, she showed that South Carolina was not yet able to control her most important harbor and Anderson had the ability to carry out his threat of closing down the harbor.[22]

Jefferson C. Davis

Jefferson Columbus Davis was born in Clark County, Indiana. Davis was a rarity in the Antebellum army. He had risen from the enlisted ranks. He had volunteered as a private in the Third Indiana during the Mexican War. He fought at the battle of Buena Vista, Zachary Taylor's great victory over Santa Anna. Davis made not only the unlikely transition from the enlisted ranks to the officer corps but the even more unlikely move from the volunteers to the regular army. By the time he was stationed at Fort Moultrie he had risen to the rank of captain.

After the events at Fort Sumter, Davis was appointed colonel of the Twenty Second Indiana. By December of 1861 he was a brigadier general of volunteers. He commanded troops at the battle of Pea Ridge in Arkansas and the siege of Corinth, Mississippi.

Davis is perhaps best known for shooting and killing a fellow general, William Nelson in the lobby of the Galt House hotel in Louisville, Kentucky. The two men had gotten into a heated argument and Nelson slapped Davis. The Indianan responded by killing Nelson. No charges were brought against Davis, military or civilian, perhaps because of his friendship with the influential governor of Indiana. Nelson also had important political connections. His family had ties to Lincoln. Although Davis continued to receive high commands and serve in important positions he only received brevet ranks. He commanded troops at Murfreesboro, Chickamauga and Atlanta. He also led one of Sherman's three divisions during the "March to the Sea."

In the post war army Davis was only a colonel and was given the unwelcome task of commanding an infantry unit in the newly acquired territory of Alaska, perhaps continued punishment for the death of Nelson. He would see action for the last time in the Modoc War in California. Jefferson C. Davis died of natural causes at the age of fifty one.

The governor was wise not to send a belligerent message. Anderson in the time it took to row across the harbor and back had regained his temper. Anderson decided to send Lieutenant Theodor Talbot, a fellow Kentuckian, to Washington to receive more direct instructions. Until then he would wait. Pickens was more than happy to give Talbot safe passage out of the state. Delay was to the governor's advantage, something an extremely frustrated Doubleday understood. The New York abolitionist was pushing for decisive action. Doubleday was also more than annoyed that Anderson allowed South Carolina to strengthen her position in the harbor. More heavy batteries were being moved to James, Morris and Sullivan's Islands. Since men and equipment could only be moved by ferry it was well within Anderson's power to stop them, but that would mean war.

Theodor Talbot

Born in Kentucky in 1825, James Theodor Talbot was the son of the prominent U.S. Senator, Isham Talbot. He was educated at a military school in Kentucky, one of many such institutions that dotted the landscape of Antebellum America.

At eighteen he joined John C. Fremont's mapping expedition to the Oregon country for the U.S. Army. Although he joined as a civilian, when war with Mexico broke out and Fremont took the expedition into California, Talbot enlisted. Fremont and his men played a key role in the capture of California during the Mexican War. Talbot ended the war as a lieutenant and would stay in the army for the rest of his life.

Talbot spent most of the late 1840's and early 50's mapping the West Coast. In 1853 he was sent east on recruiting duty. He found himself assigned to the First Artillery in 1859 and to the defenses of Charleston harbor.

After the events at Fort Sumter, Talbot was promoted to major and assigned to the Adjutant General's Office. He served mostly in Washington D.C. He died in April of 1862 from tuberculosis, a health issue he struggled with all his life. The conditions inside Fort Sumter could only have exacerbated the problem. He was thirty seven.

Although Georgia was still in the Union, at least for another eight days, the city of Savannah was kind enough to donate four abandoned ships loaded with stones for Charleston to sink in the channel to keep deep draft ships like U.S. warships from entering. However, the current quickly pushed the sunken hulks out of the way so that they did not have their desired effect, except for causing much of Charleston's ship traffic and their money to divert to Savannah.

NEGOTIATIONS WITH THE GOVERNOR

Only moments after the four ships were towed into place and sunk, the governor sent two representatives to negotiate with Anderson. Andrew Magrath, a former federal judge who resigned his post the moment he learned Lincoln had been elected, was now the Secretary of State of the Republic of South Carolina. He was accompanied by David Jamison the Secretary of War. Jamison was part of the planter elite and had served as the presiding officer of South Carolina's secession convention. Anderson met them outside the gate and escorted them to the guardroom just inside the main gate. There was no need to show the enemy any more of the fortress than was absolutely necessary. The two senior South Carolina officials had come to ask nicely for the fort's surrender.[23]

Anderson, always the officer and gentleman, politely refused, after going through the motions of consulting with his officers. He reminded them that he had sent one of his officers to Washington and he would abide by whatever instructions he returned with. That would not be acceptable to South Carolina, as they knew that Buchanan, now under the influence of his new Secretary of War, was unlikely to submit.

Magrath tried to convince Anderson and his officers that they were serving a lost cause. The old Union was disintegrating. States were leaving every day. President Buchanan was drifting into senility and there was no way he could hold the country together. Anderson and his officers needed to look after their own best interests. That was what South Carolina was doing and they would possess the fort even if that meant the "harbor waters would redden with blood."[24] It would be the humanitarian thing to do to give up the fort before thousands had to die.

Although this appeal was a direct insult to the U.S. government that Anderson so faithfully served, the humanitarian tone of Magrath's speech struck a chord with the major. His duty was clear however, he could not hand Fort Sumter over without direct orders. He appealed to Magrath to do all he could do to prevent the outbreak of violence, turning Magrath's argument back on its source. Anderson then offered that if Pickens would send a commissioner to Washington D.C., he would send one of his officers to report on the status of the fort. Anderson was attempting to buy time for the politicians to work out a peaceful solution. Had Anderson a clearer view of what was happening in Washington and the mood of the rest of the nation, he would have realized that his hopes were definitely misplaced.

When Governor Pickens received Anderson's offer, he instantly assented. Charleston was not yet in position for an armed clash with Fort Sumter or the U.S. Navy. The *Star of the West* had proven that. A truce, which was what Anderson had essentially offered, benefited the governor politically. Had Anderson responded with a simple no, the governor would have been called on to act and he was not yet ready. His bluff had not been called. Instead Pickens sent Isaac W. Hayne, South Carolina's Attorney General, to negotiate once again the peaceful handover of Fort Sumter.

THE CONFEDERATE STATES OF AMERICA

Before Hayne could make an attempt to meet with the president, he was approached by Senator Clement C. Clay of Alabama. Clay represented a cabal of Southern Senators whose goal was a new nation made up of the

Southern Slave States. They believed this could be carried out peacefully. In their ranks were men like Jefferson Davis of Mississippi, Howell Cobb of Georgia and Benjamin Fitzpatrick of Alabama. These seated Senators were using their official position to undermine the U.S. government. What these men saw as the greatest danger to the Southern cause was South Carolina taking unilateral and rash action that would start a war and end all hope of peaceful separation.[25]

Clay convinced Hayne that delivering an ultimatum to President Buchanan was not to the advantage of the South Carolina cause, which was the same as the cause of all Southern states. It would be to the best interest of South Carolina, if nothing happened until a Southern government could be formed. Hayne followed the advice and dragged his mission out for more than a month. As long as he remained in the capital, the truce in Charleston harbor remained in effect. This would allow the Southern states to strengthen their position politically and for South Carolina to strengthen her position militarily.

Buchanan was in no rush either. He had about a month and a half left in his presidency. He welcomed every day that he did not have to make the dread decision that might plunge the nation into civil war and found him one day closer to his quiet Pennsylvania home. After all, Buchanan must have thought, this was a problem created by Lincoln and his Republicans, let them deal with it.

On February 4, 1861 the decisions that controlled the fate of Fort Sumter shifted from Washington and Charleston to the more western city of Montgomery, Alabama. Although South Carolinians would never want to admit it, money, power and influence had been shifting to the Southern states of Alabama, Mississippi, Arkansas and Louisiana for the last thirty years. It was in the heart of this region that a new government for the seceding states would be formed.

The Montgomery convention worked much faster than anyone could have predicted. After only four days of meetings at the capitol building and in the boarding houses the Confederate States of America was formed. With only a few minor changes the original Constitution of the United States was provisionally adopted. Although the representatives of the six states present at Montgomery had not been empowered to go as far as to create a new government they acted aggressively because time was not on their side. Abraham Lincoln was scheduled to be inaugurated the sixteenth president of the United States in less than a month. It was the universal opinion of the Montgomery delegates that their best chance of successful secession would be while James Buchanan was still in the White House.[26]

There was also, of course, the issue of Fort Sumter. Most of the delegates strongly believed that in the face of a fully formed government of several united Southern states, the Federal government would not only relinquish Fort Sumter but would reluctantly recognize the Confederate States of America. The fear was that Governor Pickens and South Carolina would act rashly, bring about armed conflict and maybe even galvanize Northern public opinion in support of the Republicans.[27]

There was also the sense among many Southerners that the document produced by the Federal Convention should be preserved. The issue that had brought them to Montgomery was not flaws in the U.S. Constitution but that it was being corrupted by New England abolitionists, Yankee merchants and low class foreigners. These Southerners saw themselves not as leaving the United States but as excluding others.

> Besides more protections for the institution of slavery, the major change made in the Confederate Constitution was an outright ban on secession from the new Confederacy.

There were many who disagreed that the Constitution should be preserved. Just as in the original convention in Philadelphia there were those who believed the document gave too much power to the central government and those who believed it did not give enough. In the end expedience won out and the Constitution was adopted on a provisional basis. The shape the new government would take would be debated in a time of peaceful sovereignty just as it had been in 1787.

The representatives also took the radical step of naming themselves the first Confederate Congress instead of taking the time consuming step of holding elections. They also gave themselves executive power until a president and vice president could be chosen. For those positions they chose Jefferson Davis of Mississippi as president and Alexander Stephens as vice president. Although there were backroom debates and other men desperately wanted these positions the Congress wanted to show a united face to the outside world. Davis and Stephens were chosen because they would be the most acceptable to those that had not yet joined the Confederacy, primarily the Virginians, but Maryland, Kentucky and Missouri as well. A radical like Robert Barnwell Rhett of South Carolina or William Yancey of Alabama might scare off the moderate Border States.

FIRST PRESIDENT OF THE CONFEDERATE STATES OF AMERICA

Jefferson Davis had solid credentials for the position. Up until very recently Davis had been a U.S. Senator from Mississippi. Prior to that he had been

Franklin Pierce's Secretary of War. Davis graduated from West Point in 1828 and served as a colonel of a Mississippi regiment under his father-in-law Zachary Taylor during the Mexican War. He was also a slave owner and a successful cotton planter.

Alexander H. Stephens, the only vice president of the Confederacy, was a more controversial choice than Davis. He had been a Unionist until his home state of Georgia seceded. His selection had not only been a nod to the moderate Border States but also to the politically powerful state of Georgia, the Empire State of the South.

Davis was at home near Vicksburg when he learned that he had been named the provisional president of the Confederacy. To reach Montgomery Davis had to take the train north to Memphis, then to Chattanooga, south to Atlanta and then to Montgomery, more than five hundred miles that would not have been necessary had there been a direct rail line between Jackson and Montgomery. The long trip was a foreshadowing of one of the South's major problems in the years to come.[28]

Davis was sworn into office on February 18, 1861. In his inaugural address Davis called for the creation of a Confederate army and navy. On February 27, the Confederate Congress accepted his suggestion and created the provisional army of the Confederacy. There were countless political fights over the creation of the army. Not only were there debates about the size of the force or whether it should exist at all, there were also debates about who should lead this army. The governors of the seven states, Texas having just left the Union over the strong protest of the elderly governor Sam Houston, wanted to appoint generals from the state militias. Davis, the West Point graduate, preferred to have direct control over the appointment of general officers. Although Davis avoided the problems Abraham Lincoln had with politically appointed officers, the goodwill Lincoln created by allowing governors to make these appointments was invaluable to Union cause.[29]

CHARLESTON'S MILITARY COMMANDER

Davis assigned freshly commissioned brigadier general P.G.T. Beauregard to take command of all forces at Charleston. With a professional officer in charge it was much less likely that war would start before negotiations could be carried out. Governor Pickens was extremely pleased, the pressure and any criticism now belonged to the Confederate government yet he could still take credit for any success.

To the people of South Carolina, Pierre Gustave Toutant Beauregard was the ideal military commander. The forty three year old Louisianan

P.G.T. Beauregard

Pierre Gustave Toutant Beauregard was born into a wealthy plantation family just outside of New Orleans in 1818. Perhaps because of his French ancestry Beauregard was more obsessed with Napoleon than most young men of his day. Over his parents' objections, he attended West Point and graduated second in the class of 1838. He studied artillery under Robert Anderson and served as his assistant at the Academy.

On graduation he was assigned to the Army Corps of Engineers. He oversaw military and civilian projects in Rhode Island, Florida and Louisiana. With the outbreak of war with Mexico, he served on General Winfield Scott's staff. He never felt he received enough credit for his service in Mexico. This chip on his shoulder would affect the rest of his military career.

In 1841 he married into an influential Louisiana family. While their support did not help his failed attempt to become mayor of New Orleans they probably helped him secure the position of Superintendent of West Point in January 1861. His outspoken support of seceding states cost him this position within five days of taking up the post.

On joining the Confederate States Army as brigadier general, he hoped to be made commander of Louisiana state forces. Instead he was sent to Charleston. After the events of Fort Sumter, Beauregard was second in command at the First Battle of Bull Run, the first major land battle of the war. Although his contributions were dubious, the Confederates were victorious and he was promoted.

Beauregard was second in command at the Battle of Shiloh. The command devolved to him with the death of General Albert Sidney Johnston during the first day of fighting. Under Beauregard's command, Confederate forces were defeated by a Union army under Ulysses S. Grant. It was the costliest battle in U.S. history up to that point.

Beauregard was popular with the public and the Confederate Congress but could not get along with the Confederate president Jefferson Davis and many in the army high command. He was stationed in Charleston in 1862, a serious drop in status from the command in the west.

Charleston was attacked unsuccessfully by the combined Union Army and Navy while Beauregard was in command, further endearing him to the people of Charleston. In the spring of 1864 he was moved to southern Virginia to help resist General Grant's Overland Campaign to capture Richmond. Although Richmond would eventually fall, Beauregard's actions around Petersburg put off the inevitable by a year.

Beauregard was sent back to South Carolina in early 1865. Fittingly, Beauregard oversaw the evacuation of Charleston in the face of William T. Sherman's advancing army. On May 1, 1865 Beauregard surrendered to Sherman and returned to New Orleans. After the war, Beauregard spent time in Europe as an agent for a railroad company. He attempted to gain employment as a mercenary for several foreign nations to no avail. Unlike many former Confederates, Beauregard was fairly well off financially after the war. He wrote widely on the Civil War, mostly attacking Davis and his Confederate rivals. He died in 1893, one of the last Confederate generals.

had graduated second in his class at West Point. He had only risen to the rank of captain in the U.S. Army when he was offered a place in the Confederate Army. On accepting his general's stars, he first went to his tailor to have a uniform made to fit his new status.

Beauregard arrived in Charleston to take command on March 3, 1861. Almost instantly he was a favorite of the city's elite. Men wanted to serve on his staff and grew beards to match his neatly trimmed goatee. Women filled his hotel room with flowers and gifts. He was the epitome of the Southern gentleman with enough of the hint of the exotic, with jet black hair, French style goatee, olive skin and his uniform that was just a little more European than what was worn by his contemporaries, to set him apart.

Although Beauregard may have spent a disproportionate amount of time on his appearance (just as some writers have spent a disproportionate amount of time on the question of whether he dyed his hair), and socializing with the Charleston elite, he was a professional. Not only had he graduated high in his West Point class he was asked to stay on as an assistant to the instructor of artillery, Robert Anderson. He had also served in Mexico under Scott and was wounded and promoted twice.

Unlike many Confederate officers, Beauregard had no doubt where his loyalties lay. Even though he had only recently been appointed the Commandant of West Point, Beauregard instantly resigned his commission on hearing the news of Louisiana's secession. He was the most prominent officer to resign his commission until Robert E. Lee a few months later.[30]

After surveying the military situation he had two tasks. First he needed to seal off the harbor. The *Star of the West* had shown how easy it would be for a naval expedition to reinforce and resupply Fort Sumter. Beauregard also had to make preparations to retake the position. He dismissed the idea of a direct assault. He knew Anderson was a professional and would be prepared for an infantry attack. Beauregard had seen his share of attacks against stone fortresses in Mexico and knew that even when successful they carried a heavy price.

Beauregard planned to encircle Fort Sumter with heavy batteries, including as many mortars as he could procure. The mortar batteries would allow the Confederates to fire explosive shells in a high arc into the fort. The garrison inside would be unable to hold out very long against that kind of attack. Beauregard had a command of nearly nine thousand men to put his plan into effect. Over the next three months this force would put into place nearly fifty heavy guns and mortars in thirteen different batteries surrounding

By the time he was done Beauregard had thirty heavy guns and seventeen mortars facing Fort Sumter.

Fort Sumter. Major Anderson, his officers and his men, could only watch. The major described the situation as "a sheep tied watching the butcher sharpening his knife."[31]

SUFFERING INSIDE FORT SUMTER

Besides the steadily worsening strategic situation, life inside Fort Sumter continued to worsen. Even before Governor Pickens took action, Charleston merchants refused to sell supplies to the garrison, either out of patriotism to the Southern cause or out of fear of retaliation from their neighbors. The men would be without fresh meat or vegetables for nearly four months. Anderson, through a few friends in the city, was able to arrange for some fresh food to be smuggled into the fort but it was just enough to keep scurvy at bay. Their diet mostly consisted of salt pork and hard tack. The pork was stored in barrels of a salt water solution and thus would last longer than anything edible probably should. Hard tack was simply flour and water baked into a rock hard cracker. Soldiers learned to use the two together. The grease and fat of the salt pork making the hard tack a little more edible. Even this unappetizing fare had to be cut in half as the garrison ran dangerously low on rations.[32]

The daily coffee allotment was cut in half for the men, and the officers had to do completely without. This was a particularly difficult staple to relinquish during the winter. Most people think of South Carolina's weather as hot summers and mild winters. Even though there was no snow on the ground or ice in the harbor, the soldiers inside Fort Sumter spent a very uncomfortable winter. The winds off the Atlantic feel colder than a dry interior wind, regardless of what the thermometer says. Dampness permeated everywhere in the fort. The coal necessary to heat the fort quickly ran out and firewood obtained by tearing down unnecessary outbuildings was also in very short supply. The walls intended to keep out enemy gunfire also prevented direct sunlight from entering the fort for all but a few hours a day. Personal supplies and extra clothes that could have made the experience more bearable were left behind during the hurried transfer to Fort Sumter. That the enemy was now enjoying the coal and extra clothes left behind only added insult to injury.[33]

The women and children of the garrison were sent to the North in early February. Not only did their presence put them in danger if hostilities broke out but they also represented more than forty additional people that had to be fed and kept warm from the garrison's shrinking store of supplies. Governor Pickens allowed Anderson to make arrangements with a Northern steamship company still doing business in

Charleston. Although Pickens might be ruthless in his anti-Yankee language he was still a Southern gentleman, and women and children were clearly noncombatants. The U.S. Army would board the wives and children at Fort Hamilton in New York. Had it not been for Henry Ward Beecher, the famous abolitionist, and his congregation, the women and children would have suffered in the cold with lack of supplies as much as their men had.

Anderson and his officers cannot be held too much to account for being caught short of food and supplies. Their assumption was that they would be resupplied or that they would have to quickly fight a battle. That they would face a lengthy siege, unaided by their superiors, seemed highly unlikely as they transferred to Fort Sumter. That was, however, the situation they found themselves in, and in a report that reached the president's desk on March 4, Major Anderson wrote that he had supplies for less than six more weeks.[34] This was one of the last documents Buchanan read as president and one of the first that Lincoln read. This was now the Republican president's problem and the outgoing president was more than happy to let him have it.[35]

NOTES

1 W.A. Swanberg, *First Blood, The Story of Fort Sumter* (New York: Charles Scribner's Sons, 1957) 103.
2 Swanberg, *First Blood*, 134.
3 Report of John G. Foster, *The War of the Rebellion: A Compilation of the Official Records of the Union and Confederate Armies War*, hereafter cited as OR (Washington D.C.: Government Printing Office) Series 1, vol. 1, 4–5.
4 James Chester, "Inside Sumter in '61", *Battles and Leaders of the Civil War, The Opening Battles. Volume 1*, Robert Underwood Johnson and Clarence Clough Buel, Editors (New York: Castle Books, 1956) 55.
5 Chester, *Battles and Leaders*, 56–57.
6 Chester, *Battles and Leaders*, 58.
7 Chester, *Battles and Leaders*, 60.
8 Chester, *Battles and Leaders*, 60.
9 Swanberg, *First Blood*, 103–107.
10 Swanberg, *First Blood*, 152
11 Swanberg, *First Blood*, 137.
12 "Baltimore Citizen" to Robert Anderson, December 29, 1860, *Anderson Papers* (Library of Congress).
13 L.R. Hunlbruth to Robert Anderson, December 31, 1860, *Anderson Papers.*
14 A.G. Bradley to Robert Anderson, December 31, 1860, *Anderson Papers.*
15 "A Surmise" *The National Republican*, January 7, 1861.
16 Swanberg, *First Blood*, 146.

17 Swanberg, *First Blood*, 146–148.
18 Swanberg, *First Blood*, 148.
19 "By Yesterday's Evening Mail" *Anderson Intelligencer*, January 8, 1861.
20 Samuel Wyllie Crawford, *The Genesis of the Civil War, The Story of Sumter, 1860–1861* (New York: Charles L. Webster and Company, 1887) 175
21 Anderson to Pickens, January 9, 1861, OR, Series 1, vol. 1, 134.
22 Pickens to Anderson, January 9, 1861, OR, Series 1, vol. 1, 134–135.
23 Swanberg, *First Blood*, 156–158.
24 David Detzer, *Allegiance, Fort Sumter, Charleston and the Beginning of the Civil War* (New York: Harcourt, Inc., 2001) 168.
25 William C. Davis, *Look Away: A History of the Confederate States of America* (New York: Simon and Schuster: 2002) 75.
26 Jefferson Davis, *The Rise and Fall of the Confederate Government* (New York: Da Capo, 1990 reprint; Richmond: Garrett and Massie, 1938) vol. 1, 250–251.
27 Richard N. Current, *Lincoln and the First Shot* (Prospect Heights, Illinois: Waveland Press, 1990) 121–122.
28 E. Merton Coulter, *The Confederate States of America, 1861–1865. A History of the South, Volume VII* (Baton Rouge: Louisiana State University Press, 1950) 25.
29 Emory Thomas, *The Confederacy as a Revolutionary Experience* (Columbia: University of South Carolina Press, 1992) 60–62.
30 Coulter, *The Confederate States of America*, 72.
31 Robert Anderson quoted in Roy Meredith, *Storm over Sumter, the Opening Engagement of the Civil War* (New York: Simon and Schuster, 1957) 80.
32 Crawford, *Genesis of the Civil War*, 134.
33 Meredith, *Storm over Sumter*, 109–113.
34 Anderson to Cameron, March 15, 1861, OR, Series 1, vol. 1, 196–199.
35 David Herbert Donald, *Lincoln* (New York: Simon and Schuster, 1995) 285.

CHAPTER 5

Lincoln, Fox and War

PRESIDENT LINCOLN

Perhaps with only the exception of his successor Andrew Johnson no man has entered the presidency at a more difficult time than Abraham Lincoln. The country had been heading toward the ultimate crisis for as long as the new president had been alive. It came as soon as the votes in the 1860 presidential election had been counted. With three months left before he enjoyed any real power the Union was collapsing. Although the question of how he would preserve the Union was still unanswered the resolve that the American nation would survive as a whole was present.[1]

President elect Lincoln better understood the situation than anyone else on the national stage. The advice he received from so many quarters was to compromise, back down and make assurances to the Southern states that he did not really mean all the things he had said and written as far back as his famous debates with Stephen Douglas. For Lincoln any further comment on his part would only be mischaracterized as all his earlier statements had been and any change to his positions "would do positive harm." The secessionists "believing they had alarmed" him "would clamor all the louder."[2]

Although the image most of us have of Abraham Lincoln is the dignified brilliant statesman from the black and white portraits, this image did not reflect how he was viewed during his lifetime. At best he was viewed as an amiable backwoodsman at worst as an ignorant gorilla whose election proved the shortcomings of the democratic system. The man's only executive experience was running a small country post office.

William Seward, who Lincoln would ask to serve as Secretary of State, held a very low opinion of the new president. Seward believed that he should have been president and that only the location of the Republican convention in Lincoln's home state had prevented Seward from winning the highest office in the land. Seward assumed that Lincoln would only be a figurehead and that he as Secretary of State would be the power behind the throne. Of course, no one had bothered to tell the president elect.

Seward's delusions of grandeur would not have been as damaging as they turned out to be had he and Lincoln shared the same strategic outlook. Both men believed that the secessionists were a very vocal minority and eventually the Southern Unionists would rise up and restore the old order. Seward believed that the best way to bring this about was to do absolutely nothing that the secessionists could use to rally moderate Southerners to their cause. To Seward this meant giving in to South Carolina and the new Confederate government. To Lincoln, however, the solution was to stand firm. Concessions would embolden the secessionists and increase their ranks. Andrew Jackson had dealt successfully with his South Carolina crisis, a crisis very similar to Lincoln's crisis, by standing firm. Lincoln believed that if Southerners saw that their movement would not be successful without taking violent action the whole thing would collapse.

Abraham Lincoln took the oath to uphold and defend the United States Constitution on March 4, 1861. It was an inauguration day like no other before it. Sadly in our modern world it would seem very familiar. Army riflemen lined the buildings scanning for possible assassins. The Capitol Building was searched for a time bomb rumored to have been planted. A crowd control fence had even been put in place. These are security precautions that are taken for granted today, but in a time when one could still expect to bump into the chief executive on the streets of Washington D.C. this inauguration day had a very strange feel to it.[3]

After taking the oath Lincoln used his speech to very clearly spell out his philosophy toward the crisis in South Carolina. The new president promised to follow the Constitution. He would not interfere with slavery where it existed. He would, however, work to prevent its spread. The fugitive slave law would be enforced under his administration. In short, Southerners were overreacting to his election and they had no cause to fear for their domestic institutions. He argued the South had no legal right to leave the Union and only anarchy would ensue if they did.

Of the many lines from Abraham Lincoln's first inaugural address that would gain immortality the one that the people in Charleston and the garrison at Fort Sumter were most affected by was the simple "the power confided to me, will be used to hold, occupy, and possess the property and places belonging to the government."[4] There would be no war Lincoln promised unless the Southern states were the aggressors.

LINCOLN LEARNS THE REAL SITUATION AT FORT SUMTER

Lincoln made this promise confident that Fort Sumter was secure and any change to the status quo would require action by the South. It was on his first full day in office that Lincoln learned that bold immediate action was required of him. Joseph Holt had remained as the Secretary of War until Lincoln's own choice Simon Cameron from Pennsylvania could arrive. Holt forwarded to the president the most recent reports of the Fort Sumter situation. Most striking of these was the last report from Major Robert Anderson in command of Fort Sumter.

In the report, Anderson stated that, unless he was resupplied, his command would eat the last of their bread in less than thirty days. He also reported that because of the Confederate batteries being built around him his position was becoming untenable. He also included an estimate of how many men it would take to resupply, reinforce and hold Fort Sumter. The figure of twenty thousand men shocked both Holt and Lincoln. Anderson had not come to that number lightly. Before writing his report he had called a meeting of his officers. Anderson asked each to prepare a report estimating the force required to retake and hold all the positions seized by the Confederates. The numbers from his officers ranged from one thousand to ten thousand. Each of these estimates was based on the assumption that the men would be well drilled professionals and that there would be full naval support. Since Anderson knew that no such force existed, he based his estimate on the fact that most of the soldiers sent would have very little training.

Holt and Lincoln's shock and doubts about the loyalty of Major Anderson were based on misunderstandings. Holt informed the president that Anderson's earlier reports had not cited the dangers his command faced. Holt told the president that this report was the first that mentioned the problematic supply situation and that although Anderson had reported the building of the Confederate batteries, he had never before stressed the danger they presented. That Holt and the War Department viewed the document as of an "unexpected character" was not the fault of Anderson nor was Holt completely to blame.

Anderson's reports and letters were not addressed to the Secretary of War but to the Adjutant General, Samuel Cooper. Cooper had been a professional soldier since he graduated West Point in 1815. Anderson did not need to tell Cooper that a battery placed at a certain point would endanger his command, he would have known. Cooper also would have understood the supply situation without Anderson having to spell it out for him. That Cooper did not correctly translate Anderson's military reports to the civilian Holt is not surprising. Cooper resigned his commission in the U.S. Army three days after Lincoln's inauguration. He accepted the position of Inspector General in the Confederate Army and was the senior ranking general in the Southern service.

A man of no real military experience, Lincoln wisely reached out to his senior military expert, Winfield Scott, an American military hero for the last forty five years. The six foot five inch tall Scott was a graduate of William and Mary College in Virginia and was practicing law when British attacks on American ships, specifically the *Chesapeake/Leopard* affair in 1807, caused him to seek out an appointment in the U.S. Army. Commissioned a lieutenant by President Thomas Jefferson in 1808, Scott rose to the rank of general and national figure by the end of the War of 1812. The West Point Cadet uniform worn to this day honors his victory against the British at Chippewa. He commanded the army that conquered Mexico and showed such humanity to the Mexican people that he was offered the position of interim president of the Mexican government by the Mexican legislature.

At sixty five, the commanding general was as mentally sharp as ever. Physically, however, he was a wreck. A lover of fine food his weight had ballooned to over three hundred and fifty pounds and he suffered from gout and other intestinal issues.

Lincoln handed Scott the stack of papers and asked him to read them and report back. That they had not already been seen by the commanding general was evidence not only of the mess Floyd had made of the situation, but the organizational issues from which the U.S. Army had long suffered. Lincoln received Scott's professional opinion in the form of a written report that evening. Oddly it came to Lincoln through his Secretary of State, Seward.

It is understandable that Scott wanted to bypass Holt, a holdover of the Buchanan administration, and whose replacement had not yet arrived. Using Seward as an intermediary was an interesting and illustrative choice however. Not only was this the first evidence for the politically astute Lincoln that his Secretary of State thought he was running the show but it was also evidence of a view, that the Confederacy was an independent nation, that Lincoln would have to combat throughout the war. Seward was the Secretary of State. His job in the administration dealt solely with foreign nations. If this had been a crisis with Mexico or Canada it would have been quite proper for the commanding general to be communicating through the country's chief diplomat, but this was an internal matter. It is unlikely that Scott or Seward gave it that much thought but it does give evidence of their concept of the Union.

Winfield Scott

Winfield Scott was the most prominent American soldier in the Antebellum era. The vast majority of Civil War generals had attended West Point with the dream of being General Winfield Scott when they grew up. His six foot five inch frame and perfectly tailored uniform made him appear every bit the ideal warrior.

Scott was born to a moderately wealthy farming family just outside Petersburg, Virginia in 1786. His career as a lawyer was permanently sidetracked in 1808, when war with Britain seemed inevitable. He was commissioned by President Jefferson. Scott remained in the army until war did come. During the War of 1812, Scott proved himself a natural leader. He rose to the rank of major general. He mostly saw action along the Canadian frontier. His victories, while not key, occurred when politically the United States desperately needed victories. He emerged from the war as an American hero among the ranks of Andrew Jackson and William Henry Harrison.

In the 1830's, Scott commanded U.S. forces during the Second Seminole War and the Blackhawk War. He also had the extremely unpleasant task of leading the infamous Trail of Tears. In addition, he headed the diplomatic effort that prevented America's third war with Britain. Scott was also at the forefront of the Nullification Crisis. When Andrew Jackson flexed his presidential muscle to get South Carolina to submit to Federal law, it was Winfield Scott who would have carried out Jackson's threats.

In 1841, he was made commander of the entire U.S. Army. In 1846, Scott led the American invasion of Mexico. His landing at Vera Cruz was the largest American amphibious operation until D-Day in the Second World War. His capture of Mexico City with a numerically inferior force made him an international celebrity.

Unlike other great generals, he was never able to turn battlefield success into political success. In 1852, Scott made an unsuccessful run for the presidency as a Whig. The party had more success running Southern war heroes like William Henry Harrison and Zachary Taylor. Southern voters did not believe they could trust Scott with the institution of slavery.

By the time the Civil War began, Scott was seventy four years old and in physically poor shape. He weighed over three hundred and fifty pounds and suffered from gout and intestinal issues. After the events of Fort Sumter and the disaster at Bull Run Scott retired from the army. However, he was not done serving his nation. Scott toured Europe as a goodwill ambassador for the United States. He met with British and French politicians in an effort to convince them of the righteousness of the Union cause.

Scott survived to see the end of the war. He died in 1866. He was eighty years old. He was buried at his favorite spot, the United States Military Academy at West Point, New York.

Scott's report was not what Lincoln wanted to read. To Scott it was simply too late to save Fort Sumter. He had already begun drafting the order for Anderson to withdraw his garrison. His estimate of the force needed to hold the fort was larger than Anderson's and stressed the necessity of strong naval support. Scott's overall suggestion was to simply allow the South to peacefully go on its way. This was unacceptable to the president, to the majority of his cabinet and to the incoming Republican Congress. The 1860 elections and the absence of Southern congressmen, who were leaving with their states, had stiffened the resolve of the Federal government.

General Winfield Scott should not be misunderstood. He was completely loyal to the United States and would carry out with as much vigor as his body could summon the orders given to him. The first thing the Lincoln administration had asked of him was his opinion. This he delivered honestly. Holding Fort Sumter would mean not only resupplying the garrison but also capturing or destroying all the batteries that threatened Fort Sumter. This would take almost as many men as the U.S. Army had, and would take more time to organize than Major Anderson had. Scott also, like very few men in positions of influence, understood that a sectional war would be a long horrific bloodbath that, in the end, would not bring unity but a victor and a vanquished. He, in short, predicted the coming four years. What he lacked was Lincoln's conviction, and few men had that.

FOX'S PLAN

The nation, both North and South, was focused on Fort Sumter. To most Southerners, Lincoln's pledge to hold the fort was a declaration of war even worse than Anderson's initial move across the channel. Northern newspapers were full of support for Lincoln's pledge. Letters flooded newspapers and government offices with plans and suggestions for resupplying and reinforcing the garrison. The suggestions ran from the ludicrous to the practical. Two plans submitted to the War Department included supplying the fort with submarines or hot air balloons. These unsolicited ideas from the public were ignored except for the occasional one printed in a newspaper. One such strategist had an advantage over all others. He had married into one of the most politically powerful families in the country, the Blairs of Maryland. Gustavus Fox was married to the sister of Montgomery Blair, Lincoln's advisor and Post Master General. Fox had more going for him than family connections. The thirty nine year old Massachusetts born Fox was a professional naval officer. He had

Although slavery was legal in the United States, the country joined the British in an attempt to stop the international slave trade. U.S. Navy ships patrolled the coast of Africa from 1819 to 1861.

served in the U.S. Navy for fifteen years before he resigned in 1853 to seek better opportunities elsewhere, due to the incredibly slow rate of advance in the Antebellum navy. During his time in service, Fox was stationed in the Mediterranean, on the west coast of Africa and in the Caribbean. During the war with Mexico, Fox was in charge of the flow of supplies from New Orleans to Vera Cruz. If anyone knew how to resupply Fort Sumter in the face of a determined enemy it was Gustavus Fox.

In late January 1861, Fox sent the outlines of a simple and straightforward plan to Montgomery Blair. As Lincoln had not yet become president Blair was not yet a government official, but anyone who was paying attention knew that he would have a position in the new president's cabinet. When Blair approached the commanding general with his brother-in-law's plan, Scott had the political sense to give the plan a polite once over. He was impressed enough with Fox's plan and his credentials to ask Fox to come to the capital to discuss it further.[5]

Fox met with Scott, the Secretary of War, and Lieutenant Norman Hall. Hall had not been idle since Major Anderson had sent him to Washington, he was sought out by the press and political leaders as the expert on the situation inside Fort Sumter. Fox confidently wrote his wife

Gustavus Fox

Fox was the son of a Massachusetts country doctor. At sixteen, Fox joined the U.S. Navy as a midshipman. Over the next eighteen years he served on ships around the world, rising to the rank of lieutenant. In 1856, Fox resigned from the navy for the more lucrative job as an agent for a major textile manufacturer in Lawrence, Massachusetts.

With the coming of the Fort Sumter crisis, Fox used his family connections to put his plan for the relief of Fort Sumter in front of General Winfield Scott. From that point on he played a major role in U.S. naval policy in the Civil War. After the crisis, Fox was made Assistant Secretary of the Navy under Gideon Welles, a newly created position. He served in that post until 1866. After unofficially negotiating the purchase of Alaska from Russia, Fox resigned from the government and quietly returned to the textile industry. He died twenty four years later at the age of sixty two.

on February 7 that his plan would be used if Fort Sumter was reinforced but the general feeling in the capital was that it would not be necessary. He did not have the faith President Buchanan did that the situation could be worked out diplomatically.[6]

Fox's plan was rather straightforward. Fox correctly assumed that the Charleston authorities had sunk obstructions in the main ship channels. This would only keep the larger ships out of the harbor. Since all U.S. Navy ships had a deeper draft than the seven feet they would need to clear the sand bar blocking the harbor, the Confederates knew that any attempt to resupply Fort Sumter would be similar to the *Star of the West* attempt. As a navy man Fox seriously doubted the ability of shore batteries to stop ships. To Fox the *Star of the West* incident had proven that. The real threat to a relief vessel would be the armed patrol boats. To counter this threat, men and supplies would be ferried to the fort, from the large steamer that had brought them from the North to just outside the bar, by two powerful New York City tug boats. Two armed U.S. ships would come as close in as possible and, with the aid of Fort Sumter's guns, would keep the patrol boats away from the tugs.

The two ships he suggested to protect the tug boats were the *U.S.S. Pawnee* and the *Harriet Lane*. The *Pawnee* had only recently been built. She was steam powered and carried ten heavy guns. She was pushed through the water by a single underwater propeller or screw as opposed to the side paddlewheels on most steam ships. Fox was not a fan of the new design, but there were no other U.S. Navy ships available.[7]

The other ship would be the *Harriet Lane*. A relatively new steamship she was powered by the more traditional paddlewheels. She was borrowed from the Revenue Service, the precursor of the modern day Coast Guard. Built to prevent smuggling, she was fast and well-armed. Fox's plan did nothing to eliminate the threat to Fort Sumter, it was only meant to deliver reinforcements and supplies to the fort.

In trying to make an extremely difficult decision, Lincoln went to an unlikely source, Mary Doubleday. The displaced wife of Captain Abner Doubleday lived in Washington D.C. during the crisis. Lincoln came to her temporary home and asked if he might read the letters from her husband. Lincoln hoped to get an honest insider's view of the situation from these letters that were obviously not written for public consumption. Captain Doubleday, the avowed abolitionist, believed the fort was in a much better defensive position than almost anyone else and his letters were full of frustrations that Anderson and the government were not acting more aggressively. There was a germ in the letters that pushed Lincoln toward supporting Fox's plan. In one of his letters, Doubleday explained to his wife the extreme difficulty of hitting a moving ship with artillery. Not only was Doubleday a professional artillery officer but he had a front row seat to the *Star of the West* incident. Partially due to Doubleday's letters, Lincoln would present Fox's plan to his cabinet as a supporter.

The president's cabinet obviously had mixed opinions on the desirability of supplying Fort Sumter and the viability of Fox's plan. Seward was opposed to any plan. An attempt to supply the fort would "provoke combat, and probably initiate civil war."[8] Very troubling to the president was that his Secretaries of War and the Navy, the two departments which would be tasked with carrying out the plan, agreed with Seward. So too did Caleb Smith the Secretary of the Interior. Montgomery Blair obviously led the opposing view, arguing that a show of strength was needed for the morale of the North and to strengthen the will of Southern Unionists. He was supported by Salmon Chase, the Secretary of the Treasury, who believed it was highly unlikely that war would emerge from action taken at Charleston. Although the majority of the cabinet members favored doing nothing, the decision ultimately rested with the president.

Those who favored taking no action, whether in his cabinet or the many so called experts on the editorial pages, did not do so out of cowardice or disloyalty. They, for the most part, believed that the Secessionists had risen to power from fear of the Republican controlled government and that if the Lincoln administration took no action, the radical Southern leaders would lose credibility and the entire movement would fall apart. That had actually been Lincoln's original plan as spelled out in his first inaugural address. The report from Anderson had changed that. The ball was now squarely in Lincoln's court. He had to take action – either resupply the fort or evacuate it. Abandoning Fort Sumter would be a step backwards which was very different from the original plan of standing still. Seward, however, still under the delusion that he was the real power behind the throne, began laying the groundwork of a withdrawal.

THE CONFEDERATE AMBASSADORS

The Confederate government, as had South Carolina earlier, sent commissioners to Washington D.C. Considering separation a foregone conclusion, they were in the U.S. capital to work out the details. The largest detail, of course, was Fort Sumter. The Confederate representatives were Martin J. Crawford of Georgia, John Forsyth of Alabama and Andre Roman of Louisiana. They had impressive credentials. Crawford was a former judge and a longtime member of the U.S. Congress. Forsyth had been a newspaper editor in Mobile, Alabama and had served as Franklin Pierce's Ambassador to Mexico, which was a difficult post after the U.S./Mexican War. Roman was the former governor of Louisiana. Unlike the South Carolina commissioners, they were moderates. Forsyth had editorialized against secession in his newspaper and Roman had voted against secession in Louisiana's convention. Like so many Southerners, once their home states left the Union they were completely loyal to the cause. Confederate President Jefferson Davis described them as "discreet, well-informed and distinguished citizens."[9]

Crawford was the first to arrive in the capital and, through his contacts he made it public knowledge that if the government did not recognize him as the representative of the new Confederate government, there would be no way to prevent war. Seward knew that if he met with Crawford and the other representatives or communicated with them officially, it would be tantamount to recognition of the Confederacy as a foreign nation. He did not, however, want to pass up an opportunity to calm the storm and perhaps take the leadership role in the new administration.

Through William Gwin, a former Mississippi representative, California Senator and well-known friend to the Confederacy, Seward let Crawford know that the government would not take any action that would lead to war. Even though Lincoln had promised to hold Fort Sumter, Seward would be able to convince him to take the wiser course. He also passed on his overall strategy to the Confederate diplomats. With his guidance the Lincoln administration would save "the border states to the Union by moderation and justice, the people of the cotton states, unwillingly led into secession will rebel against their leaders and reconstruction will follow."[10]

Seward's strategy worked to the benefit of the Confederacy. The commissioners' instructions were that if they could not immediately get major concessions, they were to play for time without appearing to be doing so. Since the Seward strategy seemed to be playing right into their hands, the commissioners decided to push their luck. Through Robert Hunter, the Senator from Virginia, they offered Seward and the administration twenty days before they made their demands officially if they were given a written agreement that Fort Sumter would not be reinforced or resupplied. This would take pressure off the administration to make a decision, it seemed, but if it was agreed to it would actually equal formal recognition of the Confederate government. Seward took this offer to the president. Lincoln was politically astute enough to see the obvious trap and refused.

SEWARD'S OFFER TO SURRENDER

On March 13 the commissioners sent a formal request to the U.S. State Department asking for an official meeting with the Secretary of State. Although they were playing for time, it was still, they thought, beneficial to keep pressure on the Lincoln administration. This put Seward in a very difficult position. He confided in Supreme Court Justice Samuel Nelson, a fellow New Yorker. Justice Nelson brought fellow justice John A. Campbell from Alabama into the conversation. Campbell claimed he wanted to preserve the Union but eventually he served on the Confederate Supreme Court. Nelson and Campbell tried to convince Seward that he should meet with the Confederate commissioners. Seward told them there was nothing he could do as Lincoln would not agree to it. Asking Lincoln to accept the commissioners was too much as "the evacuation of Sumter is as much as the administration can bear."[11] It seemed to the justices that Seward had just let it slip that the administration planned to evacuate Sumter.

Since this was the major concession the commissioners had come to get, Campbell believed that this news meant peace. He offered to unofficially contact the commissioners and even Confederate President Jefferson Davis. To Seward this seemed a perfect solution to his problems. He did not, however, want to pass an opportunity to calm the storm and perhaps take the leadership role of the new administration.

The Confederacy would take no actions that would embarrass him or bring about war and Lincoln would have time to come to the realization, with the help of Seward's counsel, that there was no other option but to surrender Fort Sumter. Oddly enough, Seward did not buy himself as much time as he could have. When Campbell asked what he should say to President Davis, Seward asked how long it would take for the letter to reach Montgomery, the Confederate capital. Campbell responded "in three days," and Seward told him he could tell Davis that by the time he received Campbell's letter, he would have already received a telegram informing him of the evacuation of Fort Sumter. Seward had not been pressed for a date and must have been overly confident of his ability to persuade Lincoln and the rest of the cabinet since he offered one.

After five days the commissioners telegraphed General Beauregard for confirmation that Fort Sumter had been or was in the process of being evacuated. The general's response was that not only was the fort not being evacuated, but that Anderson and his command were diligently working on its defenses. When Seward was confronted with this news, he assured Davis and the Confederate representatives through his intermediaries that Fort Sumter would be evacuated. Most historians credit Seward's strategy as his attempt to control the administration and prevent it from carrying out decisions that would lead to war. Seward's belief that he should have been president caused him to act like he actually was.

Jefferson Davis viewed Seward's actions very differently. He firmly believed Seward was intentionally misleading the Confederates in order to distract them from the operation to resupply the fort. One can easily understand how Davis came to believe this, especially after it became public knowledge that the Fox expedition was being planned and organized at the exact same time Seward was giving his word that the fort would be evacuated.

ANDERSON'S POSITION

Major Robert Anderson, commanding officer at Fort Sumter, was completely unaware of the political and diplomatic intrigues in Washington and Montgomery. The garrison was getting outside information but it was second hand at best. The newspapers and letters from family, friends and well-wishers they received, all painted contrasting pictures of events outside their fortress island. There was frustratingly little official word from the army high command or the Lincoln administration. The fate of the nation had been placed on Robert Anderson, a man whose military training and experience had not prepared him for such a complicated situation, although in fairness to the major it is highly unlikely that there was anyone in the nation prepared to handle such a state of affairs. A poor or rash decision or even indecisiveness on his part could have plunged the nation into a bloody civil war and put the North in a position in which it would be impossible or difficult to win that conflict. Instructions or at least words of support from the new administration would probably have gone a long way to relieving some of the great stress he was under. It also did not help that it had been over two months since Anderson, an extremely devoted family man, had seen any of his family.

MRS. ANDERSON'S MISSION

Eliza Anderson was an officer's daughter and an officer's wife. Sitting in a New York City hotel room reading inaccurate newspaper articles and waiting for the mail was insufficient for her. She had traveled to Washington to plead with President Buchanan to protect her husband. The next month the sickly Mrs. Anderson traveled to Charleston to see her husband. She did not come alone. She brought her husband's brother,

Larz Anderson. A prominent Cincinnati politician, he brought his brother the information that he was supported in the North, at least outside of Washington D.C. She also brought Peter Hart. Hart had served under Anderson during the Mexican War. He was a New York City police officer when Mrs. Anderson convinced him to go to Charleston to serve once again with her husband. She could not be with him, but at least she could make sure he had someone with him who was completely loyal to him. She was only able to stay a few hours and even that short visit would not have been possible had she not been the daughter of General Duncan Clinch who had been a prominent Georgia planter and general before his death. The militia patrol boat that guarded the harbor was named in his honor. This visit had occurred nearly two months earlier and the effects of Anderson's lonely and stressful position were setting in again.

PHYSICAL PRIVATIONS INSIDE FORT SUMTER

The garrison and its command faced physical privations as well as mental. The winter and early spring of 1861 was unusually cold. The old Southern cliché "it's not the heat it is the humidity" is doubly true in the winter as the cold wet air can be as brutal as anything the Midwest can offer. This was especially true on an island in the middle of the bay where the high walls of the fort prevented the sun from reaching most of the interior. The garrison had not brought sufficient heating fuel or extra clothes or blankets. They had not predicted a long siege unaided by the government. The garrison was reduced to tearing down unused buildings, breaking apart furniture and anything else they could scrounge to burn. The fort was designed with a heating system to keep the men dry and warm but there was never enough fuel to run it properly.

The garrison still faced food shortages. U.S. forces had always depended on local civilian sources of supply. Even General Scott had purchased supplies from local sources as he marched his army across southern Mexico. Normally this was not a problem but these were not normal circumstances. Their normal supplier feared repercussions if he sold to the fort. Considering the situation in Charleston, this was not an unreasonable fear. Anderson had friends in Charleston who smuggled in supplies, but this was a mere trickle compared to what was needed. The men were on half rations of coffee for the last two months and the officers were doing without. Fresh vegetables were a scarce luxury and they had to settle for pork packed in barrels of salt water for longer than anyone wanted to think about. Soap and candles were also a thing of the past.

LINCOLN'S AGENTS

The general mood in Charleston had greatly improved thanks to the news from Seward and the reports from newspapers. It was generally believed that Fort Sumter would be evacuated at any moment and that the people of South Carolina were well on their way to independence. Governor Pickens sent an emissary to Major Anderson with the news. The governor was being gracious in victory. Not only would he do all he could to aid Anderson's departure but he wanted the major to know that he thought all of Anderson's actions had been just and right.

Over the next few days the presence of a number of Northern visitors in Charleston sent a mixed message to the city. Colonel George W. Lay arrived from Washington for a long meeting with Pickens and General Beauregard. Lay had recently resigned as General Winfield Scott's assistant and probably reported to them Scott's waning support of any attempt to force aid into Fort Sumter.

The following day Gustavus Fox arrived. Fox's cover was that he had come to deliver dispatches to Major Anderson and make preparations for the garrison's withdrawal. Fox's push to relieve Fort Sumter had appeared in many newspapers and Lay had obviously informed Pickens and Beauregard about the new visitor. An old navy friend of Fox's secured for him an audience with the governor. Obviously Pickens was suspicious of the peaceful nature of Fox's mission. Fox was allowed to visit Fort Sumter as long as he was escorted by his friend Captain H.J. Hartstene, formally of the U.S. Navy but now serving South Carolina. Hartstene's instructions from the governor were to not allow Fox and Anderson the opportunity to meet alone. In this the Captain failed, but the meeting did not have the detrimental effect on South Carolina that Pickens had feared.

Fox and Anderson had a short private meeting on the fort's wall. Anderson explained to Fox his belief that the only chance of securing Fort Sumter was at least capturing Morris Island to the south of the fort. Fox was only partially listening, however. In his mind Fox was seeing his tugboats run the gauntlet and unload their cargo on the fort's wharf. Once again, the two men were thinking about two different ends. Fox had not thought beyond putting extra men and supplies into the fort. To Anderson, without securing Morris Island the plan only put more targets into the fort.

Fox did not share his plan with Anderson but the major gleaned enough of the naval man's plan that he wrote a warning to the War Department that the location where Fox would have to land supplies would be under the hostile guns of Fort Moultrie. If Anderson had any doubt that his command was to be relocated, it was removed when Captain Foster, the engineer officer, received orders on what to do if the position were abandoned.

The next to arrive was Ward Lamon, a close friend and advisor to President Lincoln. He was well enough known among South Carolinians to have almost become the victim of an angry mob. Oddly enough, it was the friendly intervention of South Carolina's representative to the Confederate Congress and passionate Southern nationalist Lawrence Keitt that saved him. It would not do to have the man who had possibly come to give South Carolina all it wanted hung or beaten to death in the streets of Charleston.

Lamon met with the governor and told him that he was in South Carolina to make preparations to abandon the fort. Lamon also went to Fort Sumter where he gave Anderson the same impression that the command would soon be moved. Lamon's instructions from President Lincoln were simply to observe and report. Lamon's meeting with Anderson and the governor were completely of his own doing. Lamon was not conspiring against the president. He was caught up in his own importance and assumed the fort would be evacuated. One can easily understand why Jefferson Davis felt they had been misled by the Lincoln administration.

Lincoln had sent a second man to observe and report. Stephen Hurlbert, who arrived on the same train as Lamon, did follow his instructions. Born in Charleston, Hurlbert had a sister living in the city and was friends with Judge Pettigru, whom Hurlbert reported was the only Unionist left in Charleston. His report to Lincoln countered Seward's and many others' belief that a soft hand in South Carolina would lead to reunion.

The universal belief, strengthened by the recent visitors, in Charleston was that Fort Sumter would be evacuated. A sense of calm came over the city. Beauregard and Anderson exchanged a series of friendly letters. Rations were served regularly, the last barrel of flour was opened on March 29.

Governor Pickens' and the population of Charleston's collective patience began to wear thin. There were plenty of hints that the fort would be evacuated. U.S. officials had said so but there in the harbor sat the garrison, as menacing as always. Anderson too was growing impatient. On April 3 he wrote Secretary of War Simon Cameron asking for clear instructions. His supply of bread would only last for five more days.[12]

ORGANIZING THE RELIEF EXPEDITION

By the time Anderson had put pen to paper, the plan to relieve Fort Sumter had already been set into motion. Fox was sent to New York to make sure the preparations were moving quickly. Lincoln had also sent word to the Navy and War Departments to get men, supplies and ships ready for the expedition. The time for debates and politics was over. Both Lincoln and his cabinet had come to the conclusion that the peaceful preservation of the Union was no longer a possibility. If war was inevitable, it would be to the advantage of the Union if the war was started by the Confederacy to prevent the resupplying of the U.S. Army garrison already in place. If the South were the aggressor, it would justify all the actions the government would take to bring the seceding states back into the Union.

FORT PICKENS

Fox's Charleston expedition was not the only military operation being launched. Nor was Fort Sumter the only U.S. Army garrison under threat by Confederate forces. Fort Pickens, was named after the grandfather of South Carolina's governor. The elder Pickens had been a hero of the American Revolution as had General Thomas Sumter. Fort Pickens guarded the entrance of Pensacola bay. Pensacola, known for its lumber industry, was home to the Navy's largest base on the Gulf of Mexico and one of the few dry dock facilities in the South. Had events played out differently in Pensacola, the city would have been extremely important to the Southern cause.

Fort Pickens had a lot of similarities to Fort Sumter. It was smaller and shorter than Fort Sumter but it was part of the same fortification series. Like Fort Sumter, it was still unfinished and un-garrisoned in 1860. As well, it was part of a defensive system utilizing cross fire to keep an enemy from entering Pensacola Bay. As Fort Sumter had Fort Moultrie, Fort Pickens had Fort McCree and Fort Barrancas. Like Fort Sumter, Fort Pickens was commanded by a loyal Union man. The day before Florida seceded from the Union, Lieutenant Adam Slemmer from Pennsylvania snuck his men across the bay from Fort Barrancas to the much more tenable Fort Pickens on Santa Rosa Island. Slemmer had pressed the commander of the navy base to also act to protect the property of the U.S. government, but either through disloyalty or the lack of resoluteness that comes with age, Commodore James Armstrong allowed almost two million dollars of equipment and supplies to fall into Confederate hands. Like Anderson,

Fort Pickens

Named after Andrew Pickens, the Revolutionary War hero and grandfather of Francis Pickens, Fort Pickens guarded the entrance of Pensacola Bay. Along with Forts Barrancas and McRee, Fort Pickens made up a defensive system that kept the city of Pensacola and its naval base safe from a hostile fleet.

When Florida left the Union on January 10, 1861, the third state to do so, Governor Madison Starke Perry gave Florida's troops the order to seize all Federal installations if they were confident of success. Forts and arsenals were seized across the state with relative ease. There were three notable exceptions, Fort Jefferson, Fort Taylor and Fort Pickens.

Fort Jefferson, located on an island halfway between Cuba and the Florida mainland, was too isolated to be bothered with. Fort Taylor, on Key West and commanded by a fast acting loyal officer, was quickly put into a defensive position. No serious move, military or political, was made by the Confederates to take Key West.

Fort Pickens was a different situation. Pensacola was an important port and if its naval faculties were denied to the Confederacy it would be a major handicap in the war to come. In command at Pensacola was Lieutenant Adam J. Slemmer from Pennsylvania. He was a loyal Union man. Like Anderson in Charleston, Slemmer moved his small command across the harbor to the unfinished but more isolated and defensible Fort Pickens. He had forty six men to defend a fort built for one thousand and sixty men.

Slemmer tried to convince the commander of the Pensacola Navy Yard to take action but Commodore James Armstrong, a fifty year veteran was unmoved. He did give some assistance, it was navy boats that carried Slemmer and his command to Fort Pickens and a navy crew that spiked the guns and destroyed the gunpowder supply at Fort McRee. Thirty five sailors joined Slemmer's command at Fort Pickens as well.

Confederate representatives in Washington D.C. were able to strike what soon came to be called the Fort Pickens Truce with Buchanan. The Federal government would not reinforce the fort and the Confederates would not attack. Nothing, however, prevented them from preparing to attack. An isolated Slemmer was forced to watch train loads of Confederate troops arrive, eventually five thousand in total.

The Fort Pickens Truce, unofficial at best, caused confusion among the Confederate leadership. They assumed it covered all Federal installations in the South. Buchanan kept the truce and no reinforcements were sent except for a new commanding officer, Captain Israel Vodges, another Pennsylvanian. Vodges found the fort in an untenable position. The garrison was exhausted, the sailors were at the point of mutiny and more than half the embrasures were defended by nothing more than wooden planks nailed into place. Fort Pickens could not have stood up to an assault.

Two hundred men from the *Powhatan*, meant for Fort Sumter, were moved into Fort Pickens the day before war began in Charleston. The assault on Fort Pickens never came. The fort remained in Union hands throughout the war and because of that the important city of Pensacola played no real role in the war.

Slemmer along with a small garrison was surrounded by hostile forces without clear instructions from Washington D.C.

In spite of these similarities, there were major differences between the situations at Fort Pickens and Fort Sumter. Because of the location of Santa Rosa Island, Fort Pickens could be safely resupplied by sea. The entrance to Pensacola Bay was wide enough that Fort Pickens was not under the threat of Fort Barrancas' guns as Fort Sumter was under the threat of Fort Moultrie's. Fort Pickens was also on the periphery of national affairs so less pressure was placed on Slemmer than on Anderson, who was definitely at the center of the nation's attention.

Fort Pickens was important to Florida and the Confederate government was calling for the handover of all Federal property located in the seceding states. Although President Buchanan did not completely back down when it came to Fort Pickens, he did agree to a truce that Fort Pickens would not be resupplied or reinforced and Florida state forces would not attack.[13] One can understand the confusion of the Southern commissioners in Washington that Buchanan would enter into a truce over Fort Pickens but would deny that there was an agreement over Fort Sumter.

By March of 1861, Fort Pickens seemed the solution to Secretary of State Seward's growing problem. He had promised the South that Fort Sumter would be evacuated and now the president was set on taking action. Seward tried to convince the president that resupplying Fort Pickens would be less likely to lead to war. If Fort Sumter were abandoned and Fort Pickens resupplied, Seward's word would have been kept and Lincoln could still claim that he was keeping his inaugural promise. Seward would not present it that way to the president. In what could only be described as fuzzy logic, he argued that an attempt to resupply Fort Sumter would convince the Border States that the issue at hand was the abolition of slavery whereas the resupply of Fort Pickens would lead the Border States to believe that the only issue was the preservation of the Union. When it came down to it, Seward was still playing politics when the time for games had long passed. In the earliest days of the Lincoln administration, American political leaders, senior newsmen and foreign diplomats saw Seward as "the ablest American Statesman" and the real power behind the new Republican administration. After the events surrounding Fort Sumter, he was viewed differently. Edouard de Stoeckl, Russia's ambassador to the United States and a strong supporter of Seward, wrote in April of 1861 that Seward was only "posing as a great man" and was in actuality only a "small politician."[14]

COMPETING EXPEDITIONS

As Fox prepared the expedition to relieve Fort Sumter with the support of the Secretaries of War and the Navy, and of course the president, the expedition to relieve Fort Pickens was also underway. This expedition, also supported by the president, was being pushed by Seward. The Fort Pickens expedition was being carried out by Captain Montgomery Meigs and Colonel Erasmus Keyes, both of the U.S. Army, and Lieutenant David Dixon Porter of the U.S. Navy and son of the legendary War of 1812 commander, David Porter.

The two expeditions were both being organized in New York and both were struggling to keep their preparations out of the newspapers and away from New York's many Southern sympathizers. As had been learned during the *Star of The West* incident, Charleston was as close as the nearest telegraph office. That both expeditions were operating in secret, including from one another, and were in competition for the same scarce men, supplies and ships would lead to fatal confusion.

The Fort Pickens expedition was being carried on outside the normal chain of command. Not only was it being organized by the Secretary of State, which should have sent up red flags, but the Secretaries of War and the Navy had not been informed. Had Welles and Cameron been part of the planning, their knowledge of Fox's plan would have avoided much confusion and delay. That Lincoln had agreed to this and had given Meigs, Keyes and Porter orders that amounted to almost a blank check was a mistake. This Lincoln readily admitted to in the years to come.

> The *Harriet Lane* was named for James Buchanan's niece who served in the role of First Lady for her bachelor uncle.

Fox's expedition was given the only three available warships in the Atlantic, the *Powhatan*, *Pocahontas* and *Pawnee*, and the *Harriet Lane* of the Revenue Service. This was a bigger force than he had originally suggested but every day the force opposing him in Charleston grew.

The *Powhatan* was in the Brooklyn Navy Yard getting much needed repairs. Secretary Welles sent orders to the commandant of the yard Captain Andrew Foote that the *Powhatan* needed to be ready to sail immediately.

This was no easy task as her engines had been dismantled. Foote, who would give his life fighting for the Union cause, was only told she was needed for an important mission, he was not told what that mission was.

The *Powhatan* was as ready as she could be made on short notice when Porter, Meigs and Keyes, the commanding trio of the Fort Pickens expedition arrived with an order from the president commanding Foote to hand over the *Powhatan* to Porter. This seemed very strange to Foote as well it should have. Not only was the order not through the normal channels but the *Powhatan* already had a commander who was senior to Porter. This set off a flurry of telegrams to Washington for clarification.

Like a child caught with his hand in the cookie jar, Seward had to sheepishly go to the Secretary of the Navy and admit that he had taken authority from Secretary Welles and was fitting out his own naval expedition. It was the only way to get the *Powhatan* for the Fort Pickens expedition. Welles, who contemporaries claimed looked like a senior Neptune, the Roman god of the sea, insisted the men go see the president. Lincoln, embarrassed by the situation said he did not realize that the ship he had signed over to the Fort Pickens expedition was one Fox needed. Lincoln countermanded his order and told Seward to telegraph Porter immediately to relinquish command.

Seward did not rush and by the time the message reached the Brooklyn Navy Yard the *Powhatan* was already on its way. A fast tug was sent to catch her but when Porter read Seward's telegram, he stated his orders came from the president, not the Secretary of State, and continued on. It has often been suggested that Seward did not send the telegraph under the president's name, as he should have, because he wanted Porter to react just as he did.[15] Perhaps the worst part is that Fox was never informed. He left New York expecting the *Powhatan* to meet him at the rendezvous point eleven miles from Charleston.

Fox sailed on April 9, 1861 in the *Baltic*, a steam powered cargo ship that the expedition had leased, with great difficulty, from William Aspinwall the powerful shipping magnate. Aspinwall had been cautious about supporting an expedition against Charleston for fear it would jeopardize the Lincoln government's attempt to secure much needed funds in the New York money market. Eventually Fox would convince Aspinwall to aid him. The entire New York situation frustrated the naval man. Fox wrote Montgomery Blair on March 31 that he felt "like abandoning my country, moving off somewhere, I am sick down to my heel." Fox was upset that "in the hour of peril," so many "hands

> The *Baltic* was a luxury liner built for speed. In 1850 she broke the record for a trans-Atlantic voyage with an average speed of almost 13 knots.

and hearts that should stand by our government" were falling away. Fox was "heartsick, not discouraged at the delays, obstacles and brief time allowed for a vital measure that should have had months' careful preparation."[16] Fox was growing exasperated and he had not even received the news that the ship he planned on making his flagship and the three hundred sailors he needed were already on their way to Pensacola where they would play no role either.

On April 12 at three in the morning, Fox, on board the *Baltic*, reached the rendezvous point, eleven miles east of the extinguished Charleston lighthouse. The *Harriet Lane* was waiting and the *U.S.S. Pawnee* arrived three hours later. Fox boarded the *Pawnee* and when he informed the ship's commanding officer Stephen C. Rowan of his intentions the *Pawnee's* captain refused. He had written instructions to remain where he was until the *Powhatan* arrived and then follow her lead. Unfortunately, only Captain Samuel Mercer who should have been in command of the *Powhatan* but was left standing on the dock in New York had orders to "put yourself in communication and cooperate" with Fox "to accomplish and carry into effect its object."[17] Rowen would not take action that he believed would start a war without written orders. His service over the next four years would overshadow his timidity on this day.

The *Baltic* and the *Harriet Lane* approached Charleston on their own. When they arrived at the bar they discovered the forts and batteries were already firing at Fort Sumter and she was responding. The war had begun.

NOTES

1 David Herbert Donald, *Lincoln* (New York: Simon and Schuster, 1995) 269.
2 Lincoln to Nathaniel P. Paschall, November 16, 1860, in Basler, Roy, Editor. *Collected Works of Abraham Lincoln* (New Brunswick: Rutgers University Press, 1953) 4, 139–140.
3 Donald, *Lincoln*, 283. Richard N. Current, *Lincoln and the First Shot* (Prospect Heights, Illinois: Waveland Press, 1990) 39–40.
4 Don E. Fehrenbacher, Editor, *Abraham Lincoln: A Documentary Portrait through His Speeches and Writings* (New York: The New American Library, 1964) 154.
5 Scott to Fox, in Robert Means Thompson, Editor, *Confidential Correspondence of Gustavus Vasa Fox* (New York: The Naval Historical Society, 1920) 3.
6 Fox to wife, *Correspondence of Fox*, 6–7.
7 Foxto Winfield Scott, March 19, 1861, *Correspondence of Fox*, 8–9.
8 Seward, quoted in Douglas, *Lincoln*, 286.
9 Jefferson Davis, *The Rise and Fall of the Confederate Government* (New York: Da Capo, 1990, reprint; Richmond: Garrett and Massie, 1938) 212.
10 Seward, quoted in W.A. Swanberg, *First Blood, The Story of Fort Sumter* (New York: Charles Scribner's Sons, 1957) 227.

11 Seward, quoted in Swanberg, 230.
12 Swanberg, 252.
13 Charlton W. Tebeau, *A History of Florida* (Coral Gables: University of Miami Press, 1971) 202–204.
14 Edouard de Stoeckl, quoted in Albert Woldman, *Lincoln and the Russians, the Story of the Russian–American Diplomatic Relations during the Civil War* (Cleveland: World Publishing Company, 1952) 53–54.
15 Donald, *Lincoln*, 291.
16 Fox to Montgomery Blair, March 31, 1861, *Correspondence of Fox*, 13.
17 Navy Department to Samuel Mercer, April 5, 1861, *Correspondence of Fox*, 23–24.

CHAPTER 6

The Fall of Fort Sumter

Despite the numerous visitors from Washington D.C., Major Robert Anderson was still operating under the rules given him by Secretary of War Floyd and President Buchanan. This was not an oversight as much as a matter of trust. Between his Southern ties, and the fact that Floyd had approved of him for the position, Lincoln was afraid Anderson might sabotage any plan. It was best, the administration thought, not to give him any more information than was necessary. Considering the number of military men who left the service Lincoln should be excused for mistrusting Anderson. Lincoln would regret this and show his faith by promoting Anderson to brigadier general and giving him command of the military theater that contained Kentucky, a critical place whose loss might have doomed the Union cause.[1]

SITUATION IN CHARLESTON

The authorities in Charleston and Montgomery were better informed of the goings on in Lincoln's cabinet than the new president would have thought possible. On April 1, they received the decision that the U.S. Government would not resupply Fort Sumter without first notifying the South Carolina government. This was a major shift from the idea that the fort would be evacuated at any moment.

Beauregard and Pickens now knew more of Lincoln's thoughts on the subject than did Anderson, whose garrison had already packed their few belongings in preparation to leave. Beauregard's orders from the Confederate capital were to increase the pace of construction on the batteries that were surrounding Fort Sumter and keep out naval forces. The news, that Fort Sumter would not be reinforced without notification, confused Governor Pickens about the true intentions of Washington. On April 7, Pickens reached out to the Confederate commissioners still in the federal capital. The commissioners responded promptly the next day with out-of-date intelligence. Fort Sumter, they reported, would be evacuated at any moment. That same day, a former member of Anderson's command and newly promoted Captain Theodore Talbot returned to Charleston along with Robert L. Chew a minor clerk from the State Department. Carrying a message from the president, Chew was granted an audience with the governor. His instructions were simple. He was to inform the governor that the U.S. Government would resupply Fort Sumter with food and fuel but no men or munitions would be sent as long as South Carolina did not resist. Chew was not to accept a reply or communicate with any representative of the Confederate government. He was to deliver no honors or courtesies to the governor. The message was not even signed, it was just a statement of fact. Lincoln was making the powerful statement that he was the President of the United States and he would resupply his soldiers. That this brusque message was delivered by an unknown lowly clerk was an intentional slight to the governor.[2]

Pickens might not have believed this message was legitimate had the messenger not been escorted by Captain Talbot. If Pickens and Beauregard were not disturbed enough by this news, Talbot's request to rejoin the garrison was too much. The two men were escorted to the train station and sent out of the state.

On the same day, Anderson received his first official communication from the Lincoln administration. It was not what Anderson wanted to hear. He was now convinced that any action, besides evacuation, taken before a political solution had been worked out, would mean war. Anderson had borne insults to the flag, which as a career soldier, cut him deeply. He had kept his orders from Buchanan secret from his officers and men, and had thus lost much of their respect.[3] He was not a young man and the physical privations of his lonely vigil would cause Anderson serious health problems for the rest of his life. Now he was looking at his new orders from the Secretary of War. Orders that Anderson knew meant war, which made all of his sacrifices, in the name of peace, a wasted effort.

LINCOLN'S STRATEGY

At some point during his first troubled month in the White House, Lincoln had reached the conclusion that there was no peaceful way to preserve the Union. The disunionists would accept every concession the government offered and then use those very concessions as evidence of the weakness of the government and proof to their followers that a new government should be formed. Lincoln also held the deep conviction, as he so eloquently stated in his Gettysburg Address, that preservation of the Union and the preservation of the Constitution were the same thing and if they were not preserved America's republican form of government "would perish from the Earth."[4]

Once Lincoln had reached the conclusion that the options were only war or disunion, it was as if a switch had been flipped and he became resolute and the president that we have immortalized. On April 4, Lincoln met privately with John B. Baldwin, a member of the convention Virginia had called to discuss secession. Baldwin had Unionist leanings. He told Lincoln that if Fort Sumter were abandoned, Virginia would stay in the Union. Lincoln accepted. "If you will guarantee to me the State of Virginia I shall remove the troops. A State for a fort is no bad business."[5] As Lincoln suspected, nothing came of this offer. Some historians claim that Baldwin misunderstood, but this seems unlikely, the president's offer was clear, "a state for a fort."[6] Lincoln had simply called Baldwin's and Virginia's bluff. They would leave the Union after they had squeezed every concession politicians like Seward would give them, and no amount of appeasement would change that. Baldwin may have honestly believed his offer, but Lincoln understood Baldwin was promising something that could not be delivered.

HOW TO START A WAR?

Lincoln also knew what Anderson knew. Fox's attempt to resupply Fort Sumter would mean war. However, Lincoln was confident that there was no longer another option. The question, now, was how it should start. What would give the most political, moral and international advantage to the Union cause? Before his inauguration, Lincoln received a letter of advice from an old Illinois friend and future U.S. senator, Orville Browning. Browning had, much earlier than Lincoln, seen the inevitability of war and suggested how it should begin. "In any conflict between the Government and the seceding States, it is very important that the traitors shall be the aggressors, and that they be kept constantly and palpably in the wrong."[7]

Once Lincoln's resolve had stiffened, he took Browning's advice and turned Fort Sumter into a win/win situation. If, in the unlikely event, Fox was successful, it was a sign of strength by the new administration. If South Carolina fired on unarmed ships carrying only food, then they were the aggressors, a fact that would only help the Union cause both domestically and internationally.

THE SOUTH'S RESPONSE

To the benefit of Lincoln's new strategy, there were many influential Southerners who believed that acting aggressively on the Fort Sumter question would cement the support of the other Southern states especially the Border States like Virginia. To Jefferson Davis, the first and only president of the Confederacy, none of this really mattered. From the beginning, he believed that his new nation would have to be born in blood, that a peaceful separation would not be possible. He also strongly believed that the North had long been the aggressor in this conflict dating back more than a decade and that it would not really matter who fired the first cannon in Charleston. After all how could an attack on a military fortress with due notice given compare to the brutal cowardly invasion of John Brown and his abolitionists.[8] This would not be Davis' last major political miscalculation of the war.

Beyond the official statement delivered by Chew, Beauregard and Pickens had evidence that something major was coming. Chew's notice could have easily been about another *Star of the West* type operation, a lone unarmed ship trying to use speed and surprise to get through. The Confederates now learned that the new expedition was escorted by U.S. Navy warships and was prepared to fight its way through. Operation security, the ability to keep plans and details from the enemy, was pathetic, and the Confederate commissioners were reading details of Fox's plan in the newspapers. In defense of Fox, this was a problem commanders on both sides would struggle with throughout the war, and the political shenanigans in the capital made his task even more difficult.

Much more reliable that what was in the newspapers, were Anderson's own words. On receiving his orders from Simon Cameron, Major Anderson replied in a letter to the Secretary of War voicing his concerns about the plan. Not only would it guarantee war, which Cameron already knew, but he was convinced that the operation would fail miserably. The problem with the scheme, he did not dignify it by calling it a plan, was that even if Fox's supply boats were able to run the gauntlet of enemy fire they would be sitting ducks as they unloaded. Also, as he had long maintained, resupply was useless if the surrounding Confederate works were not captured. He also complained that he had not been informed. Had he not been under the false impression that he was to be evacuated he would have made different preparations.[9]

Anderson had sent this message through the mail, and, along with an official report from the engineer Foster describing the defensive measures of Fort Sumter, it was in the hands of General Beauregard. Instead of being sent northward, as had been done in the past, Fort Sumter's letters were, now, being forwarded to the governor's office. There Beauregard, Governor Pickens, and former federal judge Andrew Magrath each tried to pass the responsibility for opening mail not addressed to them to the others. It is odd, that after seizing Federal property and firing on ships bearing the U.S. flag, that opening the U.S. mail was a line that they were loath to cross.[10]

The debate in the Confederate president's cabinet about what to do was short and decisive. Those who feared firing the first shot would cost them support in the North were overruled by those who believed that it was necessary to "sprinkle blood in the face of the Southern people" to guarantee their support.[11] On April 10, Confederate Secretary of War Leroy Walker sent word to General Beauregard, that if he was confident that there would be an attempt to resupply Fort Sumter that he was to demand the Fort's surrender and "if this is refused, proceed in such a manner as you may determine, to reduce it."[12]

Since December, Fort Sumter's garrison had watched the Confederates prepare to attack and had made counter preparations. In the few days before war broke out, Beauregard's men revealed gun emplacements that completely changed the situation at Fort Sumter and showed that Beauregard had been paying attention to his artillery instruction at West Point. Anderson, surely, lamented his skill as a professor. On April 8, the men and officers rushed to the north wall because of an explosion on Sullivan's Island. Confederate forces had destroyed a house, and when the smoke and dust cleared there was a well-constructed four gun heavy battery. Its location would make it impossible to safely fire the guns on the top of the fort, or barbette-tier, without added protection and there was not the time or supplies to add those protections.

On the morning of April 11, the garrison discovered that the Confederates had moved into place overnight another heavy battery. The floating battery, as it quickly came to be called was constructed in Charleston's dry dock by a former U.S. Navy officer. Built of palmetto palm logs and covered in railroad iron it was one hundred feet long and twenty feet wide. It was large enough to hold four big guns and the men necessary to work them. It was based on a British concept they had used against the Russians, during the Crimean War. During the night, Beauregard had the massive floating battery towed to the west end of Sullivan's Island so its big guns would bear on the fort's weakest point and the most likely spot for Fox to unload his boats. The revelation of these two new batteries further depressed the already gloomy garrison.[13]

The only thing that kept up the spirits of the hungry garrison was the confident belief that a naval expedition was on its way. This meant men, supplies and the ability to pay back the secessionists for the many hardships and insults, and most importantly for tearing apart the country.

At 3:30 in the afternoon of April 11, a small boat approached Fort Sumter flying the white flag. Lieutenant Jefferson C. Davis met the boat at the fort's wharf. On board were three of Beauregard's staff with an important message for Anderson. Beauregard had many more aides than he probably needed, but becoming a member of the general's staff was a must among Charleston's fashionable elite. Delivering the message was Colonel A.R. Chisholm, a prominent local plantation owner who had lent his slaves to the war effort. Also on board was Colonel James Chesnut. The South Carolina born, Princeton educated, Chesnut had resigned his seat in the U.S. Senate to take part in his state's secession convention. Although he played an important role in the Confederate government he is best remembered as the husband of Mary Boykin Chesnut whose fascinating diary is mandatory reading for anyone interested in the history of Confederacy. The junior officer of the three was by far the most capable. Captain Stephen Dill Lee, no relation to Robert E. Lee, was a graduate of West Point. He resigned his commission as soon as South Carolina left the Union and would end the war as a Lieutenant General.

They were escorted into the guardroom and Anderson was summoned. The message, from Beauregard, was simple and straight to the point. Fort Sumter had to be evacuated. The Confederate government would aid them in leaving and allow the flag to be saluted as it was lowered. Anderson put the terms to his officers in another room. Unanimously they rejected the offer, generous as it might be. Even the Virginian Meade, who would later fight for the Confederacy, voted to refuse the offer.[14]

Anderson wrote a response to Beauregard politely refusing the offer. He then escorted the three men to their boat. As they walked across the wharf Anderson asked if he would be given notice before he was fired upon. Chesnut assured him he would be. It was only polite. It was then that Anderson made his other very controversial remark. In a conversational tone almost in passing Anderson said "if you do not batter us to pieces, we shall be starved out in a few days."[15]

Anderson has been much criticized for this comment. He is accused of giving key intelligence to the enemy. Sometimes this is offered as proof of Anderson's disloyalty.[16] This is rather unfair. Anderson was actually being rather sly here. Anderson was buying time. Every moment the guns were not firing was an opportunity for some other eventuality, a political solution or the fleet pushing through to his rescue. As a career army officer, he understood that this piece of information, that he had let slip, would be reported to Beauregard, passed to the governor and maybe even to the

Confederate president. It would be discussed and perhaps a new plan of action would be developed. All of this would take time and would occur while the guns were silent. As it turned out the comment only bought him the rest of the day.

General Beauregard passed this news by telegraph to the Confederate Secretary of War. An hour later Beauregard had the Secretary's response. If Anderson would "state the time at which he will evacuate and agree in the meant time he will not use his guns against us," Beauregard was authorized to disregard his earlier orders to destroy the fort.[17]

Nine hours after their first trip, the three Confederate officers returned to Fort Sumter just after midnight on April 12. There was a fourth officer on this trip, Virginia congressman Rodger Pryor. He changed his mind and decided to remain in the boat, when they reached Fort Sumter. Probably the proper decision considering he was the sitting congressman for a state that was still very much in the Union.

Chisholm, Chesnut and Lee were once again escorted into the guardroom by the fort's main gate where they presented Anderson with the new letter from Beauregard. Anderson left the three Confederates so that he could once again confer with his officers, the majority of whom were getting much needed sleep.

Anderson and his officers discussed the offer, their situation, their duty and their orders for nearly three hours. Captain Lee would later write that he felt Anderson was intentionally delaying them.[18] Perhaps Lee was correct, Anderson and his officers had no reason to rush but they also had a very difficult decision to make. It was the most important one of their lives, if not the life of their country.

Anderson put the question to the garrison doctor, Samuel Crawford: how long could the garrison remain in fighting condition with the food they now had? Five days was his answer, the last three being with no rations. Anderson's orders from Secretary Cameron were picked apart looking for an answer. It was unhelpful. They were clearly not expected to make an Alamo style last stand nor were they expected to starve to death by their guns. They were to "hold out, if possible, till the arrival of the expedition."[19] The decision was reached around three in the morning that if they held out until noon on April 15, they had done their duty.

Anderson wrote out the official reply. He would accept their offer to aid his evacuation of Fort Sumter on noon, April 15. He would not fire on Confederate forces unless they fired on Fort Sumter or "the flag it bears."[20] These last words were key. If Anderson had agreed to the terms presented, he would

The U.S. flag had thirty-three stars in 1861. It would change on July 4, 1861 when Kansas became the thirty fourth state.

Samuel Wyllie Crawford

Samuel Crawford was born in 1829 in Franklin County Pennsylvania. He graduated from the University of Pennsylvania Medical School in 1850. He accepted a position as assistant surgeon in the U.S. Army the same year. He mostly served on the western frontier until his posting in Charleston in 1860.

After the events at Fort Sumter Crawford resigned his position as an army doctor and was promoted to major in the Thirteenth United States Infantry under Colonel William T. Sherman. He served at the First Battle of Bull Run, the first major land battle of the war. Crawford was promoted brigadier general of volunteers in 1862. He saw some of the worst fighting in the war. He led a brigade at the battle of Cedar Mountain where half his men were killed or wounded. He commanded a division at Antietam and was personally wounded. He served at Gettysburg where his counter attack along the Plum Run prevented disaster. He served in every battle of Grant's Overland Campaign.

In the post Civil War army Crawford served as a lieutenant colonel on occupation duty in the South. In 1873 he retired from the army and moved to Philadelphia. In retirement he wrote *The Genesis of the Civil War*. It was not only his personal account of Fort Sumter but a history of the beginning of the war. He died in 1892 at the age of sixty-three.

have been unable to support Fox's expedition with Fort Sumter's guns. This would have been almost the same as a complete surrender.

Beauregard's aides were authorized to make a decision. They rejected Anderson's terms. That the fort would aid Fox's expedition was a deal breaker. Chesnut wrote Anderson a formal, official reply. Confederate guns would open fire in one hour. Anderson escorted the three officers to their boat. He shook their hands and offered them the nineteenth-century soldier's farewell. "If we never meet in this world again, God grant that we may meet in the next."[21] Meanwhile, Anderson's officers woke the men informing them that war was about to commence and that the soldiers were to stay where they were until further orders.

The solders, those not on watch, were sleeping in the casemates, the gun emplacements on the lower tier. That was by far the safest place in the fort. Per Anderson's orders, Fort Sumter would not return fire until daylight. With the limited supply of ammunition, firing into the darkness would do little good. The first few hours would be extremely one sided.

The four Confederates were rowed the more than two thousand yards to Fort Johnson on James Island. There, in command of the mortar battery, was Captain George S. James. He was given the order to fire the signal to the forty seven pieces of artillery surrounding Fort Sumter that war had begun. James offered the honor of firing the first shot of the Southern War of Independence to Roger Pryor. He was a great admirer of this outspoken supporter of secession. Pryor considered but refused.[22] Whether his status as a representative of a state still in the Union may have been crossing a line he was not yet willing to cross or, as Lee would later suggest, that the weight of what was to come finally settled on him is not known.

At exactly 4:30, James pulled the rope that caused the friction primer to ignite the powder whose explosion sent the ten inch mortar shell streaking across the sky to burst over Fort Sumter. In only a moment, all the guns forming an almost complete ring around the fort began firing as quickly as they could reload (Figure 6.1).

At six in the morning April 12, reveille was sounded inside Fort Sumter. It was highly unlikely that anyone was actually asleep. Roll call was done inside, since explosive shells were making the parade ground rather unsafe. After a quick, unsatisfying, breakfast of salt pork and water, their only fare for the last week, the soldiers were given their orders. The garrison was split into three details, the first under Doubleday, followed by Davis and then Crawford. It was highly unusual to give this kind of

Figure 6.1 Famous image from *Harper's Weekly* of the firing on Fort Sumter. (Courtesy of the Library of Congress)

The First Shot

The title of the man who fired the first shot of the Civil War is a dubious honor at best, considering the massive amount of bloodshed and the financial ruin of the South that followed. There is controversy over who gets to claim that title. What is defined as the start of the war obviously affects the argument. Those who consider the attack on April 12, 1861 as the start of the war generally give credit to Edmund Ruffin for pulling the first lanyard of the war. The outspoken Virginian had been a staunch supporter of Secession for decades. When the movement finally bore fruit in South Carolina he joined a Charleston militia unit, the Palmetto Guards. The sixty six year old was a celebrity in South Carolina and his fellow soldiers insisted that he have the honor, one he sorely wanted. He fired one of the big columbiads at Cumming's Point only an instant before every other Confederate gun began firing.

Although Ruffin is most often credited with firing the first shot, this claim is problematic. Captain George S. James fired the signal gun that let Ruffin know to fire his gun. This was no flare. James fired a mortar shell that exploded over the parade ground, showering the area with hot iron. Anyone in the open would most likely have been the first casualty of the war. The thirty one year old James was a veteran of the Mexican War who resigned his commission when South Carolina seceded from the Union. He did not survive the war.

It can also be argued that the first shot of the Civil War was fired at the *Star of the West* on January 9, 1861. If so, the honor falls to a cadet at the Citadel, South Carolina's military academy. Cadet George E. Haynesworth was stationed with his classmates on Morris Island. Although his shot did not even come close to the target, it was fired nearly three months before James fired his famous gun. Haynesworth served throughout the Civil War, including the Battle of Bentonville, the last major battle of the war. Haynesworth may have fired one of the last shots of the war, as well.

On January 31, 1861 Confederate gunners near Vicksburg, Mississippi fired on the paddlewheeled steamer *A.O. Taylor*. She was flying the American flag and her captain, somehow, did not know that Mississippi had left the Union. The name of the soldier who actually fired the first shot was not recorded. However, that unnamed soldier has a better claim on the honor than Ruffin.

There is also a claim that the first shots of the war were fired by Union soldiers. At midnight January 8, 1861, an unknown number of armed men tried to launch a sneak attack on Fort McRee in Pensacola, Florida. Probably with more than a couple of drinks in them, they were unable to silently approach the fort and a few shots fired by the guards sent them running back to Pensacola.

There are surely numerous other incidents that were not recorded or remembered by anyone but the participants, making it all but impossible to know who fired the first shot. How we define the start of the conflict makes this equally difficult.

command to a surgeon but Crawford would prove himself worthy of this trust in the years to come.

Anderson ordered his men to be very careful, and to remain in the casemates where they would be safe. This order had been greeted with disappointment by many of the officers and men. The fort's most powerful guns, with the longest range, were off limits. The garrison would be fighting with one hand tied behind its back.[23] Anderson had a few reasons for this order. There were one hundred and twenty eight men in the fort, forty three were loyal workmen that Pickens had refused to allow to leave so they would help eat the garrison's meager supplies. Anderson could not take casualties and continue to hold out. He was also a humanitarian who wanted to limit death. There was also the forlorn hope that even after Fort Sumter had been fired upon that there still might be the possibility of a peaceful solution. Even that slim hope would disappear if men died at Fort Sumter.

Although there is some debate about who fired the first shot of the war on the Confederate side, there is no question on the Union side. That honor went to Abner Doubleday, and he cherished it. Unlike Anderson, Doubleday entered the conflict with no moral qualms. To Doubleday "the contest was inevitable, and was not of our seeking. The United States was called upon not only to defend its sovereignty but its right to exist as a nation." Just before seven Doubleday fired the historic shot. It bounced harmlessly off the iron armor of the floating battery.[24]

Over the last several hours there had been increasing concern among the Southern soldiers and the growing crowds of civilians along the waterfront and rooftops that Fort Sumter would not return fire. The soldiers were afraid this would sully their victory and the civilians were concerned that this would spoil the show. Doubleday's shot breathed new life into the opposition.[25]

For the next thirty four hours, the two sides pounded each other with artillery. After Doubleday's first shot, Anderson's three divisions fired as quickly as they could reload. Each of the big guns took six men to reload and haul back into place after the recoil hurled it to the back of the casement. This limited the number of guns the small garrison could work.

The garrison also began with only seven hundred cartridges. Artillery cartridges were simply linen bags filled with gunpowder. The bag was rammed down the barrel of the gun followed by the projectile. Fort Sumter had plenty of gunpowder and an ample supply of shot and shell. It was the bags that were the problem. Prior to the opening of the battle, the men had been busily engaged sewing cartridges. These were made from sheets, extra clothes or anything that could be scrounged. Throughout the battle men were engaged in sewing artillery cartridges. Never more than six men, however – the other thing they were desperately short of was sewing needles.

By the middle of the day, Anderson was forced to reduce the number of guns that were being worked so that they would not run out of cartridges. Two guns fired toward Morris Island. Its battery on the northernmost point, Cummings Point, was the closest to Fort Sumter. Two guns fired toward the garrison's old home of Fort Moultrie. Although great damage was done to the interior of the old fort, the guns and their crews remained untouched. The Union gunners would later learn that the Confederates were blocking the gun ports with cotton bales between shots, a highly effective strategy. It must have been comforting to Osceola, the old Seminole chief buried outside the gate at Fort Moultrie to hear his old foes fighting one another. The last two guns fired at the western end of Sullivan's Island where the floating battery was located. They did nothing but put a few dents in the outer shell of the iron monster.

A few other targets were fired at sporadically. The Confederates had placed old ships in the main channel to set on fire, if Fox's expedition attempted to run the gauntlet at night. The garrison took a few shots at those old hulks but stopped when it became obvious that they were unoccupied. Doubleday took a couple of shots at secessionists on Sullivan's Island who came a little too close or seemed to be enjoying the display a little too much. A hotel, that had been flying the Palmetto flag proudly for the last several months, received a cannon ball from Doubleday's men, even though the flag had been lowered as soon as the shooting had started.

The physical exertions of firing the guns, after the months of frustrating inaction, lifted the spirits of the men and officers. However, as it was becoming obvious that they were doing little damage to the enemy there was growing frustration that they had been ordered not to use the upper tier guns or the makeshift mortars in the courtyard. If these guns could be worked it might be a very different fight. The big columbiads and howitzers not only would be able to reach Charleston but would have been very effective in battering Fort Moultrie and the floating battery. Those top tier guns were also the only ones capable of firing explosive shells.

This frustration was too much for some men to handle. Private John Carmody secretly climbed the stairs to the barbette-tier. The big guns were loaded and aimed in roughly the right direction. One by one Carmody fired each gun on the Fort Moultrie side before returning to his post. He probably would have continued to disobey his orders had there been any physical way for him to reload. Two sergeants secretly fired the giant columbiad aimed at Cummings Point. The first shot came so close to putting a Confederate battery out of commission that they attempted a second shot. They were amazingly able to reload but were unable to push the big gun back into place. They fired it anyway. The recoil overturned it and knocked over the neighboring gun. These shots were generally ineffective but they did cause the Confederates to redirect the fire to where there were no longer any men.[26]

Confederate shot and shell were doing little damage to the fort's twelve foot thick walls. The West Point trained Beauregard, however, knew his business and his batteries were masterfully placed. The Confederate guns were able to fire plunging shots. Coming in at a high angle they exploded on or above the ramparts and courtyard. Those areas became a no man's land. Had Anderson not given the order to stay off the ramparts the battle would have been much costlier on both sides.

Fort Sumter was designed to fight against a fleet of wooden ships. Had the British fleet that attacked Fort McHenry during the War of 1812, been reassembled to attack Fort Sumter, fifty years later, they would not have stood a chance. Cannon fire from those old ships would have been straight and would either fly over or would have harmlessly struck the fort's walls. Because of this, there was not much concern to make the interior of the fort bomb proof. This would prove to be the downfall of Fort Sumter.

The Confederates were firing hot shot, iron balls heated until they glowed red. These caused a great deal of destruction among the wooden barracks and other buildings. Peter Hart, who Mrs. Anderson had brought from New York, justified the faith she had put in him by bravely leading the men who fought these fires as Confederate shells still fell.

At around one o'clock, three ships appeared outside the bar. It was obvious to everyone that unlike the *Star of the West*, these were warships. What they were going to do was anyone's guess. Anderson gave the order to decrease the rate of fire. Each gun would now only fire once every ten minutes. If Fox's fleet was going to fight their way into the harbor, Anderson wanted to make sure he had enough ammunition to support them.[27]

The arrival of the ships was no surprise to Beauregard. Not only had he been informed of their departure from New York, but small craft had been watching the approaches to Charleston since the *Star of the West* incident. However, the sight of the American flag cheered the garrison of Fort Sumter. With fresh supplies and more men they believed they could hold out indefinitely. If they could work all of the fort's guns they could give as good as they had been receiving for the last eight hours. This, however, was a forlorn hope. Although the commander of the *Pawnee* wanted to fight his way into the harbor in broad daylight and share the fate of the Fort Sumter garrison, he was stopped by Fox who was still vainly waiting for the rest of his fleet to arrive.[28]

Commander Stephen C. Rowan was the first of many examples of the power that the events of Fort Sumter would have on the American public. The night before, Rowan had refused to enter the harbor. He would only strictly follow his written orders that with the absence of the *Powhatan* allowed him to do nothing. Now as he watched U.S. soldiers being fired upon, he was ready to enter the fight with the probable outcome that his ship would be battered to pieces. The night before, the crew of the *Harriet Lane* had been on the point of mutiny when they learned what was expected of them. After the Confederates began firing on Fort Sumter the same crew began pressuring their officers to accept any risk in order to relieve Fort Sumter.[29]

Fox was still hopeful that he could successfully carry out his mission. He just needed four more ships to arrive. One was the *Powhatan*, which unknown to Fox, was already in the Gulf of Mexico along with the sailors and small boats he needed. The other three were the tugboats that were key to his plan. Of the three, two had been delayed by storms and would never arrive. The owners of the third tugboat had lost their nerve and backed out of the project at the last minute. Fox and Rowan came up with a counter plan, while they waited. Stumbling into the wrong place at the wrong time were a couple of ice ships. Carrying ice to Southern ports was, generally, a pretty lucrative business in the days before icemakers. The benefit for a naval operation was that these two particular ships were small enough to cross the bar, and because they were filled with ice they would continue to float no matter how many holes were shot through them. How seriously this plan was considered is not known. Rain and poor visibility kept them from doing anything. Fox remained hopeful that his missing ships would arrive.[30]

Darkness and the storm were welcomed by Anderson and his men. The rain extinguished the barracks fires they had been fighting for most of the day. They also believed that the stormy weather and poor visibility that it brought, would make it easier for the relief expedition to make it in – another example of the disconnect between soldiers and sailors that marred the Fort Sumter situation from the beginning. The Confederates had sent out small boats with torches to ensure Fox did not sneak through, but they were struggling. It did not matter though, no ship's officer was going to enter a harbor they did not know in darkness. That was just begging to run aground.

Both naval and army officers used the events at Fort Sumter to argue that their service was more powerful than their rivals'.

Anderson ordered his guns to stop firing. Shooting into the darkness was an unnecessary waste of his precious supply of ammunition. Although he tried to rest as many men as he could, he also maintained a close and careful watch. When Fox made his move, Fort Sumter's garrison would have to act quickly to get men and supplies inside the fort and get the ships moving again before the Confederates could target them. They also had to be watchful for a Confederate storming party. The dark night would offer a good opportunity for Beauregard to try to overrun Fort Sumter.

The major concern would be that if armed men from small boats landed on the wharf in the night, could they tell if they were friendly or hostile? Obviously, setting off the explosives, that the garrison had planted under the wharf, to stop an assault would be disastrous if it were U.S. soldiers landing. It would be equally bad if they were slow to react to a Confederate attack.[31]

Beauregard slowed his fire to a mortar shell every fifteen minutes. After the day's long fight, the night was relatively quiet. Everyone watched and waited. The quiet night could, at any moment, bring the need for fast decisive action and the potential for slaughter. Fox scanned the horizon for any signs of the ships that would allow him to finally carry out his mission. Beauregard, his gunners and the people of Charleston watched for Fox to try and make his run. Anderson and his men watched hopefully for Fox and nervously for a Confederate assault.

When the sun rose nothing had changed. The storm had cleared but to the great frustration of Fox, no ships had arrived and to the even greater frustration of the Fort Sumter garrison the three ships still sat where they had been the day before, watching but it seemed doing little else. Beauregard was pleased with the inactivity but knew that he might not have another day before the navy tried to fight their way through. His batteries began firing with as much speed as possible at daylight on the morning of April 13.

After an unsatisfying breakfast of salt pork, the soldiers of Fort Sumter went back to their guns. They concentrated their fire on Fort Moultrie. It was the target they felt they were having the most success against. At around eight, Fort Sumter's barracks caught on fire again. Peter Hart, once again, led a group of men in putting out the fire. The smoke caught the attention of Fort Moultrie's gunners who concentrated on the barracks with hot shot. It was not long before the buildings were aflame once more. The soldiers tried to save the barracks as the enemy fire continued to pour in. Anderson realized the barracks could not be saved, and that it was too dangerous to try. He ordered his men back into the relative safety of the casemates.

Although they had been designed to be fireproof, the barracks had become a raging inferno. Anderson, who throughout the battle had kept his military bearing, calmly informed the men that the powder magazine was in danger of exploding. There were almost three hundred barrels of gunpowder inside, enough to level the fort. Per Anderson's orders, enough men remained at the guns to fire a shot every five minutes. The rest tried to clear pieces of the burning barracks away from the magazine doors, but this proved impossible. Anderson ordered the magazine emptied. Barrel after barrel was rolled out and stored in the casemates. They were covered in wet blankets to protect them from fire. Only about fifty were moved, before the fire and incoming Confederate shots made rolling barrels of explosives across the courtyard much too dangerous a task. Anderson ordered the big metal doors shut and a few brave men dug a shallow trench to prevent loose powder trails leading into the magazine from exploding. It was not long before a cannon ball struck the door making it impossible to open. They would have to fight with only what was in the casemates.[32]

As the fire spread even some of that powder had to be thrown out so that the heat would not cause the barrels to explode. Because it was low tide, the barrels landed on solid ground instead of floating away. Confederate gunners witnessed this and began targeting the barrels. One, very accurate shot, set off one. The explosion came through an embrasure dismounting one of the cannon.

The firing was also causing the hand grenades the garrison had made and stored at strategic points to explode, adding to the danger and misery of those inside the fort. When the wind would shift, heavy black smoke would pour into the casemates making it nearly impossible to breath. Men laid on the ground with wet cloths over their mouths and noses. Others got much closer to the embrasures than was prudent, in their quest for breathable air.

In those impossible conditions the gun crews kept to their work. Confederate soldiers and civilians watching from shore saw Fort Sumter fully ablaze. They expected surrender at any moment. The flag continued to fly, however. Conditions had become so bad that the garrison could only occasionally return fire. When one of the guns boomed the Southerners cheered. This unbelievable resistance in the face of hellish conditions won the respect of the soldiers and civilians watching. They also jeered at the navy sitting idly and powerless outside the harbor.[33]

At around one in the afternoon, a shot tore off the top of the flag pole. With the ropes cut the American flag floated to the ground. Lieutenant Norman Hall rushed into the flames to save the flag. He returned dirty and singed with the flag ripped and burnt on the edges.

George W. Snyder

Snyder was born in upstate New York in 1833. He graduated at the top of his class in West Point in 1856. He was assigned to the engineers, as were all the top students. He served in Mobile, Alabama on that port's defenses. He also spent a short time as an Assistant Professor of Engineering at West Point. He was assigned to the fortifications of Charleston harbor as assistant engineer in September of 1860.

After the events at Fort Sumter he was promoted to first lieutenant and assigned to the construction of the defenses around Washington D.C. He served in the First Battle of Bull Run, the first major land battle of the war. He was honored with the rank of Brevet Major for his service in the battle. Soon afterwards Snyder contracted typhoid fever, a common ailment among large armies in camp. He died on November 17, 1861 at the age of twenty eight.

Along with Peter Hart, Lieutenant Snyder and Captain Seymour, Hall made his way to the parapet and with a makeshift pole raised the flag. The garrison cheered as the men risked their lives on the open parapet in this patriotic act.

On Cumming's Point, the former Texas Senator and current Confederate colonel Louis Wigfall saw the flag go down but did not see the heroic raising. Without orders, Wigfall, along with a private, and two slaves to row the boat, crossed over to Fort Sumter. They were not seen and Wigfall landed safely. It was good that he brought Private Young with him because as soon as Wigfall stepped out of the boat the two slaves tried to row away. Confederate gunners were still targeting the fort. A rowboat floating by the fort was not a safe place to be. Young held them at gunpoint until Wigfall returned.

With the gate burning and off its hinges, Wigfall had to climb through a window, much to the surprise of Private Thompson, the first to see him. Wigfall was waving a white flag at the end of his sword. When Lieutenant Davis arrived, Wigfall shouted over the roar "your flag is down, you are on fire, and you are not firing your guns. General Beauregard desires to stop this." Davis corrected him. The flag was flying and they were still firing, not much but the occasional forty two pound projectile was still being fired at Fort Moultrie. Wigfall continued. "Let us stop this firing. Will you hoist this?" Meaning his white flag. Davis refused. It was Wigfall's flag he could fly it. Wigfall squeezed past the gun and waved the flag out the embrasure. The gunners at Fort Moultrie did not notice and continued firing. The American flag flying on the parapet was what mattered. As long as it was flying the battle still continued.[34]

When Major Anderson arrived, Wigfall introduced himself and repeated his plea. Anderson understood that it was over. Relief was not coming. "I have already stated the terms to General Beauregard. Instead of noon on the fifteenth, I will go now." These terms were accepted, the U.S. flag came down and was replaced by a white sheet. Wigfall returned to Morris Island, confident that he had secured his place in history. The problem was that Wigfall, unbeknownst to Anderson, had no authority to offer or accept terms. This became embarrassingly clear on the arrival of the three official representatives of the Confederate general.

Anderson met Steven D. Lee, Roger Pryor and William Porcher Miles on the wharf, with the burning fort behind him. Once Anderson learned that Wigfall did not represent General Beauregard, the major told his guests that "There is a misunderstanding on my part, and I will at once run up my flag and open fire."[35] Anderson was frustrated. Throughout this ordeal Anderson had followed strict military etiquette. Even in the blazing heat he wore his full uniform. Now Wigfall, the amateur, had clumsily introduced himself into the situation making a mockery of the protocol. Beauregard's three aides convinced Anderson to wait until they could return to Beauregard and report the situation before he took down the white flag. The four men retired to the closest casemate that was still habitable, the one converted to Dr. Crawford's quarters.

Lee set to work writing down the terms Anderson would accept and those offered by Wigfall. Because of the heat and the stress Pryor took a drink from one of Crawford's bottles assuming it was whiskey. He was quickly rewarded for his bad manners. It was not whiskey. He had downed a fatal dose of iodide of potassium. Crawford was called. He took a panicked Pryor out to the parade ground and induced vomiting, thus saving the Virginian's life. Doubleday would later write "Some of us questioned the doctor's right to interpose in a case of this kind. It was argued that if any rebel leader chose to come over to Fort Sumter and poison himself, the Medical Department had no business to interfere with such a laudable intention." Crawford offered a defense for his actions. "He, himself, was held responsible for the medicine in the hospital, and therefore he could not permit Pryor to carry any of it away."[36]

Before the trio left another representative of Beauregard arrived. Major D.R. Jones had a message from the general. Beauregard offered the same terms from two days earlier. Anderson accepted. The battle of Fort Sumter was over. No one had been killed. This was a rather amazing fact

The Union Navy and Army would attempt several times over the next four years to recapture Fort Sumter. Each attempt failed.

considering the events of the last two days. Over three thousand iron balls and explosive shells had been fired at Fort Sumter.

On April 14, 1861, the garrison was transported to Fox's fleet and carried to New York, where family and friends and a hero's welcome were waiting. It was Palm Sunday. It would be on Palm Sunday four years later that the war would end after more than a half a million deaths. Before the garrison left, the flag would be lowered and would receive a one hundred gun salute. This was a condition of surrender that Anderson demanded. They were barely able to scrape together enough cartridges. Anderson was almost overcome with emotion as the flag was lowered. He could very well have been the only man in the thousands watching the ceremony who truly understood that the flag was being lowered on more than this beat up fort. Regardless of what the next four years would bring, the country as it had existed would never be again.

Tragedy struck as the gunners loaded the fiftieth shot. A cartridge went off prematurely in the hot cannon killing the nearest man, Private Daniel Hough, immediately. Five others were wounded. Hough was the first death in what would be a long war.

The streets of Charleston took on a festive attitude, bands played and soldiers paraded. Mary Boykin Chesnut recorded in her diary that it was "the very liveliest crowd I think I ever saw." She added several lines later "We have burned our ships – we are obliged to go on now."[37] This allusion to Alexander the Great's invasion of Persia was very fitting. War had come. There was no going back.

NOTES

1 W.A. Swanberg, *First Blood, The Story of Fort Sumter* (New York: Charles Scribner's Sons, 1957) 223–224. David Herbert Donald, *Lincoln* (New York: Simon and Schuster, 1995) 300.
2 Swanberg, *First Blood*, 279–280.
3 Samuel Wyllie Crawford, *The Genesis of the Civil War, The Story of Sumter, 1860–1861* (New York: Charles L. Webster and Company, 1887) 187–189.
4 Don E. Fehrenbacher, Editor, *Abraham Lincoln: A Documentary Portrait through His Speeches and Writings* (New York: The New American Library, 1964) 244.
5 Lincoln, quoted in Donald, *Lincoln*, 290.
6 Lincoln, quoted in Donald, *Lincoln*, 290.
7 Orville Browning to Abraham Lincoln, quoted in Donald, *Lincoln*, 293.
8 E. Merton Coulter, *The Confederate States of America, 1861–1865. A History of the South, Volume VII* (Baton Rouge: Louisiana State University Press, 1950) 38.
9 Anderson to Thomas, March 22, 1861, *The War of the Rebellion: A Compilation of the Official Records of the Union and Confederate Armies War*, hereafter cited as OR (Washington D.C.: Government Printing Office) Series I, vol. 1, 211.

10 Swanberg, *First Blood*, 285.
11 Swanberg, *First Blood*, 286.
12 Walker to Beauregard, April 10, 1861, OR, Series I, vol. 1, 297.
13 Swanberg, *First Blood*, 205, 288, 294.
14 Crawford, *Genesis of the Civil War*, 423.
15 Stephen D. Lee "The First Step in the War" in Robert Underwood Johnson and Clarence Clough Buel, Editors, *Battles and Leaders of the Civil War, the Opening Battles* (New York: Castle Books, 1956) I, 75.
16 Abner Doubleday, *Reminiscences of Forts Sumter and Moultrie in 1860–'61* (New York: Harper Brothers, Publishers, 1876) 141.
17 Walker to Beauregard, April 11, 1861, OR, Series I, vol. 1, 301.
18 Lee, *Battles and Leaders*, I, 75.
19 Cameron to Anderson, April 4, 1861, OR, Series I, vol. 1, 235.
20 Anderson, OR, Series I, vol. 1, 14.
21 Anderson, quoted in Lee, *Battles and Leaders*, I, 76.
22 Lee, *Battles and Leaders*, 76.
23 Doubleday, *Reminiscences of Forts Sumter and Moultrie*, 140.
24 Doubleday, *Reminiscences of Forts Sumter and Moultrie*, 145–146.
25 Swanberg, *First Blood*, 301.
26 Chester, *Battles and Leaders*, I, 69–70.
27 Roy Meredith, *Storm over Sumter, the Opening Engagement of the Civil War* (New York: Simon and Schuster, 1957) 174–175.
28 Fox to Montgomery Blair, April 17, 1861, in Robert Means Thompson, Editor, *Confidential Correspondence of Gustavus Vasa Fox* (New York: The Naval Historical Society, 1920) 33–36.
29 B.S. Osborne, *A Sailor of Fortune* (New York: McClure, Phillips and Co., 1906), 119–120.
30 Fox to Montgomery Blair, April 17, 1861, *Confidential Correspondence*, 33–36.
31 Chester, *Battles and Leaders*, 70–71.
32 Chester, *Battles and Leaders*, 71–72.
33 Swanberg, *First Blood*, 314–315.
34 Doubleday, *Reminiscences of Fort Sumter and Moultrie*, 163–164.
35 Lee, *Battles and Leaders*, 79.
36 Doubleday, *Reminiscences of Fort Sumter and Moultrie*, 169–170.
37 Chesnut, April 15, 1861, in C. Vann Woodward, Editor, *Mary Chesnut's Civil War* (New Haven: Yale University Press, 1981) 50.

Epilogue

One of the great traps that historians are susceptible to is the idea of inevitability. We, of course, know what happened and are in a position to judge their consequences. The danger is that we unwittingly assume that this was the only real possible outcome and that the participants realized this as well. In trying to avoid that danger, we need to be very careful that we do not wander too deeply into the swamps of "what if" history. We must get our feet a little wet to understand the consequences of what did happen. However, to risk overusing the metaphor, we should not wade much deeper into that swamp than "the flow of events would have been greatly changed had certain events occurred differently." The Civil War would have been greatly different had the events at Fort Sumter not occurred as they did.

The first shot at Fort Sumter simplified the conflict for people on both sides. For Northerners, questions of politics, economics and human bondage were set aside, at least temporarily. The United States had been attacked. Her brave soldiers and flag had come under assault. Newspapers, across the North, praised the heroes of Fort Sumter and condemned the traitors who had attacked them. In one article, very representative of most journalists, a Cincinnati reporter wrote of his city "The military spirit of the city is thoroughly aroused. The States and Stripes wave from every point. The people to a man will sustain the administration."[1] Stephen Douglas, President Lincoln's longtime rival, declared "Everyman must be for the United States or against it; there can be no neutrals in this war – only patriots and traitors."[2] Douglas spent the last two months of his life campaigning vigorously for the Union in the Border States. He died a worn out man in Chicago two months after the fall of Fort Sumter.

Anderson and his men were greeted as great heroes when they arrived in New York City. The city's population, which until very recently had serious Southern sympathies, were now as patriotically Union men as could be found in the country. Even Mayor Fernando Wood, one of the most outspoken critics of the war in the years to come, praised the men of Fort Sumter and pledged his loyalty to the Union cause.[3]

New York City was not alone in her new found support for the Union. Cincinnati businessmen pledged to stop all trade with the Southern states the moment they heard about the attack on Fort Sumter.[4] This was not a pledge they kept for very long, as the city soon became the center for illicit smuggling between the two sides. New York and her mayor would also be a problem for the Union war effort soon, peaking in the horrific 1863 Draft Riots.

Northern support for the war rose and fell over the next four years but it was almost universal in the few months that followed the fall of Fort Sumter. Those few months were critical for Lincoln politically and militarily to get the country on a war footing. The first congressional session after Fort Sumter gave Lincoln almost everything he asked for. This would have been an unlikely scenario had the conflict had a less dramatic start.

The groundswell of emotion and support for the Union cause may have been a negative as well. As the shells were crashing into Fort Sumter, Lincoln and his cabinet were developing a war plan. It was a plan of limited warfare. There would be no grand invasion. The forts would be recaptured and that might mean the occasional amphibious landing. The navy would be used to collect taxes offshore. The president's advisors debated whether to take the more dramatic steps of a complete blockade, seizing the Mississippi River and cutting off the U.S. Mail.[5]

This plan was never made public. After Fort Sumter the people of the North wanted a blow struck. "On to Richmond" was about to become the battle cry of the press and the public. When Winfield Scott put forward his plan that was more aggressive than Lincoln's, his loyalty was questioned and he was derided as a weak old man unable to do what needed to be done. While the events at Fort Sumter guaranteed Lincoln the support of the North it may have forced him to take more aggressive action than he may have wanted.

Considering how the firing on Fort Sumter electrified the North during the critical first year of the war it is tempting to view it as a huge mistake. This overlooks the fact that the violent expelling of Robert Anderson and his "Yankee horde" from Charleston harbor also electrified the South. Newspapers across the South were calling for war. The Union defeat at Fort Sumter was proof that they were not prepared to fight and now was the time to strike the final blow for Southern independence.

On April 15, the Virginia convention voted to leave the United States of America. The coup that was being planned proved unnecessary. Along with Virginia, Tennessee, North Carolina and Arkansas changed their minds after the events at Charleston and seceded from the Union.

With the exception of South Carolina, those states that had seceded in January and early February had not done so with strong support. In each convention there had been votes and passionate pleas against secession. In Texas, the great Governor Sam Houston, father of Texas independence who had worked so hard to get Texas into the Union, pleaded with his state legislature to remain in the Union. After the attack on Fort Sumter the half-heartedness that had existed disappeared.[6]

For both sides the effect of Fort Sumter was to bring clarity to the issue. The uncertainty was gone. Since Thomas Jefferson's warning that the Missouri Comprise in 1819 guaranteed war, the question that brought about Civil War had been pondered and debated. After the attack on Fort Sumter the issues were clear. That uncertainty had been replaced by a need for action was relieving to most. When Lincoln issued his call for seventy five thousand troops, the maximum allowed by law, the response in Northern states was to attempt to make the Federal government accept more than they had asked for.[7] The Southerners' response was that Lincoln's call was all the evidence they needed that he was a dictator who should be resisted with as much vigor as if he were George III or Santa Anna.[8] It is highly unlikely that both regions would have so universally taken those positions had it not been for the dramatic events at Fort Sumter. Reasons and motivations would shift as the war went on but for the men who took up arms in 1861, fought and died, the events at Fort Sumter greatly affected their decision. Those men set the nature of the war and guaranteed that the Civil War would be a bloody contest decided on countless battlefields across the divided nation.

NOTES

1 "Cincinnati" *New York Sun*, April 15, 1861.

2 Bruce Catton, *The Coming Fury, The Centennial History of the Civil War* (New York: Doubleday, 1967, reprint; New York: Doubleday, 1961) 396.

3 "Great Union Meetings, New York and Chicago"*Daily Ohio Statesman*, April 22, 1861.

4 "Cincinnati" *New York Sun*, April 15, 1861.

5 Richard N. Current, *Lincoln and the First Shot* (Prospect Heights, Illinois: Waveland Press, 1990)157–158.

6 E. Merton Coulter, *The Confederate States of America, 1861–1865. A History of the South, Volume VII* (Baton Rouge: Louisiana State University Press, 1950) 39–40.

7 David Herbert Donald, *Lincoln* (New York: Simon and Schuster, 1995) 295–296.

8 "The Civil War" *The Richmond Daily Dispatch*, April 16, 1861.

Documents

DOCUMENT 1

Declaration of the Immediate Causes which Induce and Justify the Secession of South Carolina from the Federal Union

The people of the State of South Carolina, in Convention assembled, on the 26th day of December, A.D., 1860, declared that the frequent violations of the Constitution of the United States, by the Federal Government, and its encroachments upon the reserved rights of the States, fully justified this State in then withdrawing from the Federal Union; but in deference to the opinions and wishes of the other slaveholding States, she forbore at that time to exercise this right. Since that time, these encroachments have continued to increase, and further forbearance ceases to be a virtue.

And now the State of South Carolina having resumed her separate and equal place among nations, deems it due to herself, to the remaining United States of America, and to the nations of the world, that she should declare the immediate causes which have led to this act.

In the year 1765, that portion of the British Empire embracing Great Britain, undertook to make laws for the government of that portion composed of the thirteen American Colonies. A struggle for the right of self-government ensued, which resulted, on the 4th of July, 1776, in a Declaration, by the Colonies, "that they are, and of right ought to be, FREE AND INDEPENDENT STATES; and that, as free and independent States, they have full power to levy war, conclude peace, contract alliances, establish commerce, and to do all other acts and things which independent States may of right do."

They further solemnly declared that whenever any "form of government becomes destructive of the ends for which it was established, it is the right of the people to alter or abolish it, and to institute a new government." Deeming the Government of Great Britain to have become destructive of these ends, they declared that the Colonies "are absolved from all allegiance to the British Crown, and that all political connection between them and the State of Great Britain is, and ought to be, totally dissolved."

In pursuance of this Declaration of Independence, each of the thirteen States proceeded to exercise its separate sovereignty; adopted for itself a Constitution, and appointed officers for the administration of government in all its departments – Legislative, Executive and Judicial. For purposes of defense, they united their arms and their counsels; and, in 1778, they entered into a League known as the Articles of Confederation, whereby they agreed to entrust the administration of their external relations to a common agent, known as the Congress of the United States, expressly declaring, in the first Article "that each State retains its sovereignty, freedom and independence, and every power, jurisdiction and right which is not, by this Confederation, expressly delegated to the United States in Congress assembled."

Under this Confederation the war of the Revolution was carried on, and on the 3rd of September, 1783, the contest ended, and a definite Treaty was signed by Great Britain, in which she acknowledged the independence of the Colonies in the following terms: "ARTICLE 1 – His Britannic Majesty acknowledges the said United States, viz: New Hampshire, Massachusetts Bay, Rhode Island and Providence Plantations, Connecticut, New York, New Jersey, Pennsylvania, Delaware, Maryland, Virginia, North Carolina, South Carolina and Georgia, to be FREE, SOVEREIGN AND INDEPENDENT STATES; that he treats with them as such; and for himself, his heirs and successors, relinquishes all claims to the government, propriety and territorial rights of the same and every part thereof."

Thus were established the two great principles asserted by the Colonies, namely: the right of a State to govern itself; and the right of a people to abolish a Government when it becomes destructive of the ends for which it was instituted. And concurrent with the establishment of these principles, was the fact that each Colony became and was recognized by the mother Country a FREE, SOVEREIGN AND INDEPENDENT STATE.

In 1787, Deputies were appointed by the States to revise the Articles of Confederation, and on 17th September, 1787, these Deputies recommended for the adoption of the States, the Articles of Union, known as the Constitution of the United States.

The parties to whom this Constitution was submitted, were the several sovereign States; they were to agree or disagree, and when nine of them agreed the compact was to take effect among those concurring;

and the General Government, as the common agent, was then invested with their authority.

If only nine of the thirteen States had concurred, the other four would have remained as they then were – separate, sovereign States, independent of any of the provisions of the Constitution. In fact, two of the States did not accede to the Constitution until long after it had gone into operation among the other eleven; and during that interval, they each exercised the functions of an independent nation.

By this Constitution, certain duties were imposed upon the several States, and the exercise of certain of their powers was restrained, which necessarily implied their continued existence as sovereign States. But to remove all doubt, an amendment was added, which declared that the powers not delegated to the United States by the Constitution, nor prohibited by it to the States, are reserved to the States, respectively, or to the people. On the 23d May, 1788, South Carolina, by a Convention of her People, passed an Ordinance assenting to this Constitution, and afterwards altered her own Constitution, to conform herself to the obligations she had undertaken.

Thus was established, by compact between the States, a Government with definite objects and powers, limited to the express words of the grant. This limitation left the whole remaining mass of power subject to the clause reserving it to the States or to the people, and rendered unnecessary any specification of reserved rights.

We hold that the Government thus established is subject to the two great principles asserted in the Declaration of Independence; and we hold further, that the mode of its formation subjects it to a third fundamental principle, namely: the law of compact. We maintain that in every compact between two or more parties, the obligation is mutual; that the failure of one of the contracting parties to perform a material part of the agreement, entirely releases the obligation of the other; and that where no arbiter is provided, each party is remitted to his own judgment to determine the fact of failure, with all its consequences.

In the present case, that fact is established with certainty. We assert that fourteen of the States have deliberately refused, for years past, to fulfill their constitutional obligations, and we refer to their own Statutes for the proof.

The Constitution of the United States, in its fourth Article, provides as follows: "No person held to service or labor in one State, under the laws thereof, escaping into another, shall, in consequence of any law or regulation therein, be discharged from such service or labor, but shall be delivered up, on claim of the party to whom such service or labor may be due."

This stipulation was so material to the compact that without it that compact would not have been made. The greater number of the contracting parties held slaves, and they had previously evinced their estimate of the value of such a stipulation by making it a condition in the Ordinance for the government of the territory ceded by Virginia, which now composes the States north of the Ohio River.

The same article of the Constitution stipulates also for rendition by the several States of fugitives from justice from the other States.

The General Government, as the common agent, passed laws to carry into effect these stipulations of the States. For many years these laws were executed. But an increasing hostility on the part of the non-slaveholding States to the institution of slavery, has led to a disregard of their obligations, and the laws of the General Government have ceased to effect the objects of the Constitution. The States of Maine, New Hampshire, Vermont, Massachusetts, Connecticut, Rhode Island, New York, Pennsylvania, Illinois, Indiana, Michigan, Wisconsin and Iowa, have enacted laws which either nullify the Acts of Congress or render useless any attempt to execute them. In many of these States the fugitive is discharged from service or labor claimed, and in none of them has the State Government complied with the stipulation made in the Constitution. The State of New Jersey, at an early day, passed a law in conformity with her constitutional obligation; but the current of anti-slavery feeling has led her more recently to enact laws which render inoperative the remedies provided by her own law and by the laws of Congress. In the State of New York even the right of transit for a slave has been denied by her tribunals; and the States of Ohio and Iowa have refused to surrender to justice fugitives charged with murder, and with inciting servile insurrection in the State of Virginia. Thus the constituted compact has been deliberately broken and disregarded by the non-slaveholding States, and the consequence follows that South Carolina is released from her obligation.

The ends for which the Constitution was framed are declared by itself to be "to form a more perfect union, establish justice, insure domestic tranquility, provide for the common defence, promote the general welfare, and secure the blessings of liberty to ourselves and our posterity."

These ends it endeavored to accomplish by a Federal Government, in which each State was recognized as an equal, and had separate control over its own institutions. The right of property in slaves was recognized by giving to free persons distinct political rights, by giving them the right to represent, and burthening them with direct taxes for three-fifths of their slaves; by authorizing the importation of slaves for twenty years; and by stipulating for the rendition of fugitives from labor.

We affirm that these ends for which this Government was instituted have been defeated, and the Government itself has been made destructive of them by the action of the non-slaveholding States. Those States have assume the right of deciding upon the propriety of our domestic institutions; and have denied the rights of property established in fifteen of the States and recognized by the Constitution; they have denounced as sinful the institution of slavery; they have permitted open establishment among them of societies, whose avowed object is to disturb the peace and to eloign the property of the citizens of other States. They have encouraged and assisted thousands of our slaves to leave their homes; and those who remain, have been incited by emissaries, books and pictures to servile insurrection.

For twenty-five years this agitation has been steadily increasing, until it has now secured to its aid the power of the common Government. Observing the forms of the Constitution, a sectional party has found within that Article establishing the Executive Department, the means of subverting the Constitution itself. A geographical line has been drawn across the Union, and all the States north of that line have united in the election of a man to the high office of President of the United States, whose opinions and purposes are hostile to slavery. He is to be entrusted with the administration of the common Government, because he has declared that that "Government cannot endure permanently half slave, half free," and that the public mind must rest in the belief that slavery is in the course of ultimate extinction.

This sectional combination for the submersion of the Constitution, has been aided in some of the States by elevating to citizenship, persons who, by the supreme law of the land, are incapable of becoming citizens; and their votes have been used to inaugurate a new policy, hostile to the South, and destructive of its beliefs and safety.

On the 4th day of March next, this party will take possession of the Government. It has announced that the South shall be excluded from the common territory, that the judicial tribunals shall be made sectional, and that a war must be waged against slavery until it shall cease throughout the United States.

The guaranties of the Constitution will then no longer exist; the equal rights of the States will be lost. The slaveholding States will no longer have the power of self-government, or self-protection, and the Federal Government will have become their enemy.

Sectional interest and animosity will deepen the irritation, and all hope of remedy is rendered vain, by the fact that public opinion at the North has invested a great political error with the sanction of more erroneous religious belief.

We, therefore, the People of South Carolina, by our delegates in Convention assembled, appealing to the Supreme Judge of the world for the rectitude of our intentions, have solemnly declared that the Union heretofore existing between this State and the other States of North America, is dissolved, and that the State of South Carolina has resumed her position among the nations of the world, as a separate and independent State; with full power to levy war, conclude peace, contract alliances, establish commerce, and to do all other acts and things which independent States may of right do.

Adopted December 24, 1860

Source: Web, Watson J. *Declaration of the Immediate Causes which Induce and Justify the Secession of South Carolina from the Federal Union*. Charleston, SC: Evans & Cogswell, Printers to the Convention, 1860.

DOCUMENT 2

Letter from Abraham Lincoln to Lyman Trumbull in Response to Calls that He Compromise His Positions to Prevent Secession

Springfield, Ills. December 10, 1860
Hon. L. Trumbull.

My dear Sir: Let there be no compromise on the question of extending slavery. If there be, all our labor is lost, and ere long, must be done again. The dangerous ground – that into which some of our friends have a hankering to run – is Pop. Sov. Have none of it. Stand firm. The tug has to come, & better now, than any time hereafter. Yours as ever,

A. Lincoln.

Source: *Abraham Lincoln: A Documentary Portrait through His Speeches and Writing*, Don E. Fehrenbacher, Editor. New York, NY: Signet, 1964, 146–147.

DOCUMENT 3

Verbal Instructions to Major Anderson Delivered by Assistant Adjutant General Don Carlos Buell

Fort Moultrie, S.C. December 11, 1860

You are aware of the great anxiety of the Secretary of War that a collision of the troops with the people of this State shall be avoided, and of his studied determination to pursue a course with reference to the military force and forts in this harbor which shall guard against such a collision. He has therefore carefully abstained from increasing the force at this point, or taking any measures which might add to the present excited state of the public mind, or which would throw any doubt on the confidence he feels that South Carolina will not attempt, by violence, to obtain possession of the public works or interfere with their occupancy. But as the counsel and acts of rash and impulsive persons may possibly disappoint those expectations of the Government, he deems it proper that you should be prepared with instructions to meet so unhappy a contingency. He has therefore directed me verbally to give you such instructions.

You are carefully to avoid every act which would needlessly tend to provoke aggression; and for that reason you are not, without evident and imminent necessity, to take up any position which could be construed into the assumption of a hostile attitude. But you are to hold possession of the forts in this harbor, and if attacked you are to defend yourself to the last extremity. The smallness of your force will not permit you, perhaps, to occupy more than one of the three forts, but an attack on or attempt to take possession of any one of them will be regarded as an act of hostility, and you may then put your command into either of them which you may deem most proper to increase its power of resistance. You are also authorized to take similar steps whenever you have tangible evidence of a design to proceed to a hostile act.

D.C. Buell
Assistant Adjutant General.

Source: Scott, Robert N., Editor. *The War of the Rebellion, a Compilation of the Official Records of the Union and Confederate Armies*. Washington D.C.: Government Printing Office, 1880. Series 1, vol. 1, 90.

DOCUMENT 4

Letter from Abraham Lincoln to John A. Gilmer on Dealing with the South

Strictly Confidential
December 15, 1860
Hon. Jon A. Gilmer:

My dear Sir – Yours of the 10th is received. I am greatly disinclined to write a letter on the subject embraced in yours; and I would not do so, even privately as I do, were it not that I fear you might misconstrue my silence. Is it desired that I shall shift the ground upon which I have been elected? I can not do it. You need only to acquaint yourself with that ground, and press it on the attention of the South. It is all in print and easy of access. May I be pardoned if I ask whether even you have attempted to procure the reading of the Republican platform, or my speeches, by the Southern people? If not, what reason have I to expect that any additional production of mine would meet a better fate? It would make me appear as if I repented for the crime of having been elected, and was anxious to apologize and beg forgiveness. To so represent me, would be the principal use made of any letter I might now thrust upon the public. My old record cannot be so used; and that is precisely the reason that some new declaration is much sought.

Now, my dear sir, be assured, that I am not questioning your candor; I am only pointing out, that, while a new letter would hurt the cause which I think a just one, you can quite as well effect every patriotic object with the old record. Carefully read pages 18, 19, 74, 75, 88, 89, & 267 of the volume of Joint Debates between Senator Douglas and myself, with the Republican Platform adopted at Chicago, and all your questions will be substantially answered. I have no thought of recommending the abolition of slavery in the District of Columbia, nor the slave trade among the slave states, even on the conditions indicated; and if I were to make such recommendations, it is quite clear Congress would not follow it.

As to employing slaves in Arsenals and Dockyards, it is a thing I never thought of in my life, to my recollection, till I saw your letter; and I may say of it, precisely as I have said of the two points above.

As to the use of patronage in the slave states, where there are few or no Republicans, I do not expect to inquire for the politics of the appointee, or whether he does or not own slaves. I intend in that matter to accommodate the people in the several localities, if they themselves will allow me to accommodate them. In one word, I never have been, am not now, and probably never shall be, in a mood of harassing the people, either North or South.

On the territorial question, I am inflexible, as you see my position in the book. On that, there is a difference between you and us; and it is the only substantial difference. You think slavery is right and ought to be extended; we think it is wrong and ought to be restricted. For this, neither has any just occasion to be angry with the other.

As to the state laws, mentioned in your sixth question, I really know very little of them. I never have read one. If any of them are in conflict with the fugitive slave clause, or any other part of the constitution, I certainly should be glad of their repeal; but I could hardly be justified, as a citizen of Illinois, or as President of the United States, to recommend the repeal of a statute of Vermont, or South Carolina.

With the assurance of my highest regards I subscribe myself Your obt. Servt.,

A. Lincoln.

Source: *Abraham Lincoln: A Documentary Portrait Through His Speeches and Writing*, Don E. Fehrenbacher, Editor. New York, NY: The New American Library, 1964, 148–149.

DOCUMENT 5

Exchange of Letters between Major Anderson and Washington D.C.

Fort Sumter, S.C. December 26, 1860
(Received Adjutant General's Office, December 29.)

Colonel: I have the honor to report that I have just completed by the blessing of God, the removal of this fort of all of my garrison, except the surgeon, four non-commissioned officers, and seven men. We have one year's supply of hospital stores and about four months' supply of provisions for my command. I left orders to have all the guns at Fort Moultrie spiked, and the carriages of the 32-pounders, which are old, destroyed. I have sent orders to Captain Foster, who remains at Fort Moultrie, to destroy all the ammunition which he can not send over. The step which I have taken was, in my opinion, necessary to prevent the effusion of blood.

Respectfully, your obedient servant,

Robert Anderson
Major, First Artillery, Commanding.
Col. S. Cooper, Adjutant-General.

War Department,
Adjutant-General's Office, December 27, 1860.
Major Anderson, Fort Moultrie:

Intelligence has reached here this morning that you have abandoned Fort Moultrie, spiked your guns, burned the carriages, and gone to Fort Sumter. It is not believed, because there is no order for any such movement. Explain the meaning of this report.

J.B. Floyd
Secretary of War
Charleston, December 27, 1860.

Hon. J.B. Floyd, Secretary of War:

The telegram is correct. I abandoned Fort Moultrie because I was certain that if attacked my men must have been sacrificed, and the command of the harbor lost. I spiked the guns and destroyed the carriages to keep the guns from being used against us.

If attacked, the garrison would never have surrendered without a fight.

Robert Anderson.
Major, First Artillery.

Fort Sumter, S.C., December 27, 1860.
(Received December 31, 1860)

Colonel: I had the honor to reply this afternoon to the telegram of the honorable Secretary of War in reference to the abandonment of Fort Moultrie. In addition to the reasons given in my telegram and in my letter of last night, I will add as my opinion that many things convinced me that the authorities of the State designed to proceed to a hostile act. Under this impression I could not hesitate that it was my solemn duty to move my command from a fort which we could not probably have held longer than forty-eight or sixty hours, to this one, where my power of resistance is increased to a very great degree. The governor of this State sent down one of his aides to-day and demanded, "courteously, but peremptorily," that I should return my command to Fort Moultrie. I replied that I could not and would not do so. He stated that when the governor came into office he found that there was an understanding between his predecessor and the President that no re-enforcements were to be sent to any of these forts, and particularly to this one, and that I had violated this agreement by having re-enforced this fort. I remarked that I had not re-enforced this command, but that I had merely transferred my garrison from one fort to another, and that, as the commander of this harbor, I had a right to move my men into any fort I deemed proper. I told him that the removal was made on my responsibility, and that I did it because we were in a position that we could not defend, and also under the firm belief that it was the best means of preventing bloodshed. This afternoon an armed steamer, one of two which have been watching these two forts, between which they have been passing to and fro or anchored for the last ten nights, took possession by escalade of Castle Pinckney. Lieutenant Meade made no resistance. He is with us tonight. They also took possession tonight of Fort Moultrie, from which I withdrew the remainder of my men this afternoon, leaving the fort in charge of the overseer of the men employed by the Engineer Department. We have left about one month's and a half provisions in that fort; also some wood and coal and a small quantity of ammunition. We are engaged here today in mounting guns and in closing up some of the openings for the embrasures – temporarily closed by light boards, but which would offer but slight resistance to persons seeking entrance. If the workmen return to their work, which I doubt, we shall be enabled in three of four days to have a sufficient number of our guns mounted, and be ready for anything that may occur.

I am colonel, very respectfully, your obedient servant,

Robert Anderson
Major, First Artillery, Commanding.
Col. S. Cooper, Adjutant-General.

Fort Sumter, S.C., December 28, 1860
(Received A.G.O., January 1, 1861.)
Col. S. Cooper, Adjutant-General:

Colonel: I have the honor to send herewith a copy of a memorandum received today from the governor of South Carolina, in reply to a message from me, which shows that for the present we are treated as enemies. I sent my post-adjutant this morning with a message to the commanding officer of Fort Moultrie asking by what authority he held possession of that work, and desiring to know whether he would make any opposition to my sending for some property, public and private, left there. He replied to my first question that he held that post by the orders of the governor. To the second, that his orders were not to permit public property of any kind to be removed on any pretext whatever; that he was directed to take an inventory of the same, and to send it to the governor; that he would with pleasure assist in recovering and restoring all private property that was left. This decision about the public property shows that South Carolina is acting in this matter also toward us as if we were her enemy. The amount of public property thus left is not great, as I merely retained enough to prevent my movement from being suspected. He requested Lieutenant Hall to say that at a government meeting of the officers, the military move I made was unanimously pronounced to have been one of consummate wisdom; that it was the best one that could have been made, and that if I had not effected it things would have been very different. Speaking of his own position, he remarked that the guns of Fort Sumter looked into his guns, and said that he ought not to have been ordered to fire upon me, because if I returned his fire he would be compelled to retire to the sand hills. There were yesterday, two regiments to guard the island. The remark about his orders looks like an intention to attack me here. I must confess that I feel highly complimented by the expression of position I felt bound to take to save my command and to prevent the shedding of blood. In a few days I hope, God willing, that I shall be so strong here that they will hardly be foolish enough to attack me. I must confess that we have yet something to do before, with my small force, I shall feel quite independent, as this work is not impregnable, as I have heard it spoken of.

Trusting that something may occur which will lead to a peaceful solution of the questions between the General Government and South Carolina,

I am, colonel, very respectfully, your obedient servant,

Robert Anderson,
Major, First Artillery, Commanding.

P.S. – I do not feel authorized to reply to the memorandum of the governor, but shall regret very deeply his persistence in the course he has taken. He knows know how entirely the city of Charleston is in my power. I can cut his communication off from the sea, and thereby prevent the reception of supplies, and close the harbor, even at night, by destroying the light-houses. These things, of course, I would never do, unless to do so is in self-defense.

Source: Scott, Robert N., Editor. *The War of the Rebellion, a Compilation of the Official Records of the Union and Confederate Armies*. Washington D.C.: Government Printing Office, 1880. Series 1, vol. 1, 4.

DOCUMENT 6

South Carolina Representatives to Lincoln Asking for the Withdrawal of Anderson

Washington, December 28, 1860.
The President of the United States:

Sir: We have the honor to transmit to you a copy of the full powers from the Convention of the People of South Carolina, under which we are "authorized and empowered to treat with the Government of the United States for the delivery of the forts, magazines, light houses, and other real estate, with their appurtenances, within the limits of South Carolina; and also for an apportionment of the public debt and a division of all other property held by the Government of the United States as agent of the confederated States, of which South Carolina was recently a member; and, generally, to negotiate as to all other measures and arrangements proper to be made and adopted in the existing relations of the parties, and for the continuance of peace and amity between this Commonwealth and the Government at Washington."

In the execution of this trust it is our duty to furnish you, as we now do, with an official copy of the ordinance of secession, by which, the State of South Carolina has resumed the powers she delegated to the Government of the United States, and has declared her perfect sovereignty and independence.

It would also have been our duty to have informed you that we were ready to negotiate with you upon all such questions as are necessarily raised by the adoption of this ordinance, and that we were prepared to enter upon this negotiation with the earnest desire to avoid all unnecessary and hostile collision, and so to inaugurate our new relations as to secure mutual respect, general advantage, and a future of good will and harmony, beneficial to all the parties concerned. But the events of the last twenty-four hours render such an assurance impossible. We came here, the representatives of an authority which could at any time within the past sixty days have taken possession of the forts in Charleston Harbor, but which, upon pledges given in a manner that we cannot doubt, determined to trust to your honor rather than to its own power. Since our arrival an officer of the United States acting, as we are assured, not only without but against your orders, has dismantled one fort and occupied another, thus altering to a most important extent the condition of affairs under which we came.

Until those circumstances are explained in a manner which relieves us of all doubt as to the spirit in which these negotiations shall be conducted, we are forced to suspend all discussion as to any arrangements by which our mutual interests might be amicably adjusted.

And, in conclusion, we would urge upon you the immediate withdrawal of the troops from the harbor of Charleston. Under present circumstances they are a standing menace which renders negotiations impossible, and, as our recent experience shows, threatens speedily to bring to a bloody issue questions which ought to be settled with temperance and judgement.

We have the honor to be, sir, very respectfully, your obedient servants,

R.W. Barnwell,
J.H. Adams
James L. Orr
Commissioners

ENCLOSURES

The State of South Carolina:

At a Convention of the People of the State of South Carolina, begun and holden at Columbia on the seventeenth day of December, in the year of our Lord one thousand eight hundred and sixty, and thence continued by adjournment to Charleston, and there, by divers adjournments, to the twentieth of December in the same year:

AN ORDINANCE to dissolve the union between the State of South Carolina and other States united with her under the compact entitled "The Constitution of the United States of America":

We, the People of the State of South Carolina in convention assembled, do declare and ordain, and it is hereby declared and ordained, that the ordinance adopted by us in convention on the twenty-third day of May, in the year of our Lord one thousand seven hundred and eighty-eight, whereby the Constitution of the United States of America was ratified, and also all acts and parts of acts of the general assembly repealed; and that the union now subsisting between South Carolina and other States, under the name of the "United States of America," is hereby dissolved.

Done at Charleston the twentieth day of December, in the year of our Lord one thousand eight hundred and sixty.

D.F. Jamison,
Delegate from Barnwell, and
President of the Convention, and others.

Published in *The New York Times*, January 8, 1861. Source: Scott, Robert N., Editor. *The War of the Rebellion, a Compilation of the Official Records of the Union and Confederate Armies*. Washington D.C.: Government Printing Office, 1880. Series 1, vol. 1, 110–111.

DOCUMENT 7

Letter from the War Department to Robert Anderson's Brother about the Situation at Fort Sumter

Washington, December 29, 1860.
Larz Anderson, Esq., Cincinnati:

Sir: General Scott has been hoping for two or three days to find himself well enough to answer your letter, but is too much prostrated by diarrhea. He has done everything in his power to support your brother in his command, repeating with what effect remains to be seen, within the last twenty-four hours, an urgent recommendation, long since made, to the President to re-enforce the major.

The War Department has kept secret from the General the instructions sent to the major, but the General, in common with the whole Army, has admired and vindicated as a defensive measure the masterly transfer of the garrison from Fort Moultrie to the position of Fort Sumter.

G.W. Lay

Source: Scott, Robert N., Editor. *The War of the Rebellion, a Compilation of the Official Records of the Union and Confederate Armies*. Washington D.C.: Government Printing Office, 1880. Series 1, vol. 1, 113.

DOCUMENT 8

Scott's Plan to Save Fort Sumter

Washington, December 30, 1860
The President of the United States:

Lieutenant-General Scott begs the President of the United States to pardon the irregularity of this communication.

It is Sunday; the weather is bad, and General Scott is not well enough to go to church. But matters of the highest national importance seem to forbid a moments delay, and if mislead by zeal, he hopes for the President's forgiveness.

Will the President permit General Scott, without reference to the War Department and otherwise, as secretly as possible, to send two hundred and fifty recruits from New York Harbor to re-enforce Fort Sumter, together with some extra muskets or rifles, ammunition, and subsistence stores?

It is hoped that a sloop of war and cutter may be ordered for the same purpose as early as tomorrow.

General Scott will wait upon the President at any moment he may be called for.

The President's most obedient servant,

Winfield Scott

Source: Scott, Robert N., Editor. *The War of the Rebellion, a Compilation of the Official Records of the Union and Confederate Armies*. Washington D.C.: Government Printing Office, 1880. Series 1, vol. 1, 114.

DOCUMENT 9

Lincoln's Request for Advice from the Secretary of War on the Fort Sumter Question

Executive Mansion, March 15, 1861.
The Honorable Secretary of War:

My Dear Sir: Assuming it to be possible to now provision Fort Sumter, under all the circumstances is it wise to attempt it? Please give me your opinion in writing on this question.

Your Obedient Servant,

A. Lincoln.

Source: Basler, Roy, Editor. *Collected Works of Abraham Lincoln.* New Brunswick, NJ: Rutgers University Press, 1953, vol. 4, 284.

DOCUMENT 10

Simon Cameron's Answer

[The following report is Simon Cameron's answer to the above request of the president. Cameron placed it directly in the hands of the president who used it make his decision]

ANSWER

In reply to the letter of inquiry addressed to me by the President, whether, "assuming it to be possible now to provision Fort Sumter, under all the circumstances is it wise to attempt it," I beg leave to say that it has received the careful consideration, in the limited time I could bestow upon it, which its very grave importance demands, and that my mind has been most reluctantly forced to the conclusion that it would be unwise now to make such an attempt.

In coming to this conclusion I am free to say I am greatly influenced by the opinions of the Army officers who have expressed themselves on the subject, and who seem to concur that it is, perhaps, now impossible to succor that fort substantially, if at all, without capturing, by means of a large expedition of ships of war and troops, all the opposing batteries of South Carolina. All the officers within Fort Sumter, together with Generals Scott and Totten, express this opinion, and it would seem to me that the President would not be justified to disregard such high authority without overruling consideration of public policy.

Major Anderson, in his report of the 28th ultimo says:

"I confess that I would not be willing to risk my reputation on an attempt to throw re-enforcement into this harbor, within the time for our relief rendered necessary by the limited supply of our provisions, and with a view of holding possession of the same with a force of less than twenty thousand good and well-disciplined men."

In this opinion Major Anderson is substantially sustained by the reports of all the other officers within the fort, one of whom, Captain Seymour, speaks thus emphatically on the subject:

"It is not more than possible to supply this fort by ruse with a few men or a small amount of provisions, such is the unceasing vigilance employed to prevent it. To do so openly by vessels alone, unless they are shot-proof, is virtually impossible, so numerous and powerful are the opposing batteries. No vessel can lay near the fort without being exposed to continual fire, and the harbor could, and probably would, whenever necessary, be effectually closed, as one channel has already been. A projected attack in large force would draw to this harbor all the available resources in men and material of the contiguous States. Batteries of guns of heavy caliber would be multiplied rapidly and indefinitely. At least twenty thousand men, good marksmen and trained for months past with a view to this very contingency, would be concentrated here before the attacking force could leave Northern ports. The harbor would be closed. A landing must be effected at some distance from our guns, which could give no aid. Charleston Harbor would be a Sebastopol in such a conflict, and unlimited means would probably be required to insure success, before which time the garrison of Fort Sumter would be starved out."

General Scott, in his reply to the question addressed to him by the President, on the 12th instant, what amount of means and of what description, in addition to those already at command, it would require to supply and re-enforce the fort, says:

"I should need a fleet of war vessels and transports which, in the scattered disposition of the Navy (as understood), could not be collected in less than four months; 5,000 additional regular troops and 20,000 volunteers; that is, a force sufficient to take all the batteries, both in the harbor (including Fort Moultrie), as well as in the approach or outer bay. To raise, organize, and discipline such an army (not to speak of necessary legislation by Congress, not now in session) would require from six to eight months. As a practical military question the time for succoring Fort Sumter with any means at hand had passed away nearly a month ago. Since then a surrender under assault or from starvation has been merely a question of time."

It is true there are those, whose opinions are entitled to respectful consideration, who entertain the belief that Fort Sumter could yet be succored to a limited extent without the employment of the large army and naval forces believed to be necessary by the Army officers whose opinions I have already quoted.

Captain Ward, of the Navy, an officer of acknowledged merit, a month ago believed it to be practicable to supply the fort with men and provisions to a limited extent without the employment of any very large military or naval force. He then proposed to employ four or more small steamers belonging to the Coast Survey to accomplish the purpose, and we have the opinion of General Scott that he has no doubt that Captain Ward at the time would have succeeded with his proposed expedition, but was not allowed by the late President to attempt the execution of his plan. Now it is pronounced from the change of circumstance impracticable by Major Anderson and all the other officers of the fort, as well as by Generals Scott and Totten, and in this opinion Captain Ward, after full consultation with latter-named officers and the Superintendent of the Coast Survey, I understand now reluctantly concurs.

Mr. Fox, another gentleman of experience as a seaman, who, having formerly been engaged on the Coast Survey, is familiar with the waters of the Charleston Harbor, has proposed to make the attempt to supply the fort with cutters of light draught and large dimensions, and his proposal has in a measure been approved by Commodore Stringham, but he does not suppose or propose or profess to believe that provisions for more than one or two months could be furnished at a time.

There is no doubt whatever in my mind that when Major Anderson first took possession of Fort Sumter he could have been easily supplied with men and provisions, and that when Captain Ward, with the concurrence of General Scott, a month ago proposed his expedition he would have succeeded had he been allowed to attempt it, as I think he should have been. A different state of things now, however, exists. Fort Moultrie is now rearmed and strengthened in every way; many new land batteries have been constructed; the principal channel has been obstructed; in short, the difficulty of re-enforcing the fort has been increased ten if not twenty fold.

Whatever might have been done as late as a month ago, it is too sadly evident that it cannot now be done without the sacrifice of life and treasure not at all commensurate with the object to be attained; and as the abandonment of the fort in a few weeks, sooner or later, appears to be an inevitable necessity, it seems to me that the sooner it be done the better.

The proposition presented by Mr. Fox, so sincerely entertained and ably advocated, would be entitled to my favorable consideration if, with all the light before me and in the face of so many distinguished military authorities on the other side, I did not believe that the attempt to carry it into effect would initiate a bloody and protracted conflict. Should he succeed in relieving Fort Sumter, which is doubted by many of our most experienced soldiers and seamen, would that enable us to maintain our authority against the troops and fortifications of South Carolina? Sumter could not now contend against these formidable adversaries if filled with provisions and men. That fortress was intended, as her position on the map will show, rather to repel an invading foe. It is equally clear from repeated investigations and trials that the range of her guns is too limited to reach the city of Charleston, if that were desirable.

No practical benefit will result to the country or the Government by accepting the proposal alluded to, and I am therefore of the opinion that the cause of humanity and the highest obligation to the public interest would be best promoted by adopting the counsels of those brave and experienced men whose suggestions I have laid before you.

Simon Cameron

ENCLOSURE A

Brigadier General Joseph G. Totten, Chief of Engineers.

The obstacles to the relief of Fort Sumter are natural or artificial obstacles to navigation, and military opposition.

The main channel in its best natural state would not admit the passage of vessels larger than sloops of war; so that before it was obstructed, a naval attack, to be very formidable, must have consisted of many vessels of this kind.

In designing the defenses of Charleston Harbor, therefore, it was considered that Fort Sumter, Castle Pinckney, would suffice, with some improvement of Fort Moultrie, and the erection of batteries in time of war on James Island at the position called Fort Johnson. A deeper entrance would have demanded a stronger system.

The South Carolina troops have strengthened Fort Moultrie and added batteries thereto; they possess Castle Pinckney; they have erected batteries at Fort Johnson, and, not having Fort Sumter, they have planted a number of guns (number not known) on Morris Island

These last do not, certainly, bring their system up to that which included Fort Sumter; but they, as is represented, have also so blocked the main channel, or made its navigation so intricate, that only vessels light in draught can enter – vessels unavoidably weak to resist and impotent to assail.

If we suppose a squadron of war vessels as large as can be forced through the impediments of the main bar to have to overcome that difficulty, and, under pressure of steam, to advance in daylight (as I think would be indispensable), they would suffer greatly from the fire of Morris Island, Fort Moultrie, and its adjacent batteries – but they would suffer much less than the small vessels, because much stronger and with vital parts better secured, and because their own fire would, to a certain extent keep under, and to a great degree, render uncertain the fire of the batteries. But whether larger or smaller, the vessels have not merely to pass the fire of the batteries – they must remain exposed to it. Because, before getting beyond the fire of Fort Moultrie, they come within scope of Fort Johnson, and while yet under the guns of these batteries they will be reached by Castle Pinckney. There is no point of shelter within these waters; and although the squadron of heavy sloops might survive the dangers of the passage, they could not long endure the cannonade that would be concentrated on any anchorage. In these very waters, this problem was settled in the Revolutionary War by the contest between the squadron of Sir Peter Parker and the single work of Fort Moultrie – then certainly not more powerful than now.

To enable the supposed squadron to remain, it is indispensable that a military force should capture the batteries from the land, and be strong enough, besides, to hold possession against the troops now assembled in and around them, and those that would rapidly come from the interior.

Should small vessels attempt this entrance by daylight, their destruction would be inevitable; at any rate, the chances of getting through would be too slender to justify any such enterprise. We have certain information that there is much practice with these guns, and that the practice now is good. If this risk were to be run by daylight, the vessels might have a draught of about eight feet, and could use the "Swash Channel," or passage between this and the main channel, or, finally, the latter. But I must repeat that unless we were to find a degree of inaptness and imbecility, and a want of vigilance and courage that we have no right to assume, this attempt by daylight with small vessels, even of great speed, must fail.

There remains another project, namely, to enter at night by the "Swash Channel" with a few (two or three) fast steam-tugs, having a draught of only (or about) five feet. To do this it will be necessary to take position before dark off this channel, so as to get upon the proper leading line to be followed after dark by the ascertained course, or, possibly, by the bearing of the lights of Fort Sumter. With proper precautions in screening the lights and fires of the boats, &c., I think the risk would not be so great, *considering only the batteries*, as to deter from this attempt provided the object were of very great importance. I should expect one or two, perhaps all, of these vessels to reach Fort Sumter, and the shoal upon which they must be grounded – provided no other impediments awaited them.

But, in the first place, it is a necessary condition that the boats arrive off the harbor before night. If they can see to take these bearings, they can be seen from the shore. In the next place, it seems impossible to fit out any expedition, however small and unobtrusive, without arousing inquiry, and causing the intelligence to be transmitted by telegraph. We may be certain, therefore, that these tugs will be waited for by steamers lying in the channelway, full of men.

This mode of relieving Fort Sumter, or another by men in rowboats passing up the same channel, is so obvious that it is unreasonable to suppose it has not been duly considered and provided for, where so much intelligence and resource in military means have been displayed in the scheme of defense, and so much earnestness and energy in execution. We know that guard rowboats and steamers are active during the night; and that they have all the means of intercepting with certainty this little expedition, and overpowering it, by boarding – a commencement of war.

This attempt, like any other, will inevitably involve a collision.

This raises a question that I am not called on to discuss, but as to which I may say that if the General Government adopts a course that must be attended with this result, its first measure should not be one so likely to meet disaster and defeat; nor one, I may add, which, even if successful, would give but momentary relief, while it would open all the powers of attack upon the fort, certainly reducing it before the means of recovering Charleston Harbor, with all its forts and batteries and environs, can possibly be concentrated there.

Respectfully submitted.

JGT

ENCLOSURE B

General Winfield Scott, General of the Army.

It seems from the opinions of the Army officers who have expressed themselves on the subject – all within Fort Sumter, together with Generals Scott and Totten – that it is perhaps now impossible to succor that fort substantially, if at all, without capturing, by means of a large expedition of ships of war and troops, all the opposing batteries of South Carolina. In the mean time – six or ten months – Major Anderson would almost certainly have been obliged to surrender under assault or the approach of starvation; for even if an expedition like that proposed by G.V. Fox should succeed once in throwing in the succor of a few men and few weeks' provisions, the necessity of repeating the later supply would return again and again, including the yellow fever season. An abandonment of the fort in a few weeks, sooner or later, would appear, therefore, to be a sure necessity, and if so, the sooner the more graceful on the part of the Government.

It is doubtful, however, according to recent information from the South, whether the voluntary evacuation of Fort Sumter alone would have a decisive effect upon the States now wavering between adherence to the Union and secession. It is known, indeed, that it would be charged to necessity, and the holding of Fort Pickens would be adduced in support of that view. Our Southern friends, however, are clear that the evacuation of both the forts would instantly soothe and give confidence to the eight remaining slaveholding States, and render their cordial adherence to this Union perpetual.

The holding of Forts Jefferson and Taylor, on the ocean keys, depends on entirely different principles, and should never be abandoned; and, indeed, the giving up of Forts Sumter and Pickens may be best justified by the hope that we should thereby recover the State to which they geographically belong by the liberality of the act, besides retaining the eight doubtful States.

ENCLOSURE C

Lieutenant Hall's notes:

I have the honor to state that I could not concur with Captain Rodgers, with whom I was directed to confer, in his plan for the entrance of the harbor of Charleston with men and provisions for Fort Sumter. He proposes to procure a vessel (steamboat), with a draught of not over six and one-half feet, in some Northern port, and with the cargo to be cleared for Charleston, letting it be known, as if in confidence, that the design is to force a landing on the southern extreme of Morris Island; to carry the batteries by the rear and destroy the channel; to bring in the vessel, the vessel to regulate her speed as to arrive off the bar in a dark night and at high tide, and to proceed through the Swash Channel with her lights extinguished; in case of discovery and being fired at, to drop a cork with a light in it, which would deceive the gunners. If the batteries are lighted up the men cannot see in the distance; if they are not, the lights will not be visible. The commander is to be allowed to back his vessel in case of a storm on the way down.

My objections to this plan are very numerous. In the first place, the deception would be apparent, as no one would attempt a forced landing with means possible to such a vessel. Secondly, not being a sea-going vessel the danger to life and the success of the undertaking is so great as to appear imprudent at best. Thirdly, it is unsafe to calculate upon not being seen off the bar, as a number of watch vessels, some with troops and cannon, are stationed off and along the entrance. Fourthly, even though the above dangers should all be safely passed and it should prove a moonless night and high tide at a proper time, still a chance shot through the machinery would defeat the enterprise.

The plan is grounded upon the most fortunate and improbable circumstances. It might succeed; but I think failure would be the rule. By an examination of the chart of the harbor of Charleston it will be seen that the Swash Channel passes outside the range of all the batteries erected along the entrance, except, perhaps the small one near Cummings Point (of one 32-pounder and one 12-pounder), and this can be safely neglected. Fort Moultrie can bring several guns to bear for a mile and a half (not ten minutes), but their field has been greatly reduced by the traverse with small embrasures lately thrown up on the parapet. Considering as effective all the means in the hands of those hostile to the undertakings, the following are at present to be noticed: The channel will not admit of more than six and one-half feet draught with ease in sailing; at least one steamer with troops and field guns will be near the bar; a line of pilot schooners and signal vessels form a cordon outside the bar; the main ship channel is obstructed with sunken ships; Maffitt's Channel is raked and crossed by the fires of Moultrie and batteries placed along Sullivan's Island; the buoys and range lights are removed; the anchorage, except a small area, is under the fire of guns from the several fortified points; the Swash Channel is readily followed by ranging Fort Sumter on St. Michael's till within five hundred yards of the fort, where a detour to the right will be necessary. Carefully navigated, passing very near the north side of the fort, the vessel may be brought to the wharf at high tide. If not successful, small boats may be furnished by the fort. The only effective guns are those of Fort Moultrie on this entrance. I have the honor to propose that a war vessel (the *Brooklyn* best) be dispatched with two schooners and two ordinary steam-tugs, each of not more than six feet and a half draught, and under the same pretension as that first proposed, and this combination will give color to the rumor. One of the schooners to be loaded with provisions entirely, and the hay is to be stored on the starboard. The other, with some provisions, is to carry the troops. The vessels arrived off the bar, the *Brooklyn* can keep all hostile vessels at a distance and make the following arrangement:

The vessel with provisions is to be placed upon the right, next a screw-tug, next the vessel with troops, and again a tug. The right-hand vessel will cover those on the left, protecting from fire the troops and means of locomotion. The vessels should arrive off the bar two hours before high tide, so that the tide will be rising all the way in, and if grounded may be floated off in a short time. To prevent vessels from the city and the cutters inside the harbor from interfering, the fort shall be signaled, and will reply by lowering its flag or showing a light, and will prevent any vessel going out. Signals should be agreed upon, and the time, day or night, also. Two field pieces, loaded with canister, might be used to meet a desperate attempt to board the vessels. The hay in bales should be wet, to prevent heated balls from setting fire to the vessels.

ENCLOSURE D

Opinions of Various Officers:

George W. Snyder, lieutenant of Engineers, February 28, 1861: 4 regiments, or 4,000 men; 4 vessels of war.

R.K. Meade, jr., second lieutenant of Engineers, February 28, 1861: 5,000 men, at least; supported by gunboats.

S.W. Crawford, February 28, 1861: 4,000 men supported by the Navy.

Norman J. Hall, second lieutenant, First Artillery, February 28, 1861: 3,500 men; 7 war vessels.

J.C. Davis, first lieutenant, First Artillery, February 28, 1861: 3,000 men; 6 war vessels.

Theodore Talbot, first lieutenant, First Artillery, February 28, 1861: 3,000 men and naval vessels.

A. Doubleday, captain, First Artillery, February 28, 1861: 10,000 men and Navy.

J. G. Foster, captain of Engineers, February 28, 1861: 6,000 regulars or 20,000 volunteers to take them; 10,000 regulars or 30,000 volunteers to hold them.

Captain Ward, who came here believing it practicable, abandoned it after consultation with General Scott. General Scott and the Chief of the Coast Survey, Mr. Foster, evidently a man of sound sense and experience as a seaman, who is acquainted with the waters, having formerly been attached to the Coast Survey, proposed to make the attempt with cutters of light draught and large dimensions. He was in a measure sustained by Commodore Stringham, but did not suppose provisions for more than one or two months could be furnished at a time.

ENCLOSURE E

Memorandum of Capt. G.V. Fox.
February 8, 1861.
Lieut. Gen. Winfield Scott, U.S. Army, Washington D.C.:
General: The proposition which I had the honor to submit fully in person

is herewith presented in writing. Lieutenant Hall and myself have had several free conferences, and if he is permitted by the South Carolina authorities to re-enter Fort Sumter, Major Anderson will comprehend the plan for his relief. I consider myself very fortunate in having proposed a project which meets the approval of the General-in-chief, and I ask no reward but the entire conduct of the part, exclusive of the armed vessels. The commander of these should be ordered to co-operate with me, by affording protection and destroying their naval preparations near the bar, leaving to me as the author of the plan, the actual operations of relief. I suggest that the *Pawnee* be immediately sent to the Delaware Breakwater to await orders; the *Harriet Lane* to be ready for sea, and some arrangement entered into by which the requisite steamer and tugs should be engaged, at least so far as not to excite suspicion. I would prefer one of the Collins steamers. They are now being prepared for sea, and are of such a size and power as to able to fearlessly to run down any vessels which might attempt to capture us outside by a *coup de main*. I could quietly engage one and have her ready to start in twenty-four hours' notice, without exciting suspicion. I shall leave for New York at 3:10 p.m., and any communication previous will find me at Judge Blair's. If the *Pawnee* pivot-gun is landed it should certainly be remounted.

I have the honor to be, with great respect, your obedient servant.

G.V. Fox

ENCLOSURE F

New York, February 6, 1861.

Since the repulse of the steamer *Star of the West* at Charleston it may be assumed that all the channels over the bar are obstructed, but as the bar is more than four miles in length the spaces between these channels are too extensive to be closed; therefore at high water and smooth sea the harbor is perfectly accessible to vessels drawing, say, seven feet of water. The United States have no steamers of this draught. The skillful officers at Charleston, aware of this fact, will conclude that relief must go in at high water in boats or light-draught steamers, incapable of bearing a very offensive armament. They will be perfectly prepared for such attempts by arming and heavily manning all the steamers they possess, and at the critical moment will throw themselves alongside of the relief vessels, and thus jeopardize the movement by the very detention of the conflict. To elude their vigilance or attempt a stratagem, however ingenious, I consider too liable to failure. I propose to put the troops on board of a large, comfortable sea steamer, and hire two powerful light-draught New York tug-boats, having the necessary stores on board; these to be convoyed by the U.S. steamer *Pawnee,* now at Philadelphia, and the revenue cutter *Harriet Lane.* (The *Pawnee* is the only available steam vessel of war north of the Gulf of Mexico, draws twelve feet of water, and has seven heavy guns. As a steamer, she seems to be a failure, but may be got ready for this emergency; at least she is, unfortunately, our only resource.) The *Harriet Lane* I understand to be an excellent and efficient vessel; but either of these steamers alone may be liable to capture by an overwhelming force.

Arriving off the bar I propose to examine by day the naval preparations and obstructions. If their vessels determine to oppose our entrance (and a feint or flag of truce would ascertain this) the armed ships must approach the bar and destroy or drive them on shore. Major Anderson would do the same upon any vessels within the range of his guns, and would also prevent any naval succor being sent down from the city. Having dispersed this force the only obstacles are the forts on Cummings Point and Fort Moultrie, and whatever adjacent batteries they may have erected distant on either hand from midchannel about three-quarters of a mile. At night, two hours before high water, with half the force on board of each tug within relieving distance of each other, I should run in to Fort Sumter.

G.V. Fox

Source: Scott, Robert N., Editor. *The War of the Rebellion, a Compilation of the Official Records of the Union and Confederate Armies*. Washington D.C.: Government Printing Office, 1880. Series 1, vol. 1, 194–196.

DOCUMENT 11

Memorandum of Fort Sumter by Abraham Lincoln, March 18, 1861

Some considerations in favor of withdrawing the Troops from Fort Sumpter, by President Lincoln.

1st. The Fort cannot be permanently held without reinforcement.

This point is too apparent to need proof.

The cutting off supplies and consequent starvation, not to mention disease, would compel surrender in a few months at farthest, without firing a gun.

2. The Fort cannot now be re-enforced without a large armament, involving of course a bloody conflict and great exasperation on both sides, and when re-enforced can only be held by sufficient number to garrison the post and to keep open communication with it by means of the harbor.

3. The Fort in the present condition of affairs is of inconsiderable military value, for: It is not necessary for the Federal Government to hold it in order to protect the City of Charleston from foreign invasion, nor: Is it available under existing circumstances for the purpose of collecting the revenue: and, It is difficult to see how the possession of the Fort by the Secessionists can be rendered a means of annoyance to the Federal Government. Every purpose for which the fort can now be made available would be better subserved by Ships of War, outside the harbor.

4. The abandonment of the Post would remove a source of irritation to the Southern people and deprive the secession movement of one of its most powerful stimulants.

5. It would indicate both an independent and a conservative position on part of the new administration, and would gratify and encourage those, who while friendly to the Union are yet reluctant to see extreme measures pursued.

6. It would tend to confound and embarrass those enemies of the Union both at the North and South who have relied on the cry of

"Coercion" as a means of keeping up the excitement against the Republican Party.

7. If the garrison should, while in an enfeebled condition be successfully attacked, or from want of proper supplies should be cut off by disuse the administration would be held responsible for it and this would be used by their opponents with great effect.

8. The moral advantage to the Secessionists of a successful attack would be very great.

Objections

1st The danger of demoralizing the Republican Party by a measure which might seem to many to indicate timidity or in common parlance, "want of pluck."

That this may be the first impression is probable but if the measure is justified upon the double ground of the small importance of the post in a military point of view and the desire to conciliate wherever this can be safely done a second thought will discover the wisdom of the course, and increase rather than diminish the confidence of the party in its leaders.

2d The danger of the movement being construed by the Secessionists as a yielding from necessity, and in so far a victory on their part.

Source: Basler, Roy, Editor. *Collected Works of Abraham Lincoln.* New Brunswick, NJ: Rutgers University Press, 1953, vol. IV, 290.

DOCUMENT 12

Letters exchanged between Anderson and Beauregard on the Subject of Surrendering Fort Sumter

To – Maj. Robert Anderson, Commanding at Fort Sumter, Charleston Harbor, S.C.
Headquarters Provisional Army C.S.A.,
Charleston, S.C., April 11, 1861.

Sir: The Government of the Confederate States has hitherto forborne from any hostile demonstration against Fort Sumter, in the hope that the Government of the United States, with a view to the amicable adjustment of all questions between the two Governments, and to avert the calamities of war, would voluntarily evacuate it.

There was reason at one time to believe that such would be the course pursued by the Government of the United States, and under that impression my Government has refrained from making any demand for the surrender of the fort. But the Confederate States can no longer delay assuming actual possession of a fortification commanding the entrance of one of their harbors, and necessary to its defense and security.

I am ordered by the Government of the Confederate States to demand the evacuation of Fort Sumter. My aides, Colonel Chesnut and Captain Lee, are authorized to make such demand of you. All proper facilities will be afforded for the removal of yourself and command, together with company arms and property, and all private property, to any post in the United States which you may select. The flag which you have upheld so long and with so much fortitude, under the most trying circumstances, may be saluted by you on taking it down.

Colonel Chesnut and Captain Lee will, for a reasonable time, await your answer.

I am, sir, very respectfully, your obedient servant,
G.T. Beauregard,
Brigadier-General, Commanding.

To Brig. Gen. Beauregard, Commanding Provisional Army
Fort Sumter, S.C., April 11, 1861.

General: I have the honor to acknowledge the receipt of your communication demanding the evacuation of this fort, and to say, in reply thereto, that it is a demand with which I regret that my sense of honor, and of my obligations to my Government, prevent my compliance. Thanking you for the fair, manly, and courteous terms proposed, and for the high compliment paid me,

I am, general, very respectfully, your obedient servant,

Robert Anderson,
Major, First Artillery, Commanding.

To Maj. Robert Anderson, Commanding Fort Sumter, Charleston Harbor, S.C.
Headquarters Provisional Army, C.S.A.,
Charleston, S.C., April 11, 1861.

Major: In consequence of the verbal observation made by you to my aides, Messrs. Chesnut and Lee, in relation to the condition of your supplies, and that you would in a few days be starved out if our guns did not batter you to pieces, or words to that effect, and desiring no useless effusion of blood, I communicated both the verbal observations and your written answer to my communications to my Government.

If you will state the time at which you will evacuate Fort Sumter, and agree that in the mean time you will not use your guns against us unless ours shall be employed against Fort Sumter, we will abstain from opening fire upon you. Colonel Chesnut and Captain Lee are authorized by me to enter into such an agreement with you. You are, therefore, requested to communicate to them an open answer.

I remain, major, very respectfully, your obedient servant,

G.T. Beauregard,
Brigadier-General, Commanding.

To Brig. Gen. Beauregard, Commanding
Fort Sumter, S.C., April 12, 1861.

General: I have the honor to acknowledge the receipt by Colonel Chesnut of your second communication of the 11th instant, and to state in reply that, cordially uniting with you in the desire to avoid the useless effusion of blood, I will, if provided with the proper and necessary means of transportation, evacuate Fort Sumter by noon on the 15th instant, and that I will not in the mean time open my fires upon your forces unless compelled to do so by some hostile act against this fort or the flag it bears, should I not receive prior to that time controlling instructions from my Government or additional supplies.

I am, general, very respectfully, your obedient servant,

Robert Anderson,
Major, First Artillery, Commanding.

To Maj. Robert Anderson, U.S. Army, Commanding Fort Sumter.
Fort Sumter, S.C., April 12, 1861 – 3.20 a.m.

Sir: By Authority of Brigadier-General Beauregard, commanding the Provisional Forces of the Confederate States, we have the honor to notify you that he will open the fire of his batteries on Fort Sumter in one hour from this time.

We have the honor to be, very respectfully, your obedient servants,

James Chesnut, JR.,
Aide-de-Camp
Stephen D. Lee,
Captain, C.S. Army, Aide-de-Camp.

To Brig. Gen. G.T. Beauregard, Charleston, S.C.
Fort Sumter, S.C., April 13, 1861 – 20 min. past 2 o'clock.

General: I thank you for your kindness in having sent your aide to me with an offer of assistance upon your having observed that our flag was down. – it being a down a few moments, and merely long enough to enable us to replace it on another staff. Your aides will inform you of the circumstance of the visit to my fort by General Wigfall, who said that he came with a message from yourself.

In the peculiar circumstances in which I am now placed in consequence of that message, and of my reply thereto, I will now state that I am willing to evacuate this fort upon the terms and conditions offered, by yourself on the 11th instant, at any hour you may name to-morrow, or as soon as we can arrange means of transportation. I will not replace my flag until the return of your messenger.

I have the honor to remain, very respectfully, your obedient servant,

Robert Anderson,
Major, First Artillery, Commanding.

To Maj. R. Anderson, First Artillery, Commanding Fort Sumter, S.C.
Headquarters Provisional Army, C.S.A.,
April 13, 1861 – 5 min. to 6 o'clock p.m.

Sir: On being informed that you were in distress, caused by a conflagration in Fort Sumter, I immediately dispatched my aides, Colonels Miles and Pryor, and Captain Lee, to offer you any assistance in my power to give.

Learning a few moments afterwards that a white flag was waving on your ramparts, I sent two others of my aides, Colonel Allston and Major Jones, to offer you the following terms of evacuation: All proper facilities for the removal of yourself and command, together with company arms and private property, to any point within the United States you may select.

Apprised that you desire the privilege of saluting your flag on retiring, I cheerfully concede it, in consideration of the gallantry with which you have defended the place under your charge.

The Catawba steamer will be at the landing of Sumter to-morrow morning at any hour you may designate for the purpose of transporting you whither you may desire.

I remain, sir, very respectfully, your obedient servant,

G.T. Beauregard,
Brigadier-General, Commanding.

To Brig. Gen. G.T. Beauregard, Commanding Provisional Army, C.S.
Headquarters, Fort Sumter, S.C.,
April 13, 1861 – 7.50 p.m.

General: I have the honor to acknowledge the receipt of your communication of this evening, and to express my gratification at its contents.

Should it be convenient, I would like to have the Catawba here at about nine o'clock to-morrow morning.

With sentiments of the highest regard and esteem, I am, general, very respectfully, your obedient servant,

Robert Anderson,
Major, U.S. Army, Commanding.

Source: Scott, Robert N., Editor. *The War of the Rebellion, a Compilation of the Official Records of the Union and Confederate Armies*. Washington D.C.: Government Printing Office, 1880. Series 1, vol. 1, 14–18.

DOCUMENT 13

Journal Entries of Mary Chesnut, Wife of Colonel Chesnut, for April 12–15, 1861

APRIL 12, 1861. – ANDERSON WILL NOT CAPITULATE

Yesterday was the merriest, maddest dinner we have had yet. Men were more audaciously wise and witty. We had an unspoken foreboding it was to be our last pleasant meeting. Mr. Miles dined with us today. Mrs. Henry King rushed in: "The news, I come for the latest news – all of the men of the King family are on the island" – of which fact she seemed proud.

While she was here, our peace negotiator – or envoy – came in. That is, Mr. Chesnut returned – his interview with Colonel Anderson had been deeply interesting – but was not inclined to be communicative, wanted his dinner. Felt for Anderson. Had telegraphed to President Davis for instructions. What answer to give Anderson, &c &c. He has gone back to Fort Sumter, with additional instructions.

I do not pretend to go to sleep. How can I? If Anderson does not accept terms – at four – the orders are – he shall be fired upon.

I count four – St. Michael chimes. I begin to hope. At half-past four, the heavy booming of a cannon.

I sprang out of bed. And on my knees – prostrate – I prayed as I never prayed before.

There was a sound of stir all over the house – pattering of feet in the corridor – all seemed hurrying one way. I put on my double gown and a shawl and went, too. It was to the housetop.

The shells were bursting. In the dark I heard a man say "waste of ammunition."

I knew my husband was rowing about in a boat somewhere in that dark bay. And that the shells were roofing it over – bursting toward the fort. If Anderson was obstinate – he was to order the forts on our side to open fire. Certainly fire had begun. The regular roar of the cannon – there it was. And who could tell what each volley accomplished of death and destruction.

The women were wild, there on the housetop. Prayers from the women and imprecations from the men, and then a shell would light up the scene. Tonight, they say, the forces are to attempt to land.

The *Harriet Lane* had her wheelhouse smashed and put back to sea.

We watched up there – everybody wondered. Fort Sumter did not fire a shot.

Do you know, after all that noise and our tears and prayers, nobody has been hurt. Sound and fury, signifying nothing. A delusion and a snare.

Louisa Hamilton comes here now. This is a sort of news center. Jack Hamilton, her handsome young husband, has all the credit for the famous battery which is made of RR iron. Mr. Petigru calls it the boomerang because it throws the balls back the way they come – so Lou Hamilton tells us. She had no children during her first marriage. Hence the value of this lately achieved baby. To divert Louisa from the glories of "the battery," of which she raves, we asked if the baby could talk yet.

"No – not exactly – but he imitates the big gun. When he hears that, he claps his hands and cries "boom boom." Her mind is distinctly occupied by three things – Lieutenant Hamilton, whom she calls Randolph, the baby and "the big gun" – and it refuses to hold more.

Pryor of Virginia spoke from the piazza of the Charleston Hotel.

I asked what he said, an irreverent woman replied: "Oh, they all say the same thing, but he made great play with that long hair of his, which he is always tossing aside."

Somebody came in just now and reported Colonel Chesnut asleep on the sofa in General Beauregard's room. After two such nights he must be so tired as to be able to sleep anywhere.

I do not wonder at Louisa Hamilton's baby. We hear nothing, can listen to nothing. Boom, boom, goes the cannon – all the time. The nervous strain is awful, alone in the darkened room.

"Richmond and Washington ablaze," say the papers. Blazing with excitement. Why not? To us these last days' events seem frightfully great.

We were all on that iron balcony. Women – men we only see at a distance now. Stark Means, marching under the piazza at the head of his regiment, held his cap in his hand all the time he was in sight.

Mrs. Means leaning over, looking with tearful eyes.

"Why did he take his hat off?" said an unknown creature. Mrs. Means stood straight up.

"He did that in honor of his mother – he saw me." She is a proud mother – and at the same time most unhappy. Her lovely daughter Emma is dying in there, before her eyes – consumption. At that moment I am sure Mrs. Means had a spasm of the heart. At least, she looked as I feel sometimes. She took my arm, and we came in.

APRIL 13, 1861

Nobody hurt after all. How gay we were last night. Reaction after the dread of all the slaughter we thought those dreadful cannons were making such a noise in doing. Not even a battery the worse for wear.

Fort Sumter has been on fire. He has not yet silenced any of our guns. So the aides – still with swords and red sashes by way of uniform – tell us.

But the sound of those guns makes regular meals impossible. None of us go to table. But tea trays pervade the corridors, going everywhere.

Some of the anxious hearts lie on their beds and moan in solitary misery. Mrs. Wigfall and I solace ourselves with tea in my room.

These women have all a satisfying faith. "God is on our side," they cry. When we are shut in, we (Mrs. Wigfall and I) ask, "Why?" We are told: "Of course He hates the Yankees."

"You'll think that well of Him."

Not by one word or look can we detect any change in the demeanor of these negro servants. Laurence sits at our door, as sleepy and as respectful and as profoundly indifferent. So are they all. They carry it too far. You could not tell that they hear even the awful row that is going on in the bay, though it is dinning in their ears night and day. And people talk before them as if they were chairs and tables. And they make no sign. Are they stolidly stupid or wiser than we are, silent and strong, biding their time?

So tea and toast come. Also came Colonel Manning, A.D.C. – red sash and sword – to announce that he has been under fire and didn't mind. He said gaily, "It is one of those things – a fellow never knows how he will come out of it until he is tried. Now I know. I am a worthy descendant of my old Irish hero of an ancestor who held the British officer before him as a shield in the Revolution. And backed out of danger gracefully. (Everybody laughs at John Manning's brag.) We talked of *St. Valentines Eve*; or *The Maid of Perth* and the drop of the white doe's blood that sometimes spoiled all.

The war steamers are still there, outside the bar. And there were people who thought the Charleston bar "no good" to Charleston. The bar is our silent partner, sleeping partner, and yet in this fray he is doing us yeoman service.

APRIL 15, 1861

I did not know that one could live such days of excitement.

They called, "Come out – there is a crowd coming."

A mob indeed, but it was headed by Colonels Chesnut and Manning.

The crowd was shouting and showing these two as messengers of good news. They were escorted to Beauregard's headquarters. Fort Sumter had surrendered.

Those up on the housetops shouted to us, "The fort is on fire." That had been the story once or twice before.

When we had calmed down, Colonel Chesnut, who had taken it all quietly enough – if anything, more unruffled than usual in his serenity – told us how the surrender came about.

Wigfall was with them on Morris Island when he saw the fire in the fort, jumped in a little boat and with his handkerchief as a white flag, rowed over to Fort Sumter. Wigfall went in through a porthole.

When Colonel Chesnut arrived shortly after and was received by the regular entrance, Colonel Anderson told him he had need to pick his way warily for it was all mined.

As far as I can make out, the fort surrendered to Wigfall.

But it is all confusion. Our flag is flying there. Fire engines have been sent to put out the fire.

Everybody tells you half of something and then rushes off to tell something else or to hear the last news. (Manning, Wigfall, John Preston, &c, men without limit, beset us at night.)

In the afternoon, Mrs. Preston, Mrs. Joe Heyward, and I drove round the Battery. We were in an open carriage. What a changed scene. The very liveliest crowd I think I ever saw. Everybody talking at once. All glasses still turned on the grim old fort.

Russell, the English reporter for the *Times*, was there. They took him everywhere. One man got out Thackeray, to converse with him on equal terms. Poor Russell was awfully bored, they say. He only wanted to see the forts, &c&c, and news that was suitable to make an interesting article. Thackeray was stale news over the water.

Mrs. Frank Hampton and I went to see the camp of the Richland troops. South Carolina had volunteered to a boy. Professor Venable intends to raise a company from among them for the war, a permanent company. This is a grand frolic. No more. For the students at least.

Even the staid and severe-of-aspect Clingman is here. He says Virginia and North Carolina are arming to come to our rescue – for now U.S.A. will swoop down on us. Of that we may be sure.

We have burned our ships – we are obliged to go on now. He calls us a poor little hot-blooded, headlong, rash, and troublesome sister state.

General McQueen is in a rage because we are to send troops to Virginia. Preston Hampton in all the flush of his youth and beauty, his six feet in stature – and after all, only in his teens – appeared in lemon-colored kid gloves to grace the scene. The camp, in a fit of horseplay, seized him and rubbed them in the mud. He fought manfully but took it all naturally as a good joke.

Mrs. Frank Hampton knows already what civil war means. Her brother was in the New York Seventh Regiment, so roughly receive in Baltimore. Frank will be in the opposite camp.

Source: Woodward, C. Vann, Editor. *Mary Chesnut's Civil War*. New Haven, CT: Yale University Press, 1981, 45–48.

DOCUMENT 14

President Lincoln's Proclamation Calling for War

April 15, 1861
By the President of the United States
A Proclamation.

Whereas the laws of the United States have been for some times past, and now are opposed, and the execution thereof obstructed, in the States of South Carolina, Georgia, Alabama, Florida, Mississippi, Louisiana and Texas, by combinations too powerful to be suppressed by the ordinary course of judicial proceedings, or by the powers vested in the Marshals by law.

Now therefore, I Abraham Lincoln, President of the United States, in virtue of the power in me vested by the Constitution, and the laws, have thought fit to call forth, and hereby do call forth, the militia of the several States of the Union, to the aggregate number of seventy-five thousand, in order to suppress said combinations, and to cause the laws to be duly executed. The details, for this object, will be immediately communicated to the State authorities through the War Department.

I appeal to all loyal citizens to favor, facilitate and aid this effort to maintain the honor, the integrity, and the existence of our National Union, and the perpetuity of popular government; and to redress wrongs already long enough endured.

I deem it proper to say that the first service assigned to the forces hereby called forth will probably be to repossess the forts, places, and property which have been seized from the Union; and in every event, the utmost care will be observed, consistently with the objects aforesaid, to avoid any devastation, any destruction of, or interference with, property, or any disturbance of peaceful citizens in any part of the country.

And I hereby command the persons composing the combinations aforesaid to disperse, and retire peaceably to their respective abodes within twenty days from this date.

Deeming that the present condition of public affairs presents an extraordinary occasion, I do hereby, in virtue of the power in me vested by the Constitution, convene both Houses of Congress. Senators and Representatives are therefore summoned to assemble at their respective chambers, at 12 o'clock, noon, on Thursday, the fourth day of July, next, then and there to consider and determine, such measures, as, in their wisdom, the public safety, and interest may seem to demand.

In Witness Whereof I have hereunto set my hand, and caused the Seal of the United States to be affixed.

Done at the city of Washington this fifteenth day of April in the year of our Lord, One thousand, Eight hundred and Sixty-one, and of the Independence of the United States the Eighty-fifth.

Abraham Lincoln

Source: Basler, Roy, Editor. *Collected Works of Abraham Lincoln*. New Brunswick, NJ: Rutgers University Press, 1953.

DOCUMENT 15

Major Anderson's Reports

Steamship *Baltic*, off Sandy Hook
April 18, (1861) – 10:30 a.m. via New York.

Having defended Fort Sumter for thirty-four hours, until the quarters were entirely burned, the main gates destroyed by fire, the gorge walls seriously injured, the magazine surrounded by flames, and its door closed from the effects of heat, four barrels and three cartridges of powder only being available, and no provisions remaining but pork, I accepted terms of evacuation offered by General Beauregard, being the same offered by him on the 11th instant, prior to the commencement of hostilities, and marched out of the fort Sunday afternoon, the 14th instant, with colors flying and drums beating, bringing away company and private property, and saluting my flag with fifty guns.

Robert Anderson
Major, First Artillery, Commanding.
Hon. S. Cameron
Secretary of War, Washington.

New York, April 19, 1861

Colonel: I have the honor to send herewith dispatches Nos. 99 and 100, written at but not mailed in Fort Sumter, and to state that I shall, at as early a date as possible forward a detailed report of the operations in the harbor of Charleston, S.C., in which my command bore a part on the 12th and 13th instants, ending with the evacuation of Fort Sumter, and the withdrawal, with the honors of war, of my garrison on the 14th instant from that harbor, after having sustained for thirty-four hours the fire from seventeen 10-inch mortars and from batteries of heavy guns, well placed and well served, by the forces under the command of Brigadier-General Beauregard. Fort Sumter is left in ruins from the effect of the shell and shot from his batteries, and officers of his army reported that our firing had destroyed most of the buildings inside Fort Moultrie. God was pleased to guard my little force from the shell and shot which were thrown into and against my work, and to Him are our thanks due that I am enabled to report that no one was seriously injured by their fire. I regret that I have to add that, in consequence of some unaccountable misfortune, one man was killed two seriously and three slightly wounded whilst saluting our flag as it was lowered. The officers and men of my command acquitted themselves in a manner which entitles them to the thanks and gratitude of their country, and I feel that I ought not to close this preliminary report without saying that I think it would be injustice to order them on duty of any kind for some months, as both officers and men need rest and the recreation of a garrison life to give them an opportunity to recover from the effects of the hardships of their three months' confinement within the walls of Fort Sumter.

I have the honor to be, very respectfully, your obedient servant.

Robert Anderson,
Major, First Regiment Artillery, &c.

P.S. I enclose herewith copies of the correspondence between General Beauregard and myself.

Source: Scott, Robert N., Editor. *The War of the Rebellion, a Compilation of the Official Records of the Union and Confederate Armies*. Washington D.C.: Government Printing Office, 1880.

DOCUMENT 16

Report of Capt. G.V. Fox, U.S. Agent, of the Second Expedition for the Relief of Fort Sumter

To: Hon. Simon Cameron,
Secretary of War, Washington.
Steamer Baltic,
New York, April 19, 1861.

Sir: I sailed from New York in this vessel Tuesday morning, the 10th instant, having dispatched one steam-tug, the *Uncle Ben*, the evening previous to rendezvous off Charleston. The *Yankee*, another chartered tug, followed us to the Hook, and I left instructions to send on the *Freeborn*.

We arrived off Charleston the 12th instant, at 3 a.m., and found only the *Harriet Lane*. Weather during the whole time a gale. At 7 a.m. the *Pawnee* arrived, and, according to his orders, Captain Rowan, anchored twelve miles east of the light, to await the arrival of the *Powhatan*. I stood in with the *Baltic* to execute orders by offering, in the first place, to carry provisions to Fort Sumter. Nearing the bar it was observed that war had commenced, and, therefore, the peaceful offer of provisions was void.

The *Pawnee* and *Lane* immediately anchored close to the bar, notwithstanding the heavy sea, and though neither tugs or *Powhatan* or *Pocahontas* had arrived, it was believed a couple of boats of provisions might be got in. The attempt was to be made in the morning, because the heavy sea and absence of the *Powhatan's* gunboats crippled the night movement. All night and the morning of the 13th instant it blew strong, with a heavy sea. The *Baltic* stood off and on, looking for the *Powhatan*, and in running in during the thick weather struck on Rattlesnake Shoal, but soon got off. The heavy sea, and not having the sailors (three hundred) asked for, rendered any attempt from the *Baltic* absurd. I only felt anxious to get in a few days' provisions to last the fort until the *Powhatan's* arrival. The *Pawnee* and *Lane* were both short of men, and were only intended to afford a base of operations whilst the tugs and three hundred sailors fought their way in.

However, the *Powhatan* and tugs not coming, Captain Rowan seized an ice schooner and offered her to me, which I accepted, and Lieutenant Hudson, of the Army, several Navy officers, and plenty of volunteers agreed to man the vessel, and go in with me the night of the 13th. The events of that day so glorious to Major Anderson and his command, are known to you. As I anticipated, the guns from Sumter dispersed their naval preparations excepting small guard-boats, so that with the *Powhatan* a re-enforcement would have been easy. The Government did not anticipate that the fort was so badly constructed as the event has shown.

I learned on the 13th instant that the *Powhatan* was withdrawn from duty off Charleston on the 7th instant, yet I was permitted to sail on the 9th, the *Pawnee* on the 9th, and the *Pocahontas* on the 10th, without intimation that the main portion – the fighting portion – of our expedition was taken away. In justice to itself as well as an acknowledgement of my earnest efforts, I trust the Government has sufficient reasons for putting me in the position they have placed me.

I have the honor to be, your obedient servant,

G.V. Fox
The *Baltic* has been chartered for one month.

Source: Thompson, Robert Means, Editor. *Confidential Correspondence of Gustavus Vasa Fox*. New York, NY: The Naval Historical Society, 1920.

DOCUMENT 17

Thank You from the War Department to Major Anderson

War Department
Washington, April 20, 1861.
Maj. Robert Anderson
Late Commanding at Fort Sumter.

My Dear Sir: I am directed by the President of the United States to communicate to you, and through you to the officers and the men under your command, at Forts Moultrie and Sumter, the approbation of the Government of your and their judicious and gallant conduct there, and to tender to you and them the thanks of the Government for the same.

I am, sir, very respectfully,

Simon Cameron,
Secretary of War.

Source: Source: Scott, Robert N., Editor. *The War of the Rebellion, a Compilation of the Official Records of the Union and Confederate Armies.* Washington D.C.: Government Printing Office, 1880.

DOCUMENT 18

Editorial from a Northern Newspaper Following the Attack on Fort Sumter

FORT SUMTER

Rebellion has triumphed. The American Flag has been lowered in the face of an enemy, the rattlesnake has struck with his poisoned fangs at the crest of the eagle. Civil war has been inaugurated by the haughty Southern slaveholders. There can now be but a single feeling with everyone not sympathizing with traitors. Or in complicity with the rebellion, and that is, that the most vigorous and efficient measures must be immediately taken that the Government receive no further harm. Treasure and life were once poured out like water to save Liberty from the teeth of the lion. Shall they be spared now, when the rattlesnake strikes at the heart of Freedom? Is not the government that cost seven years' war to create, worth another seven years' war, if need? to preserve and perpetuate? We shall need wait but a little, the domineering and exultant rebels will need wait but a day for the North, the East and the great free West to utter their voice in response. And it will come like the blast of a trumpet. A million men will spring to arms at the call of their Country. Proudly and defiantly they will "follow the Flag", and keep step to the music of the "Union," And if Southern fields should be sown with salt, and the burning plough-share of war should be run through rebellious cities, upturning them from their foundations, and leaving their smoking ruins as the only record of their existence, Slavery will have nobody but itself to blame for its mad rush upon destruction. Away now with talk of compromises. Hurl concessions to the winds. The South have chosen war. There is no longer peace or justice in forbearance. Let the gleam of every Southern bayonet be flashed back from a hundred Northern swords and God speed the right.

Source: *The Daily Green Mountain Freeman*, April 15, 1861.

DOCUMENT 19

Editorial from a Southern Newspaper Following the Attack on Fort Sumter

THE SURRENDER OF SUMTER

A bloodless victory has been obtained. No weeping wives nor desolate orphans are left to mourn the horrors of war. No plunder or ravages committed for our posterity to regret, but the God of Battles has so directed our efforts that all our ends are accomplished, and an iron ball has sealed the Independence of South Carolina.

"Who is General Beauregard?" was asked very often when his appointment was first announced. A name so unknown to us was not extant, but he has made a name and fame in the last week which will be as familiar as household words.

Our city was in a perfect ferment on Saturday. Every dispatch was eagerly read and discussed; but past experience deterred a too implicit confidence. The sense of anxiety was indescribable, and every heart beat wildly at the announcement of late news. At last the surrender was announced, and a thrill of joy flashed through our city like an electric shock. Now had been consummated the act which had been awaited with so much weary forbearance, the days and weeks which had worn so slowly away, were forgotten in the joy of the present victory. Who shall ever write the gloomy forebodings in that faithful city, as her inhabitants listened with eager ears to the sound of the deep mouthed cannon from Fort Sumter; each sound might herald the death of father, son or brother, but it is past and all is well. The first blow has been struck which will satisfy the U.S. administration that our intention is to force from them independence for the Confederate States of North American which they now deny us. Mr. Lincoln may be able to tell the Virginia commissioners that he will retake all federal property, for her procrastination has bound her in chains. Her forts are garrisoned as well as filled with food and ammunition. But with an impoverished treasury and a rebellious people to combat a foe whose million hearts beat as one, his vauntings will vanish into the air. He may say what he will do, but doing it is another thing.

Fort Pulaski, we understand, is the next point to operation, we give the fleet a cordial invitation to pay us a visit. We have been expecting them for some time, and confess to some petulance at our disappointment, our preparations have been made at some expense and we dislike the idea of not giving them a salute. Come over gentlemen and see us.

The Savannah Republican, April 15, 1861.

DOCUMENT 20

Lincoln's Message to Congress in Session, July 4, 1861

It is thus seen that the assault upon, and reduction of, Fort Sumter, was, in no sense, a matter of self-defense on the part of the assailants. They well knew that the garrison in the Fort could, by no possibility, commit aggression upon them. They knew – they were expressly notified – that the giving of bread to the few brave and hungry men of the garrison, was all which would on that occasion be attempted, unless themselves, by resisting so much, should provoke more. They knew that this Government desired to keep the garrison in the Fort, not to assail them, but merely to maintain visible possession, and thus to preserve the Union from actual, and immediate dissolution – trusting, as herein-before stated, to time, discussion, and the ballot-box, for final adjustment; and they assailed, and reduced the Fort, for precisely the reverse object – to drive out the visible authority of the Federal Union, and thus force it to immediate dissolution.

That this was their object, the Executive well understood; and having said to them in the inaugural address, "You can have no conflict without being yourselves the aggressors," he took pains, not only to keep this declaration good, but also to keep the case so free from the power of ingenious sophistry, as that the world should not be able to misunderstand it. By the affair at Fort Sumter, with its surrounding circumstances, that point was reached. Then, and thereby, the assailants of the Government, began the conflict of arms, without a gun in sight, or in expectancy, to return their fire, save only the few in the Fort, sent to that harbor, years before, for their own protection, and still ready to give that protection, in whatever was lawful. In this act, discarding all else, they have forced upon the country, the distinct issue: "Immediate dissolution, or blood."

And this issue embraces more than the fate of these United States. It presents to the whole family of man, the question, whether a constitutional republic, or a democracy – a government of the people, by the same people

– can, or cannot maintain its territorial integrity, against its own domestic foes. It presents, the question, whether discontented individuals, too few in numbers to control administration, according to organic law, in any case, can always, upon the pretenses, or arbitrarily, without any pretense, break up their Government, and thus practically put an end to free government upon the earth. It forces us to ask: "Is there, in all republics, this inherent, and fatal weakness?" "Must a government, of necessity, be too strong for the liberties of its own people, or too weak to maintain its own existence?"

So viewing the issue, no choice was left but to call out the war power of the Government; and so to resist force, employed for its destruction, by force, for its preservation.

Source: Basler, Roy, Editor. *Collected Works of Abraham Lincoln.* New Brunswick, NJ: Rutgers University Press, 1953.

Bibliography

Anderson, E.L. *Soldier and Pioneer: A Biographical Sketch of Lt.-Col. Richard C. Anderson of the Continental Army*. New York, NY: G.P. Putnam's Sons, 1879.

Anderson, Robert. *An Artillery Officer in the Mexican War, 1846–7, Letters of Robert Anderson*. New York: Books for Libraries Press, 1971, reprint; New York, NY: G.P. Putnam and Sons, 1911.

Anderson, Robert. *Anderson Papers*. Library of Congress.

Bain, David Howard. *Empire Express, Building the First Transcontinental Railroad*. New York, NY: Viking, 1999.

Basler, Roy, Editor. *Collected Works of Abraham Lincoln*. New Brunswick, NJ: Rutgers University Press, 1953.

Beard, Charles A. *America in Midpassage*. New York, NY: The Macmillan Company, 1939.

Catton, Bruce. *The Coming Fury, the Centennial History of the Civil War*. New York: Doubleday, 1967, reprint; New York, NY: Doubleday, 1961.

Channing, Steven A. *Crisis of Fear, Secession in South Carolina*. New York, NY: W.W. Norton Company, 1970.

Clayton, Andrew R.L. *The Northwest Ordinance 1787, A Bicentennial Handbook*. Indianapolis, IN: Indiana Historical Society, 1987.

Coulter, E. Merton. *The Confederate States of America, 1861–1865. A History of the South, Volume VII*. Baton Rouge, LA: Louisiana State University Press, 1950.

Crawford, Samuel Wyllie. *The Genesis of the Civil War, the Story of Sumter, 1860–1861*. New York, NY: Charles L. Webster and Company, 1887.

Current, Richard N. *Lincoln and the First Shot*. Prospect Heights, IL: Waveland Press, 1990.

Davis, Jefferson. *The Rise and Fall of the Confederate Government*. New York, NY: Da Capo, 1990, reprint; Richmond, VA: Garrett and Massie, 1938.

Davis, William C. *Look Away: A History of the Confederate States of America*. New York, NY: Simon and Schuster, 2002.

Detzer, David. *Allegiance, Fort Sumter, Charleston and the Beginning of the Civil War*. New York, NY: Harcourt, Inc., 2001.

Donald, David Herbert. *Lincoln*. New York, NY: Simon and Schuster, 1995.

Doubleday, Abner. *Reminiscences of Forts Sumter and Moultrie in 1860–'61*. New York, NY: Harper Brothers Publishers, 1876.

Eisenhower, John S.D. *Zachary Taylor, The American Presidents Series: The 12th President, 1849–1850*. New York, NY: Times Books, 2008.

Fehrenbacher, Don E., Editor. *Abraham Lincoln: A Documentary Portrait through His Speeches and Writings*. New York, NY: The New American Library, 1964.

Fraser, Walter J. *Charleston, The History of a Southern City*. Columbia, SC: University of South Carolina Press, 1991.

Freehling, William. *Prelude to Civil War, the Nullification Controversy in South Carolina 1816–1836*. New York, NY: Harper and Row, 1966.

Ginzberg, Lori D. *Women in Antebellum Reform*. Wheeling, IL: Harlan Davidson, Inc., 2000.

Hamilton, Holman. *Prologue to Conflict, the Crisis and Compromise of 1850*. Lexington, KY: University of Kentucky Press, 1966.

Hammond, James Henry. Special Collections, American Antiquarian Society, Worcester, MA.

Hinks, Peter and John McKivigan, Editors. *Encyclopedia of Antislavery and Abolition*. Westport, CT: Greenwood Press, 2007.

Hoffer, William James Hull. *The Caning of Charles Sumner, Honor, Idealism and the Origins of the Civil War*. Baltimore, MD: Johns Hopkins University Press, 2010.

Holt, Michael. *The Fate of Their Country: Politicians, Slavery Extension, and the Coming of the Civil War*. New York, NY: Hill and Wang, 2004.

Jefferson, Thomas. *Thomas Jefferson Papers*. Library of Congress.

Jewett, Clayton E. *Slavery in the South: A State by State History*. Westport, CT: Greenwood Press, 2004.

Johnson, Allen, Editor. *Dictionary of American Biography*. New York, NY: Charles Scribner's Sons, 1964.

Johnson, Charles and Patricia Smith, *Africans in America, American's Journey through Slavery*. New York, NY: Harcourt Brace and Company, 1998.

Johnson, Robert Underwood and Clarence Clough Buel, Editors. *Battles and Leaders of the Civil War, the Opening Battles*. New York, NY: Castle Books, 1956.

McCardell, John. *The Idea of a Southern Nation. Southern Nationalists and Southern Nationalism, 1830–1860*. New York, NY: W.W. Norton and Company, 1979.

McPherson, James. *This Mighty Scourge, Perspectives on the Civil War*. London, UK: Oxford University Press, 2009.

Meredith, Roy. *Storm over Sumter, the Opening Engagement of the Civil War*. New York, NY: Simon and Schuster, 1957.

Osborne, B.S. *A Sailor of Fortune*. New York, NY: McClure, Phillips and Co., 1906.

Poe, Edgar Allen. *Goldbug* in *The Works of Edgar Allan Poe in One Volume*. New York, NY: P.F. Collier and Son, 1927.

Pollard. E.A. *The Lost Cause, a New Southern History of the War of the Confederates*. New York: Gramercy Publishing, 1996, reprint; New York, NY: E.B. Treat and Co., 1866.

Quarles, Benjamin. *Frederic Douglass*. New York, NY: Athenaeum, 1970.

Randall, J.G. *The Civil War and Reconstruction*. Boston, MA: D.C. Heath and Company, 1953.

Remini, Robert V. *Andrew Jackson*. New York, NY: Twayne Publishers, 1966.

Reynolds, David S. *John Brown, Abolitionist*. New York, NY: Random House, 2003.

Scott, Robert N., Editor. *The War of the Rebellion, a Compilation of the Official Records of the Union and Confederate Armies*. Washington D.C.: Government Printing Office, 1880.

Skotheim, Robert Allen. "Notes and Documents. A Note on Historical Method: David Donald's 'Toward a Reconsideration of Abolitionists.'" *The Journal of Southern History* vol. 25, no. 3 (August, 1959).

Smith. Mark M. "Remembering Mary, Shaping Revolt: Reconsidering the Stono Rebellion." *The Journal of Southern History* vol. 67, no. 3 (August, 2001).

Stewart, James Brewer. *Holy Warriors, the Abolitionists and American Slavery*. New York, NY: Hill and Wang, 1976.

Swanberg, W.A. *First Blood, The Story of Fort Sumter*. New York, NY: Charles Scribner's Sons, 1957.

Tebeau. Charlton W. *A History of Florida*. Coral Gables, FL: University of Miami Press, 1971.

Thomas, Emory. *The Confederacy as a Revolutionary Experience*. Columbia, SC: University of South Carolina Press, 1992.

Thompson, Robert Means, Editor. *Confidential Correspondence of Gustavus Vasa Fox*. New York, NY: The Naval Historical Society, 1920.

U.S. Department of Commerce, Bureau of the Census. *Historical Statistics of the United States*. Washington D.C: U.S. Government Printing Office, 1975.

Warner, Ezra J. *Generals in Gray, Lives of Confederate Commanders*. Baton Rouge, LA: Louisiana State University Press, 1959.

Web, Watson J. *Declaration of the Immediate Causes which Induce and Justify the Secession of South Carolina from the Federal Union*. Charleston, SC: Evans and Cogswell, Printers to the Convention, 1860.

Woldman, Albert. *Lincoln and the Russians, The Story of the Russian–American Diplomatic Relations during the Civil War*. Cleveland, OH: World Publishing Company, 1952.

Woodward, C. Vann, Editor. *Mary Chesnut's Civil War*. New Haven, CT: Yale University Press, 1981.

NEWSPAPERS

Abbeville Press

Anderson Intelligencer

The Anti-Slavery Bugle

The Cincinnati Commercial Appeal

Daily Cleveland Leader

Daily Nashville Patriot

Daily Ohio Statesman.

Delaware Gazette
Memphis Daily Appeal
The National Republican
New York Daily Tribune
New York Sun
The Richmond Daily Dispatch

Index